# IGNATIAN SPIRITUALITY
# &
# INTERRELIGIOUS
# DIALOGUE

*Reading Love's Mystery*

Published by Messenger Publications, 2021

ISBN 9781788123440

Designed by Messenger Publications Design Department
Cover and inside front cover photographs, author's own
Inside back cover photograph © Cola Images / Alamy
Typeset in adobe Plantin MT Pro and Goudy Old Style
Printed by Hussar Printing

Messenger Publications,
37 Leeson Place, Dublin D02 E5V0, Ireland
www.messenger.ie

# Ignatian Spirituality & Interreligious Dialogue
## *Reading Love's Mystery*

Michael Barnes SJ

For Nick Weeks
Friend and companion

*Butterfly's shadow*
*Dancing briefly on warm earth*
*Never forgotten.*

# CONTENTS

# PREFACE

THIS BOOK consists of twelve interlinked reflections on the dialogue of religions. The main body of the text is based on lectures given at the Sion Centre for Dialogue and Encounter in Bayswater, London, in 2019 on what I then called 'new approaches to interreligious relations'. Only towards the end of that series did it dawn on me that what underpinned them was not any sort of 'newness', but the intuitions and instincts of Ignatian spirituality. As I revised those lectures, reshaping the main themes and adding material from my regular teaching and contributions to conferences and seminars over the years, I sought to make explicit the principles that underpin my experience of interreligious dialogue at a variety of levels – the same principles that form the mission of the Society of Jesus and the lives of those Christians who have been inspired by the *Spiritual Exercises* of St Ignatius Loyola.

This is not, therefore, a book about the theology of religions but a record of practice – or, to be more precise, an account of how one Jesuit's personal experience feeds back into and reinforces the Church's faith. I write as a theologian and specialist in Asian religions, specifically Theravada Buddhism, the ancient tradition now to be found in Śri Lanka, Myanmar, Thailand and Cambodia. As I sought to illustrate and expound the book's many cross-religious themes, one idea kept coming back. I found myself conscious of a sort of 'holy restlessness', a sense of being on a never-ending pilgrimage. It took me back to the *Acts of the Apostles* where the early Christians became conscious of being guided by the Holy Spirit who always went ahead of them. It also reminded me of how St Ignatius talks about himself as 'the pilgrim'.

More profoundly, I was struck by how, in the various forms of interreligious relations – people gathered for neighbourly support on behalf of a local area or sharing each other's spiritual experience in silent prayer and meditation – somehow, and so mysteriously, the Word of God goes on being spoken. That is why the title of this book brings all such activities together as 'interreligious *dialogue*', to remind us that the God of Israel, the God of Jesus of Nazareth, invites us into a life of love and learning. Dialogue is a two-way process that crosses all borders and challenges all our preconceptions about where God is at work. The teacher in me has always found it a privilege to explore the inner life that is generated by Christian faith, the more so when it engages with other religious worlds, raising questions and finding unexpected responses. If there is one principle of Ignatian spirituality that gives life to these pages it is a 'deep listening' for the movements of the Spirit of God, wherever they may be felt.

Later in the summer of 2019, when those lectures were finished, I spent a month in India, visiting centres of teaching, prayer and study. It was there that the framework for this book began to form itself. I was reminded of other visits I had made to that extraordinary part of the world, what I had seen and heard that set my academic expertise in a new light. When I joined the Society of Jesus in the heady years after the Second Vatican Council, I had very little idea of what the future held in store, except that it was going to be very different from the minutely calibrated liturgy I had known as a small boy. In my noviciate we were expected to speak Latin. That lasted precisely three weeks; modernity was beginning to invade our ecclesial hideaway. Even the mode of study of philosophy and theology changed dramatically, with less emphasis on dry-as-dust theses from ancient manuals and more attention to the sources of the Church's life in Scripture, liturgy and – most revolutionary – its relations with 'the world'.

Like all Jesuits I was expected to do studies in a non-theological discipline. I quite enjoyed theology, so I opted for the languages and culture of India – because no one else was doing it, and in the days of the hippy counter-culture 'other religions' seemed like an important area to explore. I quickly realised I was not cut out for editing obscure Sanskrit texts. But India became an object of total fascination, not least because it holds such an important place in the life and mission of the early Society of Jesus. When I eventually got there, with the time to soak myself in the rhythms of its religious life, it all seemed strangely familiar – and yet disarmingly different. I knew I could not be a missionary, dedicated forever to life in another culture, but I was also conscious that living on borders, intellectual as much as cultural, was where I was instinctively 'at home'. Most of my life I have been involved in university teaching, but I have also enjoyed opportunities for the more informal pastoral activity that spins out of parish, chaplaincy and the ever-rewarding task of spiritual accompaniment. While I include a few examples of the academic side of my work in this book, my intention is to show how conversations with people from other faith traditions are constantly nudging at concept and theory, insinuating a different vision of what God may be saying to all of us.

Jesuits are not so much expert in one thing as adept at holding all sorts of things together. St Ignatius's little text of *Spiritual Exercises* brims over with spiritual wisdom, and is nothing if not a brilliant guide to the living of the Christian life. But his discretely understated pedagogy of regularity and repetition, constantly returning to the moments that have touched us and – to use his term – brought us 'relish', is what enables that sense of a purposeful spiritual journey or pilgrimage to grow.

After a brief introductory comment on my sub-title, 'Reading Love's Mystery', the first chapter takes up the theme of Jesuit mission as illustrated through my encounter with the greatest of Jesuit missionaries, St Francis Xavier. That forms one 'bookend' and was written largely in the heart of Catholic India, the sometime Portuguese enclave of Goa. The last chapter, the other 'bookend', was written in Pune where I was a guest of the Jesuit community at De Nobili College, named after the extraordinary Roberto de Nobili who, two generations after St Francis Xavier, pioneered a new form of missionary presence to the brahmin elite of Hindu society. Linking those chapters together is another Francis, the Jesuit Pope who makes his own distinctive call to a pastoral and political evangelisation. Between them come what began life as the lectures I gave at Sion, plus some independent lectures, now revised from more halting originals to fit the shape of this book. None of this material has been published before. In terms of theological genre much of what I have written, here and in various more detailed studies, fits under the general title of comparative theology. This is more a style of theology than a school, and its origins are spelled out in the book. It was one of the 'new approaches' I examined in the original lectures. Rather like Scriptural Reasoning, with which it is often contrasted, comparative theology takes up themes, symbols and words that 'resonate' across religious traditions and which can therefore be read together.

If there is one particular resonance I seek to evoke, it is that of dialogue itself. On the inside front cover is a fifteenth-century fresco of the Annunciation by Fra Angelico; on the inside back a photograph of the great 1986 interreligious gathering in Assisi. Two very different records and two very different encounters, yet together symbolic of all those moments in human lives when difference itself, being faced with the stranger, provokes thought, decision and change.

The Preface normally ends with a list of thanks. With a book like this, essentially a gathering of new experiences, scattered memories and well-thumbed files, it could quickly get out of hand. If I mention only a few of the more immediate names, it is to acknowledge that the debts are endless, some of them deep-lying and beyond words. Among the Jesuit support team, I must single out Joe Munitiz and Tom Shufflebotham for their sage advice, Donal Neary and Paddy Carberry for their excellent editing, and Michael Kirwan and Damian Howard for judicious comments and words of encouragement which they have probably long forgotten. At the Sion Centre I am indebted to Margaret Shepherd and Jonathan Gorsky for inviting me to give those lectures in the first place, and to all those who participated in the sessions so enthusiastically. In India, I must thank all those who made me so welcome and with whom I talked at some length, especially Roy Alex in Trivandrum, my sometime pupil, Xavier Tharamel, in Kalady, Kuruvilla Pandikattu who was such a generous host in Pune, and the Jesuit community in Panaji who were mobilised to introduce me to the sights of Old Goa and to ensure I was brought up to date with the story of the extraordinary Fr Thomas Stephens SJ, the first Englishman in India. More particular debts are owed to many friends: especially Chris Roberts and Nick Weeks who offered insight and reassurance, Rachel Huckstep who commented on drafts of almost everything, and David Lonsdale for his evocative calligraphy. Finally I should mention my dear friend and mentor, Br Daniel Faivre, whose influence shines through on every page. There are, however, so many more who have accompanied me on this pilgrimage. Dialogue involves an endless array of partners, especially those persons of faith who have taught me so much and so many friends, students and colleagues with whom I have been privileged to share the wisdom of St Ignatius.

Michael Barnes SJ
London
*November 2020*

# INTRODUCTION

## Reading Love's Mystery

ON THE night the Jesuit Pope was elected, I was teaching my course at Heythrop College on the theology of religions. As I finished the first hour and announced a break, one of the students from the back of the room brandished his mobile. 'White smoke', he called out. I have to admit that my immediate reaction was to look out the window, fearing Health and Safety regulations were about to be breached. No one expected a result from the conclave to emerge so quickly. After a few minutes, we got back to the business in hand. I finished the lecture, packed my books and made to leave. 'Don't you want to know who it is?' asked the student with the mobile. The class suddenly snapped to attention. The name was called out and a certain frisson hit me. 'Bergoglio of Buenos Aires?' I said to myself. 'But he's a Jesuit.' It seemed impossible. Jesuits take a special vow to refuse ecclesiastical preferment, apart from exceptional circumstances; it isn't our way to be part of the hierarchy. Indeed we take a vow of special obedience to the pope. How can a Jesuit take a vow of obedience to himself?

I rushed home and found three calls on the answer-phone. The media were clamouring for news and information. By that time various of the brethren had answered the call and were appearing on radio and television, passing on what little they knew of this extraordinary Argentinian who had suffered such a bruising experience of Jesuit leadership in the days of the military junta. My turn was to come. A month or so later I took part in a radio programme exploring the likely impact of a Jesuit pope on the Church. It focused mainly on the historic mission of the Society of Jesus and on the *Spiritual Exercises* of its founder, St Ignatius of Loyola, since these supplied important remote background to the identity of the man now leading the Church. I thought I was managing quite well until the last question was thrown out: 'And what do you think he'll be best remembered for?' Off the top of my head, I replied: 'He'll be a good communicator.' Despite my initial confusion, on that particular point I think I have been proved right.

## Speaking and Presence

It's not that this pope is an eloquent rhetorician, injecting memorable phrases into well-crafted homilies and addresses. This is a man who commands attention because his faith has a moral integrity. When he appeared on the balcony of St Peter's later that night, I was struck by the stillness of his bearing. He radiated an austere yet gentle inner strength, an impression accentuated by the fact that he was not wearing the traditional ermine-trimmed red mozzetta. This turned out to be more than a gesture towards simplicity of lifestyle. At first I presumed the name he had taken was after St Francis Xavier, the first of St Ignatius's early companions. Some hours later I understood it was in response to words of encouragement from a fellow Latin American Cardinal sitting next to him in the Sistine Chapel: 'Do not forget the poor.'

A different Francis was to be his patron, not the restless missionary but the *poverello* of Assisi who gave everything away in order to follow Christ. This was the Francis who, in the wake of the Fifth Crusade, in a Church obsessed with the Muslim menace, proposed a mission of friendship and peace. In 1219, after the battle of Damietta in which some five thousand Christians had been killed, Francis crossed the lines separating the armies and visited the Sultan al-Malik al-Kamil. An overly romantic interpretation of the episode sees it as a model for interreligious dialogue. The truth is a little different, but no less significant. Francis presented himself as a messenger from God and spoke with no doubts about the truth of his Christian faith; his intention was to convert the Sultan to Christianity. In that he failed, but the Sultan was clearly impressed by the gentleness of his manner and the zeal of his words. They conversed together about faith and peace. And when he returned home, Francis proposed that his friars commit themselves to living peaceably among Muslims, a radical move at a time when it was exceptional for Muslims and Christians to meet anywhere but on the battlefield.

A couple of years later, Francis formulated an early rule for the order in which he distinguishes two ways for his friars to conduct their mission to Muslims. 'One way is not to engage in arguments or disputes, but to be "subject to every human creature for God's sake" (1 Pet. 2.13), and to acknowledge that they are Christians. Another way is to proclaim the word of God when they see that it pleases the Lord.' That last qualification is significant. To Francis is ascribed that admirable sentiment which should be inscribed above every pulpit: 'preach always and sometimes use words.'

No doubt, there are many links and quite a few differences between this Francis and his twenty-first-century Jesuit successor. As religious 'families', Franciscans and Jesuits follow different charisms, or gifts of the Holy Spirit. But as witnesses to the truth of the Gospel they are very much at one. There's an important place for the craft of speaking and writing in any work of communication, but it will always be the quality of a person's inner life and moral integrity that speak most clearly.

*From Francis to Francis*
This book begins, not with St Francis of Assisi, but with the first Jesuit Francis, St Francis Xavier; it ends by returning to Pope Francis and his programme for a Church engaged with the

conflicts and tensions that dominate a suffering world. If this pope has caught the public imagination, it is not because he has a radical message for change but because he speaks from the heart with a voice to which people from all religious backgrounds and none can respond. The first chapter and the last are intended to complement each other: two Jesuit Francises talking to each other across the centuries. Much has changed between one Francis and the other. What remains constant is the source of their spiritual energy, the practice and forms of prayer that come from the life and writing of St Ignatius Loyola.

Ignatian spirituality, as it is often called today, is as much a school of prayer as it is an ascetical tool for the promotion of the mission of the Church. Ignatius was an extraordinary reader of the human soul, concerned with how we are forever struggling to order and reconcile desires and longings of all kinds. My subtitle, *Reading Love's Mystery,* is intended as a metaphor for the contemplation of God's loving kindness in all its many manifestations, whether discerned in liturgy and sacraments or in the more fraught activity of interreligious dialogue. Like all Jesuits, and all who share in the Ignatian approach to Christian living, St Francis Xavier and Pope Francis are companions of Jesus – not just communicators of the truth revealed in Christ but also observers of the work the Spirit of Christ is already doing in the world. Reading in this sense means careful attention not just to the words recorded in Scripture but to the signs and traces inscribed in another text – the text that is the world of everyday experience, the beautiful yet painful world of human love that in some mysterious way reflects the abundance of the love that is God.

Towards the end of the *Spiritual Exercises,* Ignatius says that God 'labours in all created things' on the face of the earth. If that sounds at first like a bit of vapid pantheism – God identified with the 'All' – nothing could be further from the truth. What Ignatius encourages throughout the course of the four 'weeks' that it takes to pray one's way through the *Exercises* is a growing sensitivity to the God revealed in inner movements of the embodied heart as much as in the convictions of faith.

That sensitivity builds discernment, understood not as a set of rules for decision-making but, in Ignatian terms, as a virtuous quality learned in companionship with Christ that enables one to live with and find a way through the complexities of human living. As anyone who has spent time trying to understand the curious phenomenon that is 'religion' knows, not everything that touches the soul is of God. When Ignatius distinguishes two polarities of the spiritual life – consolation and desolation – he is doing more than pointing us in the direction of the one and telling us to avoid the other. 'Real life' is never that straightforward, especially when we are surrounded by many different accounts of what is true and good, from the traditional wisdom of the so-called 'World Religions' to the myriad 'isms' of secular modernity. If I put 'religion' in scare quotes, it is not to deny the existence and significance for everyday living of a plurality of 'religions'. On the contrary, it is to warn against the ease with which the many forms of life, cultures and philosophies that are to be discerned on the face of the earth are reduced to some neat 'common essence'.

## God in All Things

The 'Ignatian approach' to interreligious dialogue which I am proposing in this book begins somewhere else, with the practical wisdom of a genuine mystic of the everyday. Whatever name people give to the Holy Mystery that surrounds human beings, from the strong theism of Catholic Christianity to the critical agnosticism of early Buddhism, no arbitrary separation can be made between natural and supernatural, 'this-worldly' and 'other-worldly' or immanent and transcendent. Whatever terms we use to feel our way forward, whatever distinctions we make, the one is implicated in the other. The task – never that straightforward, whether for theologians and philosophers, on the one hand, or devout practitioners, on the other – is to make the right connections.

In what follows I do not, therefore, sketch out an 'Ignatian pro-gramme' for interreligious dialogue. There can be no such thing. I offer no more than a record of experience, held together by the central conviction of Ignatian spirituality that God is to be found 'in all things'. Once that truth becomes rooted in the heart, as a foundational principle that grants entry into the many religious and cultural boundaries that criss-cross our fascinating yet tor-tured world, everything begins to speak of the *possibility of grace*. That is not to deny that we live in the middle of many desolating examples of mendacity, corruption and horrendous violence, nor is it to make a naive wager on the power of peace-making, reconcil-iation and acts of heroic generosity to win some cosmic battle be-tween the forces of good and evil. Ignatius and Francis – and their Franciscan counterpart before them – were guided by a vision not of eschatological vindication but, more simply, of a world renewed in all its living and loving by the challenging yet ever-consoling words of Jesus, that the 'Kingdom is very near'.

This, of course, is where the Gospel begins, with the invitation of the one who invites all who would listen to 'come and see', to be touched by Love's Mystery in intimately personal terms. Reading is normally understood as engaging with a text, a book, a newspa-per article, a tiny message of endearment on a mobile phone. But it can be expanded to include any act of interpretation, any external encounter with whatever or whoever is 'other' that seeks for inner understanding. Reading entails more than attending to marks on page and screen; it demands careful attention to whatever raises a question for the mind and intrigues the soul. Whatever gives a humane flesh-and-blood reality to a community of faith – sacred pages and wise sayings, geography and architecture, images and artefacts, spontaneous conversations and moments of inter-per-sonal contact – can be *read* in the sense that they lend themselves to interpretation.

If there is one advantage of living and working on the borders between religious traditions, it is the immediacy of moments of insight and understanding. While years of study bring a learning that is gradual and incremental, the learning that takes place on the streets, in other places of worship or in fruitful conversation of all kinds is often powerful and even overwhelming. Fellow Jesuits and fellow Ignatians from all religious traditions form part of the deep structure of what follows. But their contributions cannot be easily separated from those of the many people of faith who have taught me that an arbitrary limit cannot be put on the extent of God's compassionate love for human beings. Ignatius taught his companions to *read* the world of their experience as a great dramatic scene in which God in Christ was involved, bringing creation-and-redemption to a fulness, a great movement of faith, hope and love in which the whole of humanity is caught up. In this sense Love's Mystery has no bounds. To say that God is at work *in all things* means precisely that.

# CHAPTER ONE

## With Ignatius to India

OLD GOA lies on the banks of the Mandovi river, some eight miles up the estuary from the modern state capital of Panaji. Much has changed since the day, 6 May 1542, when the first and greatest of Jesuit missionaries, Francis Xavier, arrived after a voyage from Lisbon, which had taken thirteen months to complete. Today the river is bordered by vast advertising hoardings, choked by dozens of fishing boats and cruised by creepy casino-vessels aimed at the tourist trade – a far-cry from the trading centre first established by Afonso de Albuquerque in 1510.

The Portuguese have long gone, their enclave swallowed up by the State of India since 1961. But many churches in classical Renaissance style survive, not least the Jesuit Basilica of Bom Jesus – the 'good' or infant Jesus – where Xavier's body is enshrined in a finely wrought tomb. There is a charming naivety about many of the artefacts decorating these churches. The ever-proliferating angels look more like dumb cartoon characters than unearthly divine presences. For all its generous proportions, the Bom Jesus is more understated, as if to draw attention to the magnificent baroque reredos that stands above the main altar. St Ignatius Loyola, his arms raised, looks up in ecstasy to what appears like a sunburst exploding from the three Greek letters IHS, a traditional shorthand for the name of Jesus.

Whatever else the Society of Jesus may stand for, without the

*Basilica of the Bom Jesus, Goa*

name of Jesus it would lose the heart of its charism. Officially recognised in 1540, it was expected that the new and untried religious community would call themselves Ignatians, along the lines of earlier orders – Benedictines, Franciscans, Dominicans. Ignatius insisted, however, that the true founder was Jesus; he alone was to be the inspiration that would animate his companions. That did not go down well in some ecclesiastical quarters, but Ignatius was a determined man and he got his way.

The *Spiritual Exercises*, which were forged out of the intensity of his own mystical experience, are intended as an introduction to the Christian life. They teach people how to pray, and how, in praying with the story of Jesus, to enter into the life-giving mystery of the Trinitarian God. Just as Ignatius found his deepest motivation in the experience of being placed by the Father in companionship with the Son, so everyone who prays their way through the carefully constructed dynamic pattern of the *Exercises* finds a similar sense of following in the footsteps of Christ, with that name of Jesus indelibly stamped on their hearts.

## Different Experiences

I got to know that extraordinary little book when I spent some months in India completing what Jesuits call tertianship, the third year of probation that comes at the end of a long period of training, study and ministry. Nearly two decades earlier, during the first two years of formation, I had experienced the *Spiritual Exercises* as a novice. At that time we never read the text, never even saw it. For thirty long days we were subjected to what would now be called a 'preached retreat'. Each meditation was introduced by a conference from the Novice Master before our hapless little band was sent off, for what seemed an interminable length of time, to ponder on the import of some distinctly abstract theology. This version of the *Spiritual Exercises* was not calculated to inspire a generation of restless young men more interested in the revolution of the Second Vatican Council than the dusty pedantry of sixteenth-century Spanish asceticism.

By the time I went through that thirty-day experience again, the manner of delivery, not to mention the way the text was interpreted, had changed dramatically. We still had conferences, but we were guided mainly by one-to-one individual meetings with the director, a charming and wise old bird with a great deal of experience of teaching and leadership in his beloved homeland. I had been practising yoga for some years, and it seemed entirely natural to relax into a mode of contemplative prayer that seemed appropriate to two very different cultural worlds.

For me it was India, with all its anarchic energy, that put a very different gloss on both the Society's 'manner of proceeding' – as Jesuits say – and life in the post-conciliar Church. Those long slow months in a large Jesuit community on the fringes of an unremarkable little town in the south of India allowed time and space, not just to pray over the text of the *Exercises* with the benefit of some experience of Jesuit life, but to read and study it in a very specific, and very challenging, context.

*Returning to the Sources*

That complex and contested experience of 'inculturation', to use the familiar jargon of the missiologists, forms the deep structure that runs through this book. We shall return to it in different shapes and forms at various points. Sufficient for the moment to note that faith and culture coexist, not as oppositions, but in a creative tension or dialogue. Faith is not some sort of special knowledge about divine things infused from on high, but a theological virtue that, in St Anselm's evocative little phrase, is 'seeking understanding'. Faith always demands to be spoken, to be shaped by what we say and how we say it, for human beings are nothing if not creatures who are defined by their use of language.

Culture has a history, just as any language bears the marks of the tradition that has formed it. One of the great gifts of the Second Vatican Council to the Church was to commend a return to the sources that underpin the Church's inner and outer life. That process had begun many years before Pope St John XXIII announced the calling of the Council to a stunned Church in 1959. The renewal of the liturgy, the critical-historical study of Scripture and the publication of patristic commentaries were all part of a profound movement of *ressourcement* that put the Church back in touch with its inner heart. An earlier generation of Jesuits would have used a Latin translation of the *Spiritual Exercises* which had been authorised since the middle of the nineteenth century. As a result of the conciliar reforms, it has been replaced by the original Spanish version of Ignatius.

This fascinating text, careful and precise, puts Jesuits back in touch with the history of the early Society and the life of Ignatius himself. For the depths of its meaning to emerge, it cannot be read as if it were a treatise in theology or a piece of personal devotion. It appeals to the imagination as well as the intellect, and has to be prayed, its simple yet profound themes repeated over and over again until they become rooted in the heart.

What is revealed is not an unchanging and timeless truth, a

great nugget hidden from view yet suddenly exploding into consciousness. Faith does not work like that; any proper conversion of heart takes time and perseverance. Using the analogy of physical training, Ignatius gives us plenty of ways of praying, and lots of useful advice about structuring each day. As a novice, I found it all rather pedantic. As a tertian, I began to appreciate the understated subtlety with which Ignatius commends his convictions and ideas. By the time I arrived in that Indian town, the Church itself had learned that reading any ancient text, let alone seeking to interpret its meaning for today, demands attention to the contingencies of time and place. At stake is not the appropriation of the asceticism that belongs in another world, but a carefully graduated introduction to the contemplation of *this* world in which the Spirit of Christ unfolds the mystery of what God has been doing – and goes on doing.

## Discerning the Spirit

I had to go to India to discover what a classic text of Catholic spirituality meant *in its own terms*. I had not expected to be touched in this way. My reason for choosing India for the tertianship year was that I was already committed to interreligious dialogue and wanted to explore further the Indian background to much of my work. But it was there that I began to appreciate what the broader Jesuit mission in the contemporary world is all about. Ignatius and Francis Xavier came alive. Of the first ten companions, these two dominate Jesuit history and continue to exercise an extraordinary influence over Christians everywhere.

Despite their similar backgrounds, it was an unlikely relationship. Francis was born in 1506, the youngest son of a noble family in the Pyrenean kingdom of Navarre. His early years were happy and secure, and he received a solid schooling. But, at the age of ten, his father, treasurer to the King, died and the family fortunes declined rapidly. His elder brothers became embroiled in the war between France and Spain that saw Navarre torn apart. In 1521 they were with the French army that laid siege to the citadel of Pamplona.

The town was defended – by a wonderful stroke of irony – by a Basque army, which included another nobleman who then styled himself Iñigo de Loyola. Ignatius, as he later became, was born in 1491 and was therefore Francis's senior by some fifteen years. As a young man, his was the life of a carefree nobleman at the court of the Duke of Najera, the viceroy of Ferdinand and Isabella in Navarre. There seemed no reason why he should be doing anything else. But at that fateful siege of Pamplona his leg was smashed by a French cannonball and he ended up an unwilling invalid back at the castle of Loyola.

The details of what happened there are well known. To while away the long hours of convalescence, he started reading the only books available in the castle, a life of Christ and lives of the saints. At first, he dreamed of returning to a military career, cutting a fine figure and impressing the ladies. Gradually reality broke in, however, and with it an alternative: emulation not of soldiers but saints. Where dreams of the former left him feeling dispirited and empty, the latter rendered him contented and even joyful. Such was the first experience Ignatius had of inner movements of what he came to call consolation and desolation – the sphere of the good spirit and the evil spirit respectively.

## The Wisdom of the Spirit

Since this is one of the all-pervading themes of Ignatian spirituality, it is important to pause for a moment. The consolation/desolation distinction turned out to be less straightforward than Ignatius imagined. He soon came to realise there is always the possibility that the evil spirit appears as an 'angel of light', that what we experience is an illusion, that what we take for peace is actually a self-interested satisfaction or a lazy complacency. The one he calls 'the enemy of our human nature' is a master of deception whose purpose is to produce a counterfeit sense of well-being, to disguise the morally dubious as the entirely plausible. Hence the need for discernment, a careful scrutiny of the interior feelings experienced in prayer.

According to Michael Ivens, one of the wisest of modern commentators on the *Exercises*, discernment is first and foremost a 'function of the wisdom of the Spirit'. The term was not invented in the mid-sixteenth century. The basic dynamic of testing spiritual influences is found in the Pauline and Johannine writings, where it is inseparable from the work of communicating truth. In Romans, for example, Paul agonises over the fate of his fellow-Jews, ending with that amazing outburst about the 'depths of the riches and wisdom and knowledge of God' (11:33). He then comes down to earth and exhorts the community:

> For by the grace given to me I say to everyone among you not to think of yourself more highly than you ought to think, but to think with sober judgment, each according to the measure of faith that God has assigned. (Rom 12:3)

Paul is not talking here about faith as some special revelation, such as he had experienced at Damascus. In commending a sobriety of mind – a virtue of moderation that was familiar in the Hellenistic world, not least in Plato and Aristotle – he insists on a measured response to the way the members of the community are each to perceive how God has bestowed gifts upon them individually. Good discernment begins with that self-acceptance before God that refuses to hanker after what has been given to someone else, but accepts and rejoices in the gift that has been bestowed on each one *for the sake of the wider community*.

I shall return to this theme at various points, for the work of discernment is as important to the practice of interreligious dialogue as to any aspect of human living. The word has connotations of reflective deliberation or judicious decision-making, and that is certainly the way in which I understood it when I first went to India. There, surrounded by the extraordinary complexity of an ancient yet ever-renewed civilisation, I realised that Ignatius intended something richer and more theological. The conviction that guided him from the earliest days of his convalescence was that

Christ recognises in each person the indelible image of the Father. Guided by the Spirit of Christ, he began to recognise the miracle of grace in himself – and then to see it elsewhere, in the life of others, for there can be no limit to the extent of God's grace except what human sinfulness interposes.

## Ignatius and the Companions

That was in the future, however, and Ignatius's adjustment to the new reality in his life was far from straightforward. Formally relinquishing the armour of the soldier and taking up the staff of the pilgrim was only the beginning of a quest for what God intended for him. He tells us how he let his hair and nails grow, failing to care for his appearance. Today we would probably say he had a nervous breakdown, a crisis of identity that took years of inner and outer wandering to resolve. Precisely where were those deep feelings of consolation and desolation taking him?

Francis Xavier meanwhile had no such doubts, and responded to the collapse of the family fortunes by deciding to become a priest. It took Ignatius much longer to move in that direction. When he arrived at the University of Paris in 1529, Francis had already been there some four years. He was, from all accounts, a brilliant student, self-confident and accomplished, and he rather looked down on the poverty-stricken Basque who had only just learned sufficient Latin to begin the study of theology. Francis poked fun at the plans of Ignatius and mocked the little group of devoted followers who had begun to gather round him. But somewhere between December 1532 and June 1533 there occurred an extraordinary change in Francis: he capitulated to the powerful influence of Ignatius. On 15 August 1534, the first companions took vows together at Montmartre. The next year Ignatius accompanied Francis as he made the *Spiritual Exercises*, forging a bond between them that lasted for the rest of their lives.

The friendship was all the more remarkable for being maintained almost entirely by letters, for the early Society was characterised not by the stability of the monastic life but by its opposite: an availability for mission, a willingness to be sent to the furthest reaches of the world. Ignatius himself and his companions in those formative years of the late 1530s had dreamed of one great purpose, one all-dominating goal: a pilgrimage to Jerusalem. It proved impossible. But another soon took its place: they would put themselves at the disposal of the Pope, to be directed on whatever mission he desired for them.

The Society of Jesus was given its formal seal of approval by Pope Paul III on 27 September 1540. Almost immediately the dispersal began as the first companions answered calls for work in different parts of the world. One request came from King John III of Portugal who wanted Jesuits to work as missionaries in his rapidly expanding Eastern empire. The original choice of Ignatius fell ill, and he was forced to send his closest friend in his place. So it was that, with scarcely a moment to pack his bags, Francis sailed from Lisbon on 7 April 1541, his thirty-fifth birthday. Ignatius was never to see him again.

*Encountering Francis*

Francis clearly felt uneasy with life at the centre of Portuguese power. After a few months working with the poor and rejected of Goa he took himself off to the south – which was where, in the middle of that experience as a Jesuit tertian in India, I caught up with him.

I had studied the culture and language of ancient India, had done some school teaching, lectured in Buddhism at the Gregorian University in Rome and had even enjoyed a brief period as a university chaplain. My year as a tertian was not a time to mull over the past and discern possible futures. I did not intend to deviate from a commitment to an inter-scriptural dialogue of religions. Something more subtle, however, happened within my sense of commitment to the mission of the Society. Pope John's initial vision for the Council was *aggiornamento*, and that focus on 'today' which peppers the Council documents was shifting my attention from the purely academic discipline of the history of religions to something more practically engaged.

I remember being fascinated by the local culture of Tamil Nadu and particularly by temple architecture. Alongside my study of key Jesuit texts, I began to compile a personal file, recording my visits to tiny shrines set in shady groves as well as to extremely large temples, which seemed somehow to encompass whole towns. One of my more daring expeditions was to the temple of Rameśwaram, down on the Coromandel coast opposite the northern tip of the Jaffna peninsula of Śri Lanka. In order to get to the temple it was necessary to take a train across a precarious causeway. My companion and I negotiated the outward journey easily enough, but the way back was a little more hazardous. The only space available was on the roof, jammed in alongside vast numbers of extremely cheerful returning pilgrims.

It is not a journey I would want to repeat, and it was with some relief that we made it to the local parish where we had arranged to stay the night. The next morning the two of us celebrated Mass – or, rather, my friend celebrated and I mouthed the few words of Tamil which I had picked up, trying not to look a complete idiot. The parish consisted mainly of low-caste fisher-folk and, like so many coastal communities in the deep south of India, they kept an intense memory of St Francis Xavier.

Had their ancestors been baptised by Francis himself? I don't know; certainly their extraordinary devotion spoke of a deep faith. What I do know is that it was there on the southern tip of India in the early 1540s that the infant Society of Jesus began a new and exciting approach to mission which was to have enormous consequences for the Church in Asia and South America.

## Faith and Culture

There can be little doubt that Francis is the source of inspiration for the Society as a missionary body. His letters made a profound impression on the coming generations, on men like Matteo Ricci, Roberto de Nobili, Alexandre de Rhodes and Ippolito Desideri, to name only a few of the pioneers who travelled deep into Asia. Like Francis, they were all intelligent and imaginative men, schooled both in Thomistic thought and in the humanist values of the Renaissance. Ignatius expected his Jesuits to be learned, but not walking scholastic encyclopaedias. He wanted them to be able to engage at a deep level with all manner of human culture, from the classics of Greece and Rome to other sources of human culture that were beginning to make themselves felt, not least the growing culture of science. Perhaps most importantly he expected them to be able to communicate their learning.

That may be one reason why, in a quite radical move within the lifetime of Ignatius himself, a decision was made to engage in formal education. Catechesis of young children had always been a commitment of the first companions, perhaps providing a balance to the focus on study. The founding document of the Society, the 1540 *Formula of the Institute*, concentrates on the pastoral life for the 'salvation of souls'. The sudden and extraordinary growth in numbers in that momentous first decade of the Society meant that attention had to be given to the formation of the new recruits. Colleges for their instruction were started, and that in turn led to specific requests that this energetic new enterprise should formally commit itself to education. Such, in an unexpected way, was the beginning of what was to become the work for which Jesuits have always been renowned. The Society was the first Catholic religious order to set up and run schools, as distinct from monasteries where schooling took place. Schools were the very heart of Jesuit life and mission itself.

The life of the scattered missionary, like Francis, and the ministry of the disciplined school-teacher, which I had experienced for a few of my early years as a Jesuit, may seem far apart. There is undoubtedly a tension between the two. When Ignatius came to write his *Constitutions* he had two separate sections, one to govern life in 'the Colleges', the other to guide life on 'the Missions'. What holds them together is the vision developed in the *Spiritual Exercises* of a world shot through with the glory of God, a vision that inspires myriad possible ways of working 'in companionship' with the Son. That world, whether populated by 'pagans' or young students, is not just the object of God's loving care but also the site of the transforming work of God's Spirit. To be a companion of Jesus is, very simply, to share in that vision and to play a part in that trans-formation. Education – both teaching *and* learning – is inseparable from an abiding fascination with the manifold movements of God's Spirit already at work in human hearts.

I shall return to Xavier in the last chapter of this book when we trace some of the links between the early Society's sense of mission and the vision of another Francis, the first Jesuit pope. That will be an opportunity to reflect on the contemporary demands faced by the dialogue of religions. It will also enable us to tie together some of the themes that will emerge as we proceed. Meanwhile let us stay a little longer with Ignatius and the book of *Spiritual Exercises* that brought India alive for me

*Generous Openness*
Ignatius begins the *Exercises* with a formal consideration he calls the Principle and Foundation. The first time I made what was then called the 'long retreat' this was treated as a bit of natural theology, proving God's existence and making everything that followed seem sweetly reasonable. It is anything but that. If it is an exercise in rea-son, it is to make the point that, before we human beings can ever enter into a relationship with God, we need to put everything else – our property and possessions, our gifts and talents, even our most prized aspirations and enthusiasms – firmly to one side. Everything is made subject to God's will, which is always prior.

Ignatius uses the term 'indifference', but what he commends is not an austere renunciation but a generous openness to whatever it is that life, or God, may throw at us. It does not come easily. Gradually what grows is a freedom before creation that, paradoxically enough, values *all things* precisely because one does not own them or rely on them – whether one is thinking about persons and what they say, places and what they reveal, or those complex situations of joy and sadness, reconciliation and violence, triumph and loss, that structure human living. Allow such experiences to be what they are, approach them with the wonder that respects their sheer otherness, and they become *pure gift* – and, as such, they act as channels of the very life of God in the world.

The implications of those dry little thoughts are enormous, opening up the possibility of experiencing a key 'fruit' of the *Exercises,* namely 'finding God in all things'. If it was the elusive God that consumed my adolescent search for meaning the first time I made the *Exercises,* the second time the focus was on the word 'all'. In India, I did not have to justify a religious quest in the face of secular reason. Religion was a given, part of the cultural fabric, inseparable from the round of the seasons, from traditions of custom and social interaction, from the marvel of creation itself.

One day, as the sun rose in the East and the land seemed to come alive with a great swirl of sounds, I remember listening to *bhajans,* or devotional songs, from a little temple by the railway line. 'What are they saying?' I asked one of my companions, expecting some piece of expansive mythology. 'They are waking up the god', he said. I still ponder the implications of that remark. It speaks of a religious world in which God is already part of the fabric of human living, not a distant and utterly transcendent mystery, but implicated in our everyday lives and everything we do.

Maybe that little phrase gives some indication of how finding God in *all* things can be an enormous challenge, both intellectually and existentially. India is often described as an assault on the senses, with its ever-competing noises, its vibrant colours, exotic tastes and restless energy. It cannot be domesticated or controlled by the categories of Western philosophy. And yet, if Ignatius had ever known India directly instead of reading second-hand about

*Dawn over village of Ropar, Panjab*

the experiences of Francis and the first missionaries, he would have been very straightforward about how to engage with its teeming mysteries. For the method of prayer he taught seeks to bring *all the senses* to bear on what we experience. That way, what often begins as a proposition, a truth to be pondered intellectually, becomes fixed in the heart – and, as Ignatius would say, *relished.*

### Ignatian spirituality

So far all I have sketched out is something of the practical impact the *Spiritual Exercises* have had on one person in one particular context. Others would no doubt put things differently. My intention is to show that what Ignatius is teaching is not a package of methods but, in his own phrase noted above, a 'way of proceeding'. Nowadays we might want to use the word *spirituality*. Despite being full of rules and notes and principles, the *Exercises* – as the name implies – is more like a coaching manual than a code of practice, forming the skills needed to play the game rather than defining the game itself. What Ignatius sets out to encourage in his exercitant is a certain religious sensibility, a contemplative attention to what God is doing in the world. In recent years, the term 'Ignatian spirituality' has emerged to describe this sensibility; as such it has become a useful shorthand for a particular religious ethos or attitude. It sums up a series of convictions which can be ascribed to Ignatius and account for his distinctive approach to the mysteries of human living.

Of course, much the same applies to St Bonaventure and Meister Eckhart, or St Augustine and St Teresa of Avila, and other great charismatic teachers in the Church. Something in what they say or write catches the imagination, breaks open boundaries and establishes new ways of prayerful thinking. Nor is the term to be limited to Christianity; there is a whole variety of schools or styles of Buddhist, Jewish, Hindu and Muslim spirituality. Each comes out of a tradition of religious learning and cannot be properly understood without reference to that tradition. For Ignatius, as those great baroque statues and paintings of the saint amply testify, Christ is the heart of the tradition, and entering into the spirit of the Gospel narrative is the way to establish a life-giving relationship with him. The most important meditations of the *Exercises,* from the spare Principle and Foundation at the beginning to the brilliantly evocative Contemplation for Attaining Love at the end, give that narrative a certain shape, their key phrases forming the primary features of Ignatius's own spirituality.

Sometimes such a concept as spirituality may seem too vague to be useful; it can be used to account for all manner of spiritual practice, from the Eucharist to yoga, without giving much clue as to how these practices are to be judged and differentiated. But that is only to underline the need for discernment, as we shall see in due course. The positive point to make, especially where the encounter of religions is concerned, is that a focus on spiritual practice allows for a more open-ended attention to what persons of faith *do*, how they find their way into the heart of a tradition. Practice or 'exercise' makes it live for them.

Where interreligious dialogue is concerned, this shift turns out to be crucially important. 'Religion' is itself a tricky concept, fraught with the baggage of history, and almost inevitably bound up with the hard-and-fast distinctions that attend faith traditions when they are spelled out only in terms of systems of belief. Spirituality may have its conceptual problems, but of its very nature it crosses religious boundaries. What we are used to calling 'religions' are more than creeds or codes; they are rich and diverse complexes of religious practice or *spiritualities*.

### Examples of Faith in Practice

Once that move is made, once we focus on *what people do religiously* rather than what they say about what they believe, all kinds of spiritual and social practices begin to offer themselves for attention. And many will sound echoes or resonances across the religious divide. For instance, in what follows I shall want to reflect on the practice of pilgrimage, not just because 'the pilgrim' is Ignatius's favourite self-designation, but because as religious practice it is to be found in some shape or form in almost all religious traditions. Something about that outer movement towards a goal enables people to connect with the inner movement of the heart.

That will be just one example of faith in practice which I will be introducing – some of them more towards the conceptual end of the spectrum, demanding attention to texts and tradition, some at the more practical end, where the structure of belief meets the exigencies of the everyday and the demands of life in modern pluralist society. All of them have their own integrity, taking their rise from particular religious traditions – Jewish or Muslim, Hindu or Buddhist. But dialogue between them is not a matter of subsuming one into another, a reduction of each to some common core. It is not about 'colonising' the other in order to exercise control, but a matter of *learning from* the other for the sake of the common good. That is a claim I shall be returning to throughout this book. In applying the term 'spirituality' across a wide spectrum of religious beliefs and practices, I am not suggesting that difference is not an issue, or that at some deep 'spiritual' level all religions fit into certain manageable patterns. Clearly what Christians believe is not the same as others believe. The strongly theistic narrative unfolded in the Gospels and the austere ethical and meditative practices of ancient Buddhism inhabit very different cultural and linguistic spaces. The narrative of Jesus' passion and the story of Imam Hussein's death at the massacre of Karbala are not parallel versions of some grand mythology. And the colourful images set around the Hindu *mandir* are not to be confused with the statues of Catholic saints. The different religions are sometimes very different indeed. But that does not make comparison impossible – just demanding, *and more interesting.*

My point is that difference is something to be respected, if not positively cherished. In the middle of strange language and mystifying practice, what people do and say of themselves may well set up a process of recognition, a trace of something known in the unknown. Ignatius, in a little paragraph in the *Exercises* called the Presupposition, makes the important point that 'every good Christian should be more ready to *justify* than to condemn a neighbour's statement' [22]. It's a little bit of advice to the director – to the 'one who gives the *Exercises*', to use Ignatius's language – not just to listen intently to what is being said in the spiritual conversation, but to give it the very best interpretation possible. Generosity, a counter-cultural move that runs certain risks but also yields its own rewards, is to be preferred to suspicion. Ignatius is saying that this person before me is also created in the image and likeness of God and has his or her own insights and ideas that are worthy of consideration and respect.

*Discerning a Way*

It is at this point that a distinctive characteristic of Ignatian spirituality becomes significant, especially from the interreligious perspective. Any set of spiritual or religious practices introduces people into a particular tradition and commends a practical way to make progress in the spiritual life. For Jesuits, and for Christians who follow the Ignatian approach to prayer, that tradition makes sense when its practices coalesce around the person of Christ. Indeed, as I noted in the opening paragraphs, the *Exercises* can only make complete sense when related to the Paschal Mystery of the Death and Resurrection of Christ that *is* the Gospel. Nevertheless, taken as a single pattern of open and generous self-offering that orders and channels the desires that make us most deeply human – both our basic needs for security and satisfaction and more deeply felt yearnings for understanding, wisdom and love – the text of Ignatius commends values that can be appropriated by all persons of faith.

Anyone who has made the *Exercises* in one of its traditional forms knows that they are being offered more than an 'Ignatian angle' on Christianity. If the analogy with a coaching manual holds, they are being given certain tools with which they can unpack their own unique experience of faith. Faith is already there, untested and in need of more precise focus, but *there* nonetheless. In other words, while one can identify certain ways of presenting the Christian faith that are 'typically Jesuit' or distinctive of the Ignatian world-view, the *Spiritual Exercises* also make explicit these deep movements of the human spirit, recognising them as often disordered, but taking them seriously as the very centre of the encounter with the divine. As Ignatius discovered in that disconcerting experience of dreaming about possible futures, God works through our mixed-up feelings as much as in the clear and distinct ideas of our reasoning faculties.

In the next chapter I will say more about how Ignatius's early experience of what he calls consolation and desolation – feelings of joy and peace, on the one hand, and feelings of anxiety and confusion, on the other – led to his formulation of 'Rules for Discernment'. Let me anticipate briefly by stressing they are 'rules' only in the sense that they emerge from the *regular* or regulated pattern of an ordered inner life. That acts as a reminder of the very purpose of the *Exercises*, the overcoming of disordered tendencies of all kinds. Ignatius was not a schoolteacher, but he spoke of how God worked with him in just such terms. Intellectual, moral and spiritual education are all of a piece. In the *Exercises* in particular, but also in the vast bibliography that has grown out of their influence, a well-crafted, intelligent pedagogy teaches ways of prayer and builds sound virtues of human living. As a gift to the Church, indeed to all people of good will, they encourage the wisdom that grows from a careful scrutiny of experience.

## Signs of the Times

Let me finish this chapter by returning to the statue of Ignatius in the Bom Jesus. He is totally captivated by the person of Christ. The word that translates Messiah, or 'Anointed One', is not another name for a peculiarly Jewish saviour-figure which parallels other equally 'unique' religious founders and teachers. More profoundly, this is the one who, as the incarnate Word, works to challenge and unravel all given norms of human interaction by turning persons of faith back to the implications of what is always *God's* voice sounding in our midst. The experience of Ignatius is, of course, intensely Christian. But it is also, in an important sense, a *Jewish* experience, for resonances of the Word are sounded, not just in Isaiah and Elijah and John the Baptist, but throughout creation itself. And this raises a question that in some shape or form continues to occupy Christians everywhere. How can it be possible to speak of the Word of God, incarnate in Christ, speaking in 'other voices' and 'other languages'?

Let me sketch a first response which will deepen as we proceed. Ignatius and Francis did not doubt the truth of Christianity. It

would be anachronistic to present them as anything less than zealous missionaries, deeply committed to the 'salvation of souls'. But
they and their followers were also intelligent and thoughtful men,
convinced that there is always more to be learned about the ways of
God with human beings. Rome and Goa, the two places I associate
with Ignatius and Francis, stand symbolic of the tension – between
known and unknown, central and local, universal and particular,
familiar and other – that runs through all missionary engagement.
The ideal of an eventual completion in God's good time coexists in
this present moment with all manner of difference and otherness
that remains to be explored in the company of the Spirit of Christ.
For men formed in both the scholastic method of Aquinas and the
classical culture of the Renaissance – the one commending academic rigour the other generosity of vision – it is the actual *seeking*
of a resolution, and learning to live with its ambiguities that is *now*
the immediate priority.

Any search for meaning is guided, not by cross-religious es-
sences or ideas that we imagine to be embodied in a variety of
religious traditions, but by something more intrinsic to the nature
of human beings as such. We are creatures who are formed both
by historical memories that keep alive traces of our past *and* by
the webs of meaning that continue to be carried by time-honoured
images and symbols. All of this is embodied in the use of *language*,
that capacity to address and communicate with each other which
most characterises our nature as human beings. We cannot get *outside* language any more than language itself can be reduced to a set
of marks on paper or sounds on the radio. But neither can we get
*inside* language without attending to the 'signs' of human living,
whether embodied in artefacts and architecture or in the humane
culture that grows from popular pastimes, communities of interest
and institutions of civic engagement. In short: human living bears
historical and aesthetic as well as political dimensions.

'Inculturation' begins with the crafting of words and imagery
that respond to the Word made Flesh, *the Word made visible*. But

it cannot end there. The substance of this chapter was written in sight of the river where it is still possible to imagine fleets of Portuguese galleons exploring a 'new world'. I completed it further to the north, in the modern city of Pune, the capital of the state of Maharashtra, listening to the incessant buzzing of cicadas, the constant drip of late monsoon rains, and the distant drumming which accompanies the ten-day festival known as Ganesh Chaturthi. Much of that would have been familiar to Francis; Ignatius too would have known something of the culture, customs and climate of the distant missions from the letters his Jesuits sent back home. What neither would have known is another set of 'signs', the sometimes strident political clamour that affects all interreligious dialogue nowadays, not least in today's India. I was aware of such rumblings in the background during my first period in India. The day the Falklands war erupted in earnest I visited a convent in south India. The older sisters in particular were gracious and kind to their young visitor, but I was left with no doubts about their attitude to the colonial power that had once ruled their land.

The past is never absent. The historical, the aesthetic and the political are intricately interwoven into the fabric of interreligious relations. The way we deal with memory, especially those traumatic events we would rather forget, is shaped by the predominant patterns of writing, painting, sketching and sculpting that shape our everyday experience and in turn form our politics, the implicit and explicit ways we deal with power and resources, inequalities and aspirations, difference and identity. *Reading Love's Mystery* is a demanding but exciting task. Much more is at stake than imposing a well-ordered pattern on an unruly religious pluralism. At its best, an Ignatian approach to interreligious relations is typified by a holy restlessness that feels called to explore the unknown, to discern the workings of the Spirit in the everyday, and to follow the deepest of desires that draw us into dialogue with what good Pope John at the Council called 'the signs of the times'.

# CHAPTER TWO

## Spirituality of the Pilgrim

TOWARDS THE end of his life Ignatius dictated to one of his close companions a series of reminiscences, usually known as the *Autobiography*. With the benefit of hindsight, he talks about the important moments in his life, how he has been led by God. He refers to himself in the third person as 'the pilgrim' – a touch ironic, of course, since it was Francis who was the traveller, following the Spirit of Christ into the unknown, while Ignatius ended in Rome, a reluctant Superior General, managing the administration of his rapidly expanding Society. In the story he seeks to tell about himself, Ignatius comes across as a serious searcher after truth, with occasional touches of self-deprecating humour. On the harbour-side in Barcelona he recounts how he feels embarrassed by his grand plan to go to Jerusalem, and tells a lady from whom he is begging alms that he is making for Rome. 'And she, as if horrified, said: "It's to Rome you're intending to go? Well, those who go there come back in I don't know what state".'

Later he is less reticent about pilgrimages and more realistic about life at the centre of Catholic Christianity. By then he knows from experience that nothing on life's journey is ever predictable, certainly not its intermediate destinations. When he gets to Jerusalem he thinks he has achieved the aim he has set himself. He resolves to stay, but is told in no uncertain terms by the authorities that this cannot be allowed; if he stays, they say, it's under pain of excommunication. Reluctantly he obeys. Despite all the obstacles, he knows that God in his providence has got him to Jerusalem, and the faithful God will take him further. Even when handled roughly, the pilgrim says 'he had great consolation from Our Lord, in that it seemed to him he was seeing Christ always over him'.

The *Autobiography* is a record, not just of the life of Ignatius, but of the growth of the early Society. A decade after his stay in Jerusalem, history seems to be repeating itself. The companions have made a vow to go on pilgrimage to Jerusalem. Despite waiting for the best part of a year in Venice, while they occupy themselves with preaching and pastoral ministry, this proves impossible. So they enact Plan B, turn round and travel to Rome to put themselves under the direction of the Pope himself. It's a momentous step. The *Formula of the Institute* makes explicit a special vow to the Pope with regard to the propagation of the faith, to go wherever he should see fit to send them: 'We pledge to do this whether he sends us among the Turks or to other infidels, even to the land they call India, or to any heretics or schismatics, or to any of the faithful'. For the first Jesuits the pilgrimage now takes a new form, giving them a special identity, 'being sent' to fulfil a specific task or mission.

### A Pilgrimage of Discernment

Pilgrimage is not one of the many spiritual exercises Ignatius describes in his little manual, but as a metaphor for missionary vocation it's there on every page. At the very beginning of the *Exercises* he draws an analogy between physical exercise and spiritual exercise. In the first place, he wants to show how seriously one should approach the task of ordering one's desires; one needs to be purposive and organised. At the same time, the careful consideration he gives to matters of bodily posture and breathing allows that he is thinking in more than analogical terms. In practice the physical fades into the spiritual. There's a dynamic in play here that crosses religious boundaries. Zen Buddhism, for instance, the most ascetical of all religious practices, combines long periods of *zazen*, pure sitting, with shorter bouts of *kinhin*, walking meditation. Walking is not intended as relaxation from the intensity of sitting, but as a different mode of focusing the attention. Similarly, when Ignatius talks about his experience as 'the pilgrim', he is not reminiscing about journeys from this to that centre of faith, but calling to mind all that happened during the period of pilgrimage itself, on the journey *between* one place and another. In other words, the exterior journey of faithful following of the Spirit is reflected in an interior movement of the soul, a growing intensification of mood and feeling. Pilgrimage, as I shall seek to explain later, is a privileged period of testing, when the pilgrim learns to see familiar things from another angle and the unexpected as if for the first time. For it often happens that the rhythm of movement is punctuated by encounters and chance meetings that raise questions – and even cause something of a crisis.

Early in the *Autobiography* Ignatius recounts what must rank as the most unlikely example of interreligious 'dialogue' in the history of the Society of Jesus. On the road he falls into conversation with a Muslim, 'a Moor'. They speak together of the virgin birth, about which the Muslim has some reservations. He rides on, and the impetuous soldier in Ignatius works himself into a lather of indignation about what he feels is an insult to the dignity of Our Lady. Has he let her down? Should he avenge her honour? Full of righteous zeal he follows the man and reaches a fork in the road. The Muslim has taken the road to the town in search of an inn for the night. Ignatius is faced with a dilemma, whether to confront his adversary or let him go in peace. He decides to leave it to the mule on which he is riding to choose. Mercifully – for the sake of inter-community harmony in that part of Spain and the future of the Society of Jesus – the stolid mule plods on past the town. Ignatius recounts how 'Our Lord willed that, though the town was little more than thirty or forty paces away, and the road leading to it very broad and very good, the mule took the main road, and left the one for the town behind.'

By the time we get to the end of his little text, the pilgrim – now Superior General – has mellowed somewhat; the battles he fights are focused on a very different 'other' on behalf of the Society resisting intransigent ecclesiastical authorities. So why did Ignatius remember the story of the Muslim and the mule? Maybe he thought of it as a personal cautionary tale about the potentially catastrophic results of hasty, unthinking reactions. Maybe it also reminded him of his earlier experience of the discernment of spiritual influences, how the best of intentions are sometimes subject to the corrupting influence of 'the enemy of our human nature'. And what sort of lesson is he drawing from this bizarre incident? Note how Ignatius takes for granted that this is what 'Our Lord willed'. At first it might seem he is invoking a fideistic theology of divine intervention: ignore all the subtleties of natural causality, forget responsibility for ethical decision-making, and just stick with a comforting two-tier model of the Universe. That is very far from the 'Divine Majesty' Ignatius has come to know through long years of prayer and personal discernment. The world he contemplates is the world God contemplates. The mule's world, the Moor's world, is God's world, the very same world in which he himself is immersed, a world where he has learned how to touch into the mystery of the God of mercy and compassion.

His conviction that he is caught up in what he knows is *God*'s work does not leave him any less convinced of the truth of Catholic doctrine, but it no longer makes him feel compelled literally to stick the knife into those who fail to respond to it. This is a story, not about the building up of zeal for mission, but about faith and the maturing of faith, about the foundational act behind the practice of discernment which we looked at briefly in the first chapter. Discernment is not a decision-making mechanism, still less an intuition that reveals the 'right thing to do'. On the contrary, it has more to do with a healthy reticence that learns, all too painfully and trustingly, that the way forward begins by admitting one's doubts and ignorance and putting everything back into the hands of God. A little exchange from a modern novel about a world convulsed by religious passions and political intrigue may help to illustrate the point.

Gwen Griffith Dickson's intellectual thriller, *Bleedback*, centres around a major terrorist outrage in Iraq. The TV screens are full of carnage and mayhem, and the Middle East seems ready to explode into an intra-Islamic civil war. In the UK, self-appointed anti-Muslim demagogues and lordly secularists are united in shrill condemnation, convinced that the upsurge of violence will engulf the fragile fabric of community relations in a Shi'a–Sunni rivalry that has simmered since the earliest days of the Muslim *umma*. A gentle scholar, Ayatollah Arman Rastani, recently deported from the USA, quickly assumes the role of scapegoat number one. He is no contemporary version of Ignatius's fellow-pilgrim. His questions are less about the details of faith than existential dilemmas to do with the nexus between religion and politics. Called to play a leadership role for which he feels totally unqualified, he wants nothing more than to retire back to his home in the Iranian countryside. One evening he sits talking in the home of Sami, his life-long Jewish friend:

> Sami listened with hands folded and his chin resting on his hands. He spoke with his eyes closed. 'Arman, it's not a question of whether you go there, or stay here, or run away to this country or go back to that one. It's a question of whether you are going to fight or not.'
>
> Rastani's golden-centred irises vanished back into black. 'I'm not a fighter. And the horrible truth is that you can't fight and win against something like this. I don't know why it's happening, but I do know this. Whoever they are, they will not let me win. The most one can hope for is that it's over sooner rather than later. And that there's something left of me at the end of it.'
>
> 'My point is that it's not a question of location. It's something more existential. My gut feeling is that there is

some deeper decision that you have to make. I just sense you've been on the run from something ever since you were exiled from Iran. And running hasn't answered this existential question.'

Rastani's head swayed in a movement too slow and too tired to be a shake. 'I keep trying to do the right thing … and I'm not sure I ever have. It's not that I don't want to, that I have to struggle with my conscience. I struggle with my ignorance. I'm desperate to do the right thing, if only I knew what it was.'

'Then at least you are better than the rest of us.'

Conscience is not the issue, but ignorance. Right-minded, sincere, conscientious folk want to act, but are often unsure what precisely that might mean. To avenge the honour of the Mother of God? But if so, how? To expose and face down the malign forces fomenting global terror? But if so, how? So often it is that tricky 'how' question, with its existential and ethical implications, that causes the most acute dilemma. In a complex, pluralist world, convulsed by difference and division, how can one be confident of knowing enough in order to 'do the right thing'?

I once thought Ignatius's Rules for Discernment could be adapted as a set of useful guidelines for dialogue, giving partners a clear sense of where the Spirit was at work. I have long gone off that idea, not because the reasons and motivations behind other ways of life and thought are too complex and opaque to be reduced to sets of rules. That may be so, but it misses the point. Discernment is not about developing principles that can be applied from a lordly height on to situations that are often massively complicated, even shot through with trauma and discord. What is at stake here – and what will recur at various points in this book – is an account of discernment as a *virtuous activity* that springs from the humility of ignorance. Ignatius's little story of the Moor has about it a touch of the pious fable but that should not obscure traces of Rastani's dilemma. The *Exercises* are about ordering 'disordered tendencies', building the virtues of a Christlike existence, not revealing a blueprint for Christian action. At what point does one understand enough, are the issues clear enough, to take the risk of speaking and acting in a way that is not just religiously honest, but morally defensible?

## A Missionary Church

Where are the virtues of discernment – not just humility, but patience, fortitude and generosity – to be learned? In this chapter I want to argue that it is appropriate to invoke the pilgrimage metaphor to speak about the open-ended and often unpredictable process of interreligious dialogue as a journey. What stops this familiar image from descending into cliché is the common experience of dialogue as conversation, not alternating monologues but a free-moving informal exploration of shared points of concern. Whether we are talking about a debate between experts or an open-ended conversation between friends, dialogue 'happens' not with the exchange of position papers but in the encounter of *persons,* when superficial pleasantries are raised to a more serious level and, almost despite themselves, partners are drawn into something more serious and lasting.

Even that description may seem overly romantic. The practice of dialogue is not a straightforward journey towards truth. Human beings are never entirely transparent to themselves, let alone each other. While any meeting is to be conducted with a generosity of welcome that respects the stranger, it cannot be at the expense of critical witness to the integrity of truth. Thus the four types of dialogue that have emerged in the Christian churches in recent years – theological exchange, religious experience, common action and common life – are not alternatives to the witness the Church makes to the truth that is Christ, but variations appropriate to different times and places. What we are talking about in today's post-every-thing world is a shift internal to the Church's sense of mission, not a shift away from it.

*The annual London Inter-faith Pilgrimage for Peace gathers outside
the De Nobili Centre, Southall*

One of the simplest yet most memorable statements of the
Second Vatican Council came right at the end, in the penultimate
document to be promulgated. The Decree on the Missionary
Activity of the Church, known as *Ad Gentes* – 'To the Nations' –
says that the Church is 'missionary of its very nature' because it
participates in the mission or *sending* of Son and Spirit into the world
by the Father. This vision of a world made alive by the power of the
Trinitarian God was what drew Ignatius from his personal retreat in
Manresa away on solitary pilgrimage to the Holy Land in search of
God's will. In an extraordinary moment of mystical illumination, he
became convinced that his vocation was to be a companion – 'placed
by the Father with the Son', as he described it in the *Autobiography*.
If that was what started him on his own journey of faith, what kept
him going was the constant guidance of the Spirit – much as the
Spirit in the *Acts* goes ahead of the Apostles and leads the new Jesus
communities forward.

For the Catholic Church, it was a better-known document of the Council – *Nostra Aetate,* the celebrated Declaration on other religions – which in 1965 put the dialogue of religions firmly on the missionary map. Thirty years later, the Society of Jesus at its thirty-fourth General Congregation produced a commentary with two memorable phrases that sum up this new perspective. One is the 'service of faith' which goes back to the great ferment of pastoral outreach unleashed by the Council. The other is the 'culture of dialogue' which commends, not a new method of evangelisation, but a certain capacity to draw out the implications for the present situation of what God is already doing in transforming the world. If the former takes forward the commitment to the faith that does justice in response to God's 'preferential option for the poor', the latter builds up the 'dialogical spirit' in which all human relations are to be conducted for the sake of the common good. From Paul VI in *Ecclesiam Suam* to Francis in *Evangelii Gaudium,* all popes since the Second Vatican Council have emphasised how dialogue is as much a new experience for the Church as it is a mode of witnessing to the Gospel.

## Dialogue and the Word of God

Yet dialogue is *new* only in the sense that the Second Vatican Council retrieved an older, richer and more scripturally informed way of life and action on which the Church as a people of diverse cultures and background is based. In the wake of a Council which, as John O'Malley has noted, might almost be defined by its pastoral 'style', dialogue emerges as a much broader concept than is normally allowed. As a new *experience*, it begins with the reception of the Word of God by the worshipping and praying Church, and continues in the world of human relations as Good News is communicated under the guidance of the Spirit in words and deeds of all kinds.

In this sense the document on the Church's 'missionary activity' which ended the Council cannot be separated from the difficult discussions surrounding the document on Revelation, *Dei Verbum* – 'The Word of God' – with which it began. God does not reveal truths which the Church is *then* commissioned to proclaim to others. Rather, God reveals God's own self by calling a people and inviting them into a conversation of loving friendship. To make explicit a point made at the end of the last chapter, if the Word brings intelligibility and meaning into everyday encounters, then we human beings can be defined by our capacity to use language. We are in an important sense 'linguistic beings', called not just to read the mystery but to become adept in communicating its truth.

Dialogue enters the vocabulary of the Church as a mode or form of mission, essentially a variation within the Church's basic 'mission toolkit'. But it soon shifts away from pragmatic consider-ations about what is appropriate to a particular situation, and finds itself rooted in intrinsically theological categories, specifically in the Church's faith in the Trinitarian God where is discerned a witness of mutual love and interchange. The Church is 'missionary of its very nature', not because it is forever proclaiming the Gospel 'out there', but because its inner sacramental life reflects something of the inner life of God.

Two forms of mission can therefore be distinguished, although they intermingle with each other. Mission, understood in tradi-tional terms as proclamation, is based on the premise that the Church acts as a mediator of the Word; priority is given to speaking about what is known of the God revealed in Christ. On the other hand, mission, understood as the 'new experience' of dialogue, is more sensitive to the complexities of the inter-human encounter; the Church learns how to discern the promptings of God's Word by first listening to the Spirit of Christ already at work. Where the first form communicates directly through recourse to an appropri-ate act of public speaking, the second form operates at the margins of human interaction, where for whatever reason communication and understanding are difficult. One of the most familiar texts which retrieves this more patient dialogical form of mission is to be found in the First Epistle of Peter where a community suffering persecution is told to 'be prepared to make a defence to anyone who calls you to account for the hope that is in you, but do it with gentleness and reverence' (3:15). Faithfulness and openness, clarity of purpose and gentle reverence for the other, are the twin virtues that most characterise what *Lumen Gentium,* the Council's ground-breaking Constitution on the Church, refers to as the 'pilgrim Church' (§§ 48–51).

## Archetypal Journeys

My claim is that such a virtuous activity characterises men and women who, in their journeying through a pluralist world, have learned the wisdom that comes from experience. Pilgrimage is something of a 'pan-religious practice' with powerful examples ranging from the Muslim Hajj to Makka to the Varkari Panth in Vaishnava Hinduism. But how far can pilgrimage act as a genuinely *inter*-religious metaphor for the spiritual life? Can the connotations that surround different religious accounts of journeys, path and pilgrimages be smoothed out into an overarching pattern? Or does that reduce richness of meaning to a few abstractions?

There is, for sure, no single archetypal journey. In his engagement with Western or 'Greek' philosophy, as he calls it, Emmanuel Levinas draws an interesting distinction between the journey of Abraham and that of Odysseus. The journey of Odysseus is typical of Western man, Levinas tells us, eager to try everything, to taste everything, to 'travel the universe'. Yet this same universe is also complex and ambiguous; we are surrounded on all sides by good and evil, and our desire for mastery, the desire to be in control, means taking a risk. We want adventure, but we also want security. We want to be like Odysseus on his great journey of discovery, but we also want to be sure of coming back home to something familiar. The image of Ithaca is what keeps us going, the memory of 'home'.

Abraham's journey has about it a different sort of logic, and plays with the security/risk dilemma in another way, one that is deeply counter-intuitive. Abraham sets out in answer to a call from beyond, responding to the invitation that comes from the unknown. If the journey of Odysseus takes the form of a cyclical return, Abraham's is a much more open-ended exploration of an unknown future, the truth of which lies ultimately not in his hands but with the mysterious source of one who calls. This, of course, is the tradition the people of Israel accept, what Levinas calls a 'difficult freedom'. In what sense, he asks, were the people 'free' to accept Torah? Certainly it appears at first like a constraint, an imposition. But this would be to forget the true nature of Torah as gift, a freeing grace that the people pledge to accept – and practise. And it is in the *practice,* in the daily discipline of prayer and study, that they come to understand more precisely what God is asking, indeed *what God is like.*

Just as there is some universal truth in the story of Odysseus, so in the story of Abraham human beings confront a deep truth about themselves and the God who calls them into a new freedom. Levinas makes the point that human freedom is not opposed to divine authority; more positively, freedom is something chosen, what comes with responsibility, by *responding* generously to what is given. The 'difficult freedom' of Judaism does not spring from some sort of examination of God's credentials, submitting God's Word to rational scrutiny, still less from a naive fideism. It depends on a sort of foundational trust, a basic attitude of openness and welcome that allows for – even encourages – a movement into the unknown.

Are the two stories – a cyclical movement of return to beginnings and a more linear sense of progress elsewhere – opposed to each other? Or is there, perhaps, a complementarity between them, in which the one works together with the other – a spiralling movement, perhaps, not adding a bright new idea or inner experience but a repetition and retrieval, acting as a sort of lens through which the familiar can be glimpsed from an unfamiliar angle? And if that is the case, perhaps other cultures add other lenses, other frameworks within which 'the Whole' is to be glimpsed?

I have often wondered what the archetypal Asian story would be, and how, for instance, the two great Epics of Hinduism or the enlightenment narrative of the Buddha might contribute to a richer dialogue. Rama, the great hero of the *Ramayana*, sets out on a great journey in pursuit of the wicked demon Ravana who has carried off his wife Sita. This is no tale of risk-taking revenge, but the story of an indomitable loyalty in which the demands of *dharma* – truth or justice – are served by daily acts of devotion, one step at a time. Similar tales are told in the *Mahabharata,* a massive compendium of Hindu devotional mythology that includes the single most popular of all Hindu texts, the *Bhagavad Gita.* Neither of the Epics nor the *Puranas,* the 'tales of old', are history in the ordinary sense of the term as used in the West. But that is not to say they do not give people a similar way of anchoring present reality in relation to what is known of the past, the 'deep structure' of memory that shapes the psyche of a people. If there is a Hindu counterpart to the Hebrew Abrahamic journey and the Hellenistic Odyssean journey, it has something to do with a transformative movement or reintegration into Holy Mystery or Brahman – a word from a Sanskrit root meaning growth or expansion.

## Facing the Centre

Let me give an example from the world of Tamil *bhakti* or devotional spirituality. Not far from the town where I spent those months of the Jesuit tertianship is a temple built on a steep hill called Palni, a word that means 'fruit'. The story is told of the two sons of Śiva, Ganesh and Murugan, whose father promised a special prize to whichever of the two went around the world the faster. Murugan, always determined and powerful, got on his peacock and set off as fast as he could go. Ganesh, more ponderous but also more canny, stood up and slowly trotted round his parents, saying to them, 'You are the centre of my world'. He got the prize, the 'fruit'.

When Murugan came back he was not best pleased to find what his brother had done and retired to the top of the hill where he sat and sulked, demanding to be placated by his fearful devotees.

'History' and 'mythology' fade into each other. Most pilgrims in the Hindu tradition visit the shrine of the god-figure, not in order to get in touch with the site that holds the story – as Ignatius longed to do in Jerusalem – but to have *darshan*, 'sight' or revelation of the Blessed Lord. Over the centuries a mystique has grown up around the temple itself. Like so many of the great temples of Tamil Nadu it has come to act as a microcosm of the Universe itself, ordering the dangerous spiritual forces associated with the god into a harmony. From the still centre, the very heart of the Universe itself, the divine power of creation emanates. Pilgrims, glimpsing the *gopuram* or tower appearing on the horizon as they walk across the plain, find themselves being gently beckoned towards the sacred centre.

The building itself has an integrative power, sometimes – as at the town of Palni – set on a hill, sometimes near a river, symbolising a crossing-place, and sometimes at the very centre of a great city that appears to grow out of the many sets of squares and courts that surround the still point. The architecture tells its own story, and provides its own archetype of the spiritual life. The devotee is caught into a process of emanation and return, back and forth, learning how to 'face the centre' where time appears to stand still. As massive artefacts that represent the mystery of Brahman itself, these structures seem deliberately designed to overwhelm the imagination. But maybe there is also something else – something more humane and less overwhelmingly cosmic in its dimensions – in play here.

I was once visiting a big Catholic shrine outside the city of Chennai and was intrigued to see hundreds of young men devoutly lining up to pay their respects at a prominent Marian shrine. The majority, I was told by my guide, were not Catholics. What were they doing there? What attracted them?

It seems unlikely, and even quite paradoxical, that culture-specific memories can somehow become hospitable and positively welcoming. And yet Ignatius, with his intellectual roots in the Christian humanism of the Renaissance, passed on an attitude of respectful curiosity to his companions. His metaphorical pilgrimage had Jerusalem talking to Rome, Abraham talking to Odysseus. Later generations of Jesuits broadened out that dialogue into an imaginative correlation that crossed many boundaries. Now, no doubt there is this much that all stories of journey have in common – whether, as with the people of Israel, a much-anticipated return from Exile or, as with Hindu pilgrims everywhere, a more personal pursuit of *darshan*. All are versions of that peculiar quality which makes us human: our capacity to narrate our existence, to bring order into the passing of time by piecing together the fragments of memory that give a meaningful framework to life as a whole. And yet the very journey can become strangely counter-cultural, not reimposing memories but *releasing* them. That may be because the focus on the fluidity of movement challenges the temptation to claim ownership, to insist on the dominating perspective. Being constantly on the move acts as a great leveller, bringing people from different backgrounds together to cross borders and build new relations.

That may account for the attraction of pilgrimage as a religious practice that mends Levinas's security/adventure dilemma. As a liturgy that re-enacts foundational memories, it both offers a map across a strange terrain and anchors devotees in a tangible or, to use a Catholic term that seems appropriate, sacramental form. The idea that progress is made by moving elsewhere is countered by the insistence that *this* is the place, *this* is the time. In this way, the journey and *the time it takes* often turn out to be more important than the arrival, offering a counter to the obsession with achieving fixed results.

*Pilgrimage as Interreligious Practice*

I'll come back to that last point shortly. But first I want to change tack slightly and say something about the experience of interreligious pilgrimage. The one with which I was involved for many years – the Westminster Interfaith Pilgrimage for Peace – was started by the late Brother Daniel Faivre in Southall more than three decades ago.

Those who knew Daniel will remember him as an interreligious genius with an extraordinary flair for liturgies, pilgrimages and celebrations of all kinds. A self-described 'bombastic Frenchman', he was by training and inclination a teacher. Although a very private person, but not exactly shy, he knew how to communicate, and how to catch and keep the attention of his audience. He trained as a teacher in London, became a missionary in Thailand and returned to the UK in the late 1970s where he began Westminster Interfaith, originally a parish-based group which quickly became an agency for the Roman Catholic diocese of Westminster.

What I most value from my time with Daniel was watching him build practices of faith that were genuinely and richly inclusive. He knew how to take the ordinary familiar rhythms of prayer and juxtapose them with symbols – water, candles, flowers – so as to make people from different faiths think about the interreligious significance of what they often took for granted. The annual peace pilgrimage had many such moments of 'crossing over', some planned, some spontaneous and unexpected, but always binding a motley group of people together so that they genuinely enjoyed and appreciated each other's company. Each year we visited a different part of London, wending our way from one place of worship to another, synagogue followed by mosque followed by church followed by gurdwara. It could be quite physical, and timing was everything. To be fair to our hosts we needed to be at particular places on time. Keeping an unruly gaggle of pilgrims moving together was never easy, not least when the local police, who were usually so laid-back and helpful ('Never been at such a nice demo' was one comment I

*Theravada Buddhist Vihara of Amaravati*

recall) were getting a little anxious over health and safety.

One year, Daniel proclaimed what he called a 'rally'. Packed into a fair number of cars we visited various religious sites north of London, finishing with the Buddhists at Amaravati tucked away on the top of a hill above Berkhamsted. Everything went well, apart from the tendency of the less confident drivers to follow each other into unlikely rural byways. (These were the days before the nice voice on the satnav relays the reassuring message that 'you have arrived at your destination'.) Usually, however, we walked. The main object of the exercise was to get to a strange place, to cross the threshold, and experience strangeness for its own sake. But what happened on the journey turned out to be no less important. Against the rhythm of the walk were set moments of interpersonal encounter and conversation.

If it were not for the former, the latter would not have happened. It was never a matter of sampling a bit of religious exotica. The hospitality given and received put each community we visited at the centre of the exercise, reminding everyone of the importance of that reciprocity and respect that is essential to all interreligious practice. Sometimes I am the host, sometimes the guest, and there is an appropriate mode of behaviour that goes along with each role. There is a value in the way a community is formed on the way; the pilgrimage takes on a sort of corporate personality which makes it easier to negotiate that always daunting moment of crossing the threshold into another world. One remark has always stayed with me: 'I would never have dared to go into a place like that on my own.'

Getting it right can be tricky. There was one famous occasion when we arrived at the Friends' House a little late and needed to be speedy in getting through what would in ordinary circumstances have been a relaxing period of silent contemplative prayer. The first elder told us that we would stay in silence until he shook hands with the second elder to signal the prayer was over. We sat and we sat ... and we sat. No sign of an end. We could not afford to keep our next hosts waiting. Maybe the elders had gone to sleep, or were they in a gentle ecstasy? I looked at Daniel and Daniel looked at me. Eventually, I took the initiative and said a spontaneous prayer; we got up and left as graciously as possible. As we walked quickly down the hill to the last visit, a Quaker from the group caught up with me, smiled and said, 'Nice try, Michael; almost right'. I don't think offence was taken.

*Times and Places*

It is telling that the first response of Ignatius to that early experience of conversion was to go on pilgrimage. Jerusalem was central to his new-found but curiously ill-directed religious zeal. The same desire for the holy places caught the imagination of the first companions until they too were forced to reconsider. Did something similar happen to our interreligious pilgrims on their way round London's places of worship? I don't know, but it would be a little surprising if experience did not exceed, or at least challenge, expectations. Allowing oneself to become the guest of an unknown host can be quite disorientating. Hence the two themes which the practice of pilgrimage holds in tension: taking *time* and attending to *place*.

I started with Ignatius the pilgrim, recalling his early experience of following the life-giving Spirit of Christ. Let me finish with a thought from Michel de Certeau, a contemporary Jesuit thinker for whom life was always a voyage into the unknown. Theologian, historian of Christian mysticism, psychotherapist and cultural critic, de Certeau was fascinated by the 'inner logic' behind the ways in which people identify themselves in relationship to their environment and each other. He drew a basic contrast between a *strategic* control, which seeks to establish its own place from which it can dominate the environment and the 'others' that inhabit it, and a more open-ended, free-wheeling, *tactical* adjustment, which works with the lack of any space of its own. If the former characterises the attitude of the powerful, the latter says something about how the weak are forever working *within* the cracks and fissures that characterise their lives and which they spend their time learning how to exploit.

De Certeau's point is that the strategies of the powerful are a calculating response to the ownership of places, while the tactics of the weak depend on a careful use of time – waiting patiently, biding their time, looking out for the right moment. He is trying to expose the fallacy behind the assumption that the world 'out there' is a sort of 'arena' to be dominated by human action, with nothing hidden, a sort of grand *tabula rasa* with everything open to control. Rather, what human beings share is a much more mysterious, ill-defined environment which can never be mastered. Instead of being open to exploitation, it needs instead to be 'mapped out' in terms of the rhythms and harmonies which are *already built* into it.

This takes us back to the early Jesuits and their novel approach to mission, which we shall explore later as 'inculturation'. The first task is to understand and grow accustomed to 'places', not just sacred buildings and what goes on in them but more metaphorical places which keep the record and teach the wisdom that arises from human beings' attempts to find a way through this mysterious world. At first it sounds very straightforward: a matter of zealous engagement with the world as we encounter it, with all its darkness and danger. All very admirable. But, as Levinas reminds us, movements of domination can do violence – and the task of philosophy, he says, is to minimise violence. For philosophy let us substitute our religious visions and practices, ways of looking at the world that have a moral force. In a rapidly changing globalised world, communities of faith no longer inhabit discrete enclaves (though tragically many still try). Walking together is a more complex business than walking apart; I am less in control, less able to organise things to suit my particular interests. Careful discernment is always necessary – a matter not of getting the right answer but asking the right question. Gradually, as the pilgrim takes time to recognise echoes of the familiar built into places of all kinds – 'haunting' them, to use a very de Certeau word – so one learns a set of virtuous responses. To drop the claim to mastery and to grant a place within the space of our world to 'the other' – both other persons and the environment itself which we ignore at our peril – can be an exercise in freedom through which the most important of human and divine values begin to manifest themselves.

# CHAPTER THREE

## *Image and Interruption*

THE FIRST chapter opened in what is now known as Old Goa, the final resting place of St Francis Xavier. The second began with a reminiscence from the *Autobiography* of Ignatius, a remark on the quayside in Barcelona where 'the pilgrim' is about to embark on the next stage of his quest. This chapter will end with references to two more significant places, as if to make the point that human lives do not just begin in particular places, at particular moments in time, but are surrounded by the memories that are etched into buildings and crafted into artefacts. We exist as 'linguistic creatures', capable of shaping our environment through the places we inhabit, the things we make, the stories we tell about ourselves and the conversations that follow from encounters with others. Hindu temples, to recall the example introduced earlier, are not just places for worship, but markers on the spiritual map, providing points of focus and orientation that make 'space' habitable and secure. Something analogous can be said for the way other sacred centres can be read as traces of the human search for meaning.

Let me repeat the point made at the end of the last chapter: there is always the risk that the natural human tendency to dominate and control our environment may do unthinking violence to the life-giving rhythms already inscribed there. At their best, our religious institutions are proof against this tendency, because their first instinct is to preserve the memories that make the everyday more than a series of fleeting moments, but rather sources of hope. Of course, religions are not always at their best; they can be corrupted by our venal instincts just as all human institutions can. All the more reason to be clear about what precisely 'religion' is: not a gathering of sacred phenomena hovering untouched above the messiness of 'real life', but a *source of transformative value*. The religions embedded in local neighbourhoods are not alternative sets of ideas about ultimate truth, not even collections of ancient memories and folk culture but, more profoundly, channels for that extraordinary creative energy which flows through human lives, renewing the best of our aspirations and correcting the worst.

Later I shall have more to say about religion in such dynamic terms as a source of wise teaching and learning. I shall use the little phrase, 'the middle of things', in order to stress that all religion, and *all religions*, are not escape mechanisms into some alternative heavenly universe, but ways of enabling human beings to come to terms with what makes them most deeply human. Let me start with Ignatius as an exemplary teacher, whose particular genius was to connect memory to the present moment and to inspire others to do the same.

*Introductions to Prayer*

Ignatian spirituality is often characterised as 'imaginative contemplation'. In this kind of prayer, I read a passage from the Gospel and allow myself to be drawn into the story, listening to the words, pondering what is said, observing what happens, making a personal response to the drama. In some ways, this is no more than a variation on the medieval monastic practice of *lectio divina*, with its fourfold sequence of reading, meditation, prayer and contemplation. There are, however, many other forms of prayer recommended in the *Spiritual Exercises*, from more reasoned 'considerations' to the affective 'application of the senses'. All have a part to play in the journey of faith that gradually transforms our sense of who we are.

If prayer is like a pilgrimage, then the rhythms of its movement enable us to build a discerning sensibility by which we become attuned not just to the many ways in which the Word of God resonates between scriptural texts and the times and places of our ordinary lives. The discernment taught by Ignatius demands an *active listening* that seeks to open up new perspectives on familiar themes. But if, like Ignatius, we are seeking to follow the insistent prompting of the Spirit, how do we listen, and what precisely are we listening *for*?

In order to approach that question, let me start from the text of the *Exercises*, with the series of preliminaries or preludes with which Ignatius prefaces each meditation. Back in the heady 1960s the impatient novice in me found them a little tedious, but later I came to realise that they have an important role to play in introducing and structuring the movement of prayer. In most cases there are three such preludes. After what Ignatius calls 'the usual preliminary prayer' – that everything be directed towards the praise of God – we are to consider 'the history' (usually the content of the scriptural narrative), make a 'composition of place', and then 'ask for what I desire'.

This third preliminary acts as a constant reminder of the overall purpose of the *Exercises*, given in the very first Annotation as 'to get rid of all disordered affections'. Making the *Exercises* may lead to particular outcomes – a deepening of one's life of prayer or the making of a decision about the future – but it will always involve a conversion of heart, or what I will call in a later chapter the 'right channelling of desire'. There I open up a dialogue with Buddhism which will, I hope, bring out some powerful resonances between the Buddha's Way of Enlightenment and the pilgrimage of prayer commended by Ignatius. It would, however, be a mistake to skate over the first two preliminaries: setting out 'the history' and 'seeing the place'. Taken together, they illustrate the constant preference of Ignatius for the concrete and local over the abstract and general. He always begins where his exercitant is, in the here and now, as if to ensure that the use of the imagination is never empty self-indulgence but a rooting in the true reality of everyday existence.

These two preliminaries are not imaginative constructs but reminders that both past and present are to be taken with all seriousness as points of interaction between God and the world. For any particular individual, the first task is to effect a correlation between the two, to make the events in the life of Christ speak to the events that make up the life-story of the person making the *Exercises*. As noted earlier, the key principles of Ignatius are intended to form instinctive responses that become habituated as virtues of living and loving. What is often translated from the Latin text as 'composition of place' is more exactly rendered, according to the Spanish original, as 'composing oneself', with connotations of 'pulling oneself together' or, more simply, 'recollecting oneself'. Rather than build some sort of imaginary picture of the place – the Temple where Jesus was presented as a child or the Lake of Galilee where he preached to the people – one attends to the self-image that emerges in a particular place, the responses it provokes, the feelings that arise in this particular place. In that sense 'place' is used loosely to refer to any human experience orientated around a moment in space and time.

This comes out clearly when Ignatius uses the term for the first time. He asks us to meditate on sin, but precisely *not* to indulge in any morbid obsession with guilt. On the contrary, we are to recognise both our need for healing *and* God's offer of reconciliation. Michael Ivens comments that

> before coming to consider the effects of sin in history, one puts oneself into a situation of loneliness, irrationality, and disharmony with both self and creation, which is the situation of every human being in so far as he or she is under the thrall of sin. The imagery recalls the parable of the Prodigal Son.

The phrase Luke uses in the Gospel gets to the heart of the matter.

Sitting in the pig-sty, far from the family home, the son 'comes to himself' (15:17). This is perhaps the most powerful example in the *Exercises* of the two preliminaries of 'history' and 'composition'. A particular place evokes memory. By focusing on objective experiences of sin, failure and tragedy, I 'compose myself' by building up a deep sense of human sinfulness set within the overwhelming abundance of God's grace. This dynamic of loss and redemption which is definitive of the human condition comes back time and again in the *Exercises*, albeit less dramatically, with the repeated demand to recognise and respect the terms of the encounter with divine love, by whatever means or form it is mediated.

What Ignatius is looking for, of course, are signs of a change of heart, a resolution to order one's life by a careful attention to the destructive nature of human desire. And, as he makes clear, it is the revelation of God's love for humankind through the Word made incarnate in Christ that makes such a conversion possible. That's where his faith takes him, the direction of its fulness. Nevertheless, as *preliminary introductions* to generous and open prayer, 'history' and 'composition' are practices that all people of faith can share. They build a religious sensibility that touches the edges of another world and crosses all religious boundaries, forming a capacity to *read* the sacred.

## The Space of the World

With a touch of Ignatian spirituality by way of introduction, let me take up that theme of place. I'm thinking not just of sacred places – grand Catholic cathedrals and sprawling Hindu temples – but the backyards and the next street where those strange edges are becoming increasingly familiar. The very word 'globalisation' acts as a reminder that in the age of instant communication and ease of travel, the border lines between peoples, religions and cultures can no longer be drawn with the assurance of an earlier era. Yet for all the talk of cultural hybrids, in which ways of looking at our one world become saturated with different symbols and values, reactions to the plurality of religions and cultures are mixed and even confused. What some people find intriguing and enriching, others find threatening to their sense of security. Anyone beginning an Ignatian type of meditation with a contemporary 'composition of place' would quickly come up against a degree of ambivalence.

The Second Vatican Council was nothing if not a call to the Church to 'compose itself' in this ambivalent modern world. Its declaration on other religions, *Nostra Aetate,* has inspired Christians everywhere and many people from other faiths, not just with a new vision of the harmony of creation but with practical principles for engaging generously and judiciously with each other:

> In our time, when day by day humankind is being drawn more closely together and the ties between different peoples are becoming stronger, the Church is giving deeper attention to her relationship with non-Christian religions.

So begins this extraordinary text, which is rightly celebrated for its rapprochement with Judaism, giving rise to the affirmation – implicit in the words, the Jews 'remain most dear to God' – that the Sinai Covenant still stands. Once that move has been made, and another community of faith is accepted as legitimate in the sight of God, it is but a short step to recognising the possibility that God may be present in the world in ways of which the Church knows nothing. And yet in *our* time – in *this* time – little more than fifty years on, interreligious engagement has become more fraught. Antisemitism has not gone away; Islamophobia is on the rise; religiously-inspired violence in different parts of the world poses a serious threat to the cohesion of pluralist societies everywhere; religion itself is under severe scrutiny in a culture where the default option is rapidly becoming secular atheism. Small wonder that there are a number of theological reactions to our contemporary 'composition of place'.

Catholic Christians use the term 'inclusivism' to refer to the theological vision of *Nostra Aetate*. The beliefs of other religious traditions are contained or 'included' in what Christians confess as the Paschal Mystery of the death and resurrection of Christ. A much more sophisticated version is to be found in Karl Rahner's idea that the conscientious atheist or right-minded Buddhist is *really* an Anonymous Christian. This sounds quite patronising, but it is important to note that Rahner is not concerned in the first place with the status of other faiths, but with the *credibility of Christian faith*. How to maintain the integrity of the Church in an apparently faithless or, at any rate, increasingly post-Christian world? The concept of the Anonymous Christian is best understood, not as a bit of genial Catholic imperialism, but as arising out of Rahner's theology of the human person as intrinsically open or orientated to what he calls Holy Mystery.

Rahner's basic presupposition is that the relationship between God and humanity contains an immanent dimension; that is to say that within human experience are contained the seeds of our understanding of God. Human beings share a 'pre-apprehension' of unlimited possibility. All experiences which take us out of ourselves – most obviously that of love, knowing at the deepest level the truth revealed in another human being – act as sources of transformation. Corresponding to this human orientation towards the Divine is the Divine offer of self-communication to human beings, what Rahner calls the 'supernatural existential'. Human existence is characterised by a universal orientation towards the Divine *and* a purely gratuitous offer, an offer that is additional to what is offered to human nature as such. For Rahner, a tacit expectation of hearing God's Word in the radical openness of the human spirit's love and searching forms a sort of 'natural template' within which to understand the Paschal Mystery of Jesus Christ. Such a realisation depends, of course, upon God's initiative, but it originates as God's answer to the quest for human fulfilment implied in the structures of the human spirit. On the one hand, there is a 'categorial' or historically instantiated revelation; on the other, there is one that is unlimited and transcendental in its scope. These two dimensions of this contemporary version of what the early Fathers of the Church used to call *preparatio evangelica* – a 'preparation for the Gospel' – are not held together easily. How do we acknowledge continuity with ordinary everyday human experience while still allowing for that specificity of Christian faith which recognises that something new has been revealed in Christ?

In addressing such a question, it is important to remember that we are dealing with a *theological intuition* rather than a thesis about whether there is salvation 'outside the Church'. In speaking of the non-Christian as an 'Anonymous Christian', Rahner makes explicit a principle recognised by the Second Vatican Council: that it is important to allow for the possibility that the Spirit works in ways and forms which the Church may not know about. Rahner's later work, especially in *Foundations of Christian Faith*, is more nuanced, focusing on the action of the Spirit in bringing to fruition that truth about God which is revealed in Christ. Let me postpone that debate until the penultimate chapter of this book, and stay instead with the Ignatian preliminaries with which I began this chapter.

Like all good Ignatians, Rahner is caught up in this mystery of creation-and-redemption. I have long thought that, properly speaking, there is only one theological question: how can God enter into this world of ours and still remain God? In addressing it, theologians have developed sophisticated theologies which cover the great themes of Christian living, from Trinitarian theology and Christology to ecclesiology and missiology. Yet, in an increasingly diverse world, they have not got very far in accounting for the diversity and variety of religious culture, its complexity and richness, its sheer unremitting difference or 'otherness'. Are all the multiform things that people do in their temples and synagogues and mosques, all that goes on there, purely contingent phenomena? In other words, are they of little meaning or significance? Or, just possibly, are they to be interpreted as signs of the creating-and-redeeming God whom Christians affirm to be at work in our midst through the Spirit of Christ?

These are the questions a theology of religions seeks to address, questions that seek, not a magisterial ordering of religious phenomena, but a more humble reading of what is always an infinitely mysterious world. The point I made earlier is that 'reading the history' and 'composing oneself' are themselves spiritual exercises that are not religion-specific; Ignatius's concern is to root prayer in the concrete circumstances of the everyday, with attention being paid to context and circumstances. That history, as already noted, has a strong focus on the tradition: what has brought *me* to this position now, what *I* owe to the past and the inner life of my particular community. And the 'composition', with its focus on the present, is inseparable from life alongside other persons and communities, not to mention the secular world and popular culture. To repeat de Certeau's point again: places – and what goes on there – enable us to build some sort of 'map' with which the 'space' of the world can be appreciated.

### Memory and Remembrance

It thus makes sense to see the prayerful attention Ignatius gives to the everyday as an act of remembrance, literally *re-membering*, putting things back together again. This is less another version of 'inclusivism', with its connotations of subordinating a lesser to a more superior tradition, than a way of learning with and from the circumstances – and people – one encounters. This is where all theology, and particularly a theology of religions, begins: not with 'top-down' theory but with practice, with the observation of, and critical commentary on, what people of faith actually *do*. Ignatius was not, of course, interested in any sort of theology of religions; it would be anachronistic to expect otherwise. On the other hand, he was always attentive to the feelings and responses evoked by all manner of everyday human experiences. God, to repeat, is to be found in *all things*.

Let me give an example of the sort of thing I mean by going

*Memorial to Indian soldiers killed fighting in the First World War*

back to the pilgrimage theme. On 11 November 2018, I engaged in a personal ritual of remembrance. That morning, I took part in the national commemoration of the end of the First World War. In the afternoon, I found myself alongside gaggles of people of all ages out on the South Downs overlooking the city of Brighton, where I was born. We were looking for a war memorial called the *Chattri*, meaning 'umbrella'. It looks more like a relic from Mughal India than the standard Lutyensesque monolith, but it works well as a remembrance of a far-away land, reminding us that more than a million Indian soldiers fought for the British Empire and some seventy-five thousand were killed.

Why is it here? What resonances does this particular composition of place conjure up? During the war, wounded soldiers were brought back to hospitals all over England. Many Indians came to Brighton and those who succumbed to their wounds were cremated on a pyre set in a fold on the Downs. Opened in 1921 by the Prince of Wales, the *Chattri* is marked by a moving inscription:

> To the memory of all Indian soldiers who gave their lives for their King-Emperor in the Great War, this monument, erected on the site of the funeral pyre where the Hindus and Sikhs who died in hospital at Brighton passed through the fire, is in grateful admiration and brotherly affection dedicated.

One of the places used as a makeshift hospital was the Royal Pavilion, the most extraordinary royal palace in the UK. Built for the Prince Regent who made Brighton famous as a holiday centre, it was inherited by Queen Victoria. She was, however, not amused by it, and never went there. So it passed to the local council and was used for a variety of purposes. My father, a little boy during the First World War, retained vivid memories of Sikh soldiers, bearded and turbaned, sitting out in the sun. 'The council thought it would make them feel at home,' he mused. Possibly – but inside the Pavilion the decoration is very Chinese. It is as much a wonderful example of the Oriental Renaissance as it is a monument to colonialism. When the Romantics were not colonising foreign lands and plundering art works, they did a fairly good job of pinching ideas and domesticating exotic images for consumption 'back home'. This eccentric building makes an important statement about the British love affair with India. After the austere rationalist Enlightenment, philosophers, poets and artists turned to the 'Mysterious East' to cultivate the affective rather than the cognitive dimension of human nature. There they discovered another side of themselves mirrored in what many took to be a lost world, now created anew: Europe's 'other half'.

I suspect very few of the pilgrims traipsing the footpath to the *Chattri* that afternoon were thinking about the 'Oriental Renaissance' or the history of the Raj. A few might have been recalling an India they knew, the tourist India of Mughal palaces and the beautiful beaches of Goa. Some might have been entertaining vivid local memories, like mine, of family and childhood. All of us, I am sure, would have pondered for a moment the tragedy and waste of war, the sacrifice of all those who 'passed through the fire'. Places with their own founding memories, especially places with the tangible form of a monument, remind us that human lives are worth remembering for their own sake. And, mysteriously, they touch into something much bigger and almost overwhelming in its power. The act of remembrance, putting things back together again, takes us deep into whatever it is that makes us human – and reveals traces of the divine.

The theme of memory and remembrance runs through these chapters, not as a technical philosophical problem, but as one of the largely unregarded foundations on which culture is built. We take it for granted that we can remember the past, that we are formed by memories, that the little boy stimulated by a landscape of green hills and exotic buildings is somehow continuous with the older man who muses on more complex networks of persons, events and encounters of all kinds. I'm always fascinated by how past, present and future are brought into a correlation, how we keep faith with the past and manage somehow to remain hopeful about a future that is, strictly speaking, unknown. The challenge, it seems to me, is to allow our past to form our future without letting it dominate it; we cannot escape our past, but we can come to terms with it. Indeed, we *must* come to terms with it.

### Life in the Middle of Things

Any serious reflection on the contemporary phenomenon of religious pluralism very quickly moves from the 'problem of the other' – how 'they' can be said to relate to 'us' – to questions that affect the human condition as a whole: what makes us '*us*', how as human persons we relate to our world and each other. *Nostra Aetate*'s practical principles of 'conversation and collaboration' respond to a new context, raising complex questions about identity and belonging, and what can and cannot be shared with others. This is where Ignatius's 'composition of place' can help to build a spirituality, and thus a theology, of religions. In introducing a mood of prayerful attention to the present moment, it asks us to attend to everything that has brought us to the here and now, life in 'the middle of things'. While it is much more broadly conceived than focusing on places of worship, that is not to underestimate the power of religious places to focus the mind on the most significant questions that form and challenge all persons of faith.

Whether we are thinking about a war memorial in the shape of an Indian *chattri*, a tiny wayside shrine next to a crossroads in an Indian town, or a mosque built in memory of a Sufi sheikh somewhere in the Middle East, religious buildings take any number of forms and meet a variety of needs, practical and spiritual. While their origins may be lost in time, in all religions are to be found sites for ritual performance, spaces where a community can congregate, dwellings for holy men and women, and pilgrimage centres which preserve vital memories and attract devotees from far and wide. Hindu *mandirs* and Sikh *gurdwaras*, Buddhist *viharas* and Christian churches, are not just variations on some common cultural pattern, but icons in brick, wood and stone which speak eloquently of the key symbols and stories of faith.

It is important to relate buildings and their religious decoration to what goes on there, to the human lives they support. They witness not just to some sort of divine presence but to the identity of a community, its values and its sense of self-confidence. In the UK and Ireland in recent decades we have witnessed the building of many fine new places of worship. There is much to admire here – and learn from. Such a shift in our national cultures contributes immensely to the stock of what, to use the jargon, is called 'social capital', the glue which holds an increasingly pluralist society together. Not that everything in the relationship between religions is ever straightforward. Physical buildings do not directly contribute to interreligious dialogue; only persons can do that. Nevertheless, without the support that places provide for religious life, and the opportunities they open up for hospitality between faiths, our capacity for mutual understanding would be significantly reduced.

Being 'in the middle of things' is not just a feature of our feckless post-modern world. I have long been fascinated by a phrase I stumbled upon years ago. Gillian Rose makes a distinction between the 'holy middle', where we are all at home and secure and protected, and what she dubs 'the broken middle'. This 'middle' – what we might call the space in which human beings interact with each other – is never finished; it is always broken and therefore in need of mending. And that mending has a political face: it raises questions about how the individual relates to the communal and how the communities that constitute 'the people' relate to the State. That is not to say that the new mosques and temples are all in need of constant attention, only that the sacred landscape they support, and the wider secular dimensions of that landscape with which they are always bound up – institutions of education, commerce and the law – always demand sustained attention. The good politician is constantly attuned to such stresses and strains. The good theologian can do nothing less. In the introduction to his book *On Christian Theology*, Rowan Williams argues that the theologian's task is to observe and comment on what the community does. That includes not just the formal ritual and the religious life that flows from it, but also the ordinary ways we human beings respond to each other, and to the cultures, customs and institutions we construct to express our sense of who we are.

## Theological Hospitality

We shall keep coming back to the spiritual and theological value of places, if only to repeat the point, in good Ignatian pedagogical fashion, that they enable 'composition', the building up of the sense of self. In exploring the purposive intent of sacred structures, my aim is to relate such external manifestations of faith to the wider religious framework of spirituality, ritual, prayer, meditation and social engagement of all kinds. This, however, is not to presume upon some over-arching scheme that links religions together. Whether or not that exists is beside the point. My concern is with what the actual practice of faith, and the interaction of persons, says about the spiritual journey. If you want a theological 'model', it is that of hospitality.

*St Ethelburga's Centre for Dialogue and Reconciliation*

Let us explore that point by visiting another place. The church of St Ethelburga on Bishopsgate in the City of London is one of very few medieval churches that survived the Great Fire of 1666. Having come through the blitz with only modest damage, it was then half-destroyed by the IRA bombing of 1993. It is now an ecumenical centre for peace and reconciliation, and its events reach out beyond London to establish and promote interreligious un-derstanding at many levels. In the courtyard behind the church is a handsome Bedouin tent which is used for Scriptural Reasoning gatherings. As the name implies, Scriptural Reasoning is about cul-tivating a particular 'scriptural rationality', learning how to discern the 'logic' that is contained in scripture, how ideas and stories and symbols give rise to thought by evoking memories, challenging as-sumptions, provoking the imagination. When the groups that prac-tise Scriptural Reasoning come together, they are not interested in teasing out some theological consensus, but extending the bounds of friendship – or, as nicely put by one regular participant, 'improv-ing the quality of our disagreements'.

For a moment let us stay in the tent with its evocation of a strangely life-giving desert wilderness. Sitting here, listening to various interpretations of sacred texts, one is reminded of the pa-triarchs of Israel graciously welcoming the stranger. And it makes me think that theology should be understood in such a way: as generous, yet respectful, hospitality to what is 'other', which yet, with deeper acquaintance, appears not-so-other. Still, hospitality means taking a risk. The stranger welcomed into the tent is a po-tential friend, but may be an enemy. That does not mean that I play a game of chance, and hope for the best. We learn from our experi-ence. That's what the 'inner dialogue' that accompanies the 'outer dialogue' does for us. It's not just a matter of cultivating an intu-itive sense about the other, learning to recognise 'good vibes'. In a culture which is becoming more suspicious of people's motives, more distrustful of elites and experts, more ready to dismiss what is threatening or just inconvenient as 'fake news' and take refuge in the slogans dreamt up by populist bullies, we need something a bit more robust on which to build a culture of hospitality.

At stake is not the weight of evidence, nor the cogency of argu-ment, but something more challenging: how far we allow our inner world to be touched by the outer. This is not just a theological question. It's a moral question. I have talked about composing a sense of self around the practice of *remembering*. Let us take that word in its usual, familiar sense of calling to mind, and give it a moral focus. What debt do we owe to the past and what responsibility should we take for the future?

## *Words of Warning*

I want to address that question in company with the enigmatic Jewish philosopher, Walter Benjamin, who was born in the Berlin of the German Empire in 1892. His family consisted of well-connected businessmen who made their money in all sorts of enterprises, from antiques to ice-rinks. Benjamin talks about the Jewishness of his family life as an 'exotic aroma' hanging around a liberal upbringing that was fascinated equally by the values of a cultural Zionism as by the perennial questions raised by post-Kantian philosophy. He seems to have spent most of his life on the fringes of various philosophical circles, writing a vast amount – often in elliptical, aphoristic form – on a number of subjects, from politics to aesthetics. All his work is haunted by a spirit of foreboding, as if a Jewish prophetic voice was warning him of the dangerous pretensions of the gathering evil. Benjamin himself was not a theologian, but 'the theological' – what I think of as a 'trace' of God or 'seed of the Word' – simmers away beneath so many of his important texts. Benjamin recounts a strange little parable about a struggle between two giants:

> The weaker of the two is always just on the verge of losing when it pulls an unexpected trick and finally frees itself from the clutches of the other. The reason it can do this is that a hunchback dwarf is sitting in its giant ear, encouraging it and continually whispering new ways to resist.

The wizened little dwarf is really an expert chess player who is far more effective than the big brash giants, but he always remains hidden. In the 'great game of life', it seems as if everything is open to reasoned observation, but we never see everything, the hidden motivations and prejudices which control our interactions with the wider world. Putting it rather more positively, truth is hidden, something that only reveals itself in moments of intuition, that awakens us to the ways we tend to avoid opening ourselves to the possibility of the transcendent.

During the 1930's, with the rise of the Nazi regime in Germany, Benjamin's life as a public intellectual was always under threat. In 1940 he was in Paris, absorbed in the comfort of his writing. Eventually, in September, he was forced to flee the city and with some companions he made his way south, intending to escape into Spain and Portugal, and thence to sanctuary in the USA. He was too late. The Spanish authorities closed the border. His visa would not be recognised; he would be sent back to Paris. That night, 26 September, he took a massive overdose; one more statistic in the murderous march of the Nazi extermination programme.

But this one is especially poignant. He was neither a pious Jew nor a secular one; his life seems to have been spent in uneasy tension between exile and remembrance, between absorption in the perennial philosophical questions of the time and that uneasy awareness that history is shot through with traces of the little hidden dwarf, 'the theological', traces of the Divine. The most painful of times is subject to the corruption of the human spirit, and yet never beyond redemption. He reminds us not just that six million lives were violently expunged, but that each is to be remembered, each is a pointer to what is happening all the time throughout history.

Benjamin is a major influence on the work of the celebrated Catholic political theologian, Johann Baptist Metz, whose own work is dominated by the theme of remembrance. The political imagination, says Metz, can only resist the power of technological forces if it builds a 'moral-religious imagination'. Theology is still there, still influential, guarding the continuing influence that religion plays in our everyday living and political engagement, and reminding us of what can happen if we collude with the temptation to forget. More positively, Metz talks about theology in one word, 'interruption'. God somehow acts by cutting across the human tendency to smooth out the unacceptable, to domesticate the horror. That is the meaning of Metz's familiar term, 'the dangerous memory' of Jesus Christ. What is revealed in the Paschal Mystery of the Death and Resurrection is God's own challenge to a human history characterised by violence and forgetfulness.

Benjamin does not, of course, use such overtly Christian terminology, but he does call attention to the modern tendency to overcome painful and troubling moments in time with what Metz calls an 'evolutionary logic' that seeks to surmount the movement of time. Metz, taking inspiration from Benjamin's sense of urgency, seeks to counter the victors' uncritical optimism about the future with a more focused remembrance of the past that acknowledges the less comforting aspects of the present and builds solidarity with the victims.

## Interruptions and Signs of Hope

Once we make that move – as *Nostra Aetate* made the move from the dialogue with the Jewish people to 'conversation and collaboration' elsewhere – it becomes impossible to avoid further 'interruptions'. In a post-modern world that has grown tired of the sacred and lacks the curiosity to probe beneath the surface of human interaction, the wizened dwarf still has a role to play. This takes me back to where we began this chapter, with places, objects and artefacts that act as signs, pointing always to something deeper than mere cultural decoration. They open up a history of human interaction, a history that is pockmarked by petty mistakes and appalling acts of violence. And they raise a question: about how it is still possible to hope. How are we to remember, to put things back together, without either getting caught into a paralysing guilt trip or turning the future into some romantic and untruthful utopia?

Much depends on how we respond to the outer signs of hope that are bound up with the inner life of communities of faith – in

Catholic terms a sacramental vision. Let me repeat the great scriptural warrant for dialogue: 'Always be prepared to make a defence to anyone who calls you to make an account for the hope that is in you, yet do it with gentleness and reverence' (1 Pet. 3:15). Written for a community facing persecution, it is nothing if not a counter to the sort of other-worldly triumphalism of which Metz and Benjamin are so suspicious. Yet Metz – if not Benjamin himself – would want to emphasise the first words of the verse that are easily overlooked, 'In your hearts reverence Christ the Lord'. To Benjamin's question, Metz responds with the 'dangerous memory' that interrupts our comfortable ordering of experience. Not that this is an 'answer' in any straightforward sense. It is more an imperative, an unthreatening yet insistent invitation to 'come and see'.

And if we look, we will see, both in the ambivalence of history and in the obscurities of human encounter, what Benjamin calls fleeting 'images' that anchor us more deeply into this present moment through which past and future can be connected without forgetting the one and trivialising the other. An enigmatic thought from Benjamin's last writings may help us here:

> It is not that what is past casts its light on what is present or what is present casts its light on what is past; rather, image is that wherein what has been comes together in a flash with the now to form a constellation.

In the first half of this chapter I have been concerned with Ignatius's introductions to prayer, particularly with the 'composition of place' that anchors the searching yet disordered self in a moment of history. In the next chapter I will turn to a third preliminary, more a guiding principle of prayerful practice. We will then move towards forms of 'reverential reading' as a model for a repeated attention to what is given in the classic texts and artefacts of tradition. Reading, however, is never enough, for mere repetition risks dulling the senses, instead of attuning them to the source of a stimulus – God's own Word – that always exceeds the human capacity for response. My opening question was about what I called 'active listening', learning how to follow the Spirit that seeks to unfold the Word for us. In a pluralist world of many words, I have urged the discipline of listening to the times and places that define our lives in order to hear there the *echo* of the Word. This takes us now to another question, another stage on the journey, as it were: How can our 'reading' become more attentive, more expectant of what I have given as the title of this chapter: image and interruption?

Meaning crystallises around form or image. Benjamin recognises in all sorts of records of human experience – from texts and documents to artefacts and other sacred objects – what at a purely objective level is no more than a relic. Thus, as a moment in history it 'flashes past', always threatening to disappear for ever. But in what he calls this 'now moment' of reception, potentially it becomes a source of insight and revelation. The danger is that we build a future that is no more than a repetition of the past. Memory is always limited and can be very selective. That is not, however, to collude with the hopeless banality of the post-modern. On the contrary, if it is the case that all our remembering is limited by the contingencies of history, then we are forced to pay less attention to the grand scheme that encloses everything and more to the small-scale emergence of 'flashes' of illumination. The past is recorded not just in images lodged somewhere in our bodily selves but in the world of time and place, in nature itself and the signs of human cultivation, in the failures of the past as well as its glories, above all in the voice of the victims who interrupt the tendency to smooth away the past in favour of a narrative constructed by the victors.

# CHAPTER FOUR

## Right Channelling of Desire

I ONCE celebrated Holy Week in a large school in South India, a beautiful, peaceful spot up in the Kodai hills. On Palm Sunday we went in procession around the village carrying large bits of greenery and genuine palm leaves, and it seemed as if the entire population came out to watch. Hindus love feasts and festivals. It did not seem to matter that we were Roman Catholics led by a bespectacled white man dressed in a saffron shawl and almost completely ignorant of the local language. This was their village and these were their neighbours. What they were witnessing was less a strange cult than another aspect of an all-encompassing inclusive Hindu faith – to be interpreted, to go by comments I have heard, as the *puja* offered to *guru* Jesus. I enjoyed the occasion tremendously. After weeks stuck away in a large Jesuit community, with very little to do except read and pray, I was at the centre of things again and discovering how the ancient memories of Christian faith could be renewed by new perspectives and fresh insights.

Ignatius, of course, never deviated from his conviction that Christian faith was to be read as the record of God's revelation. Nothing needed to be added to its fullness. All he did in crafting out his *Exercises* was make some catechetical commentary on key themes and images, in order to embed them more deeply into the psyche of his exercitants. I am sure he would have relished that Palm Sunday, with happy crowds waving us on our way. And he would most probably have approved of the Passion story being acted out by local children, with plenty of imaginative improvisation and scant attention paid to the niceties of convention. God is present to human beings at the level of our affective as well as our intellective nature; indeed the way to the latter is often through the former, as the senses gradually become attuned to what is 'given' in the present moment. In terms of *content* the Christian faith of Ignatius is poles apart from anything Hindu; in terms of manner of expression there are all sorts of 'echoes' that sound across the boundaries.

It is hardly surprising, therefore, that outsiders to the practices of faith can sometimes feel 'at home' in other conceptual worlds, even if the depths of its mystery remain beyond comprehension. But 'insiders' too have much to learn. Later that afternoon an Indian sister from the school, an amazing young woman who seemed to know everyone and missed nothing, asked me if I would like to go for a walk to visit a family. I was delighted; another chance to see a bit more of the real India. We set off and wound our way up the dusty path, through the banana plantation and the paddyfields until we got to a tiny dwelling patched together with rough bricks and a rudimentary covering of palm leaves. Inside, it was neat and tidy, sparsely decorated with a low table and a few kitchen implements. It was not a scene of ghastly poverty; just simplicity of life. As my eyes adjusted to the gloom I could see an old woman lying on a tiny bed, perfectly still, with a younger woman squatting by her side. The sister introduced me. My hands were kissed reverently by the old woman's daughter. I sat there attentively without saying a word, feeling a bit of an intruder, if not an outsider, while the sister spoke to the old woman who, I realised, was quietly dying.

I remember a solitary fly settling on her forehead. She blinked but hadn't the strength to swat it away. Before we left, I was asked for a blessing. It was a touching moment, an encounter with an honest and ordinary holiness. A little plastic crucifix and a mass-produced image of the Sacred Heart told me they were Christians.

But religious affiliation seemed not to matter. It was so ordinary, yet extraordinary; about as different from the morning's liturgy as could be imagined. It was an important little corrective to any pretension to interreligious significance I might have entertained. I do not know the reason the sister took me on this trip; I think she was just keen to show me another side of village life. But it made me wonder if Jesus was not doing something similar as he entered the Holy City, filled with the overwhelming joy of that moment, yet aware of a much more tragic story waiting to be told.

## Consolation and Desolation

We human beings are often unaware how short-term and partial our needs and desires really are. On Sunday, the Messiah-figure is welcomed with joy as just the person to sort out the mess; by Friday he has already disappointed, with the result we know so well. That shift could be dismissed as another example of the fickleness of human nature. Not for Ignatius. He always asks us to stop and think, to examine more carefully what is happening beneath the surface, as it were. We are all dominated by aspirations, hopes, longings and wishes of all kinds which act as a sort of energy that propels us on our way. Whatever we call them, desires are morally neutral, at least until they acquire creative or destructive power when directed towards particular ends. At that point they all demand a degree of ordering, or they may order or *dis*order us.

It is relatively straightforward to distinguish between needs and 'wants', opening up a whole spectrum, from the satisfaction of appetites to more specific actions like preparing a meal or getting a piece of writing finished. But once we move into the world of religious belief and the search for ultimate meaning, it becomes more complex and raises difficult yet life-giving questions. Are our hopes and expectations mere wish-fulfilment? Are we just filling up the human void with self-serving make-believe? Is religion doing more than managing something pathological about human desire?

Ignatius does not ask such questions. Living in a religiously more homogeneous age, he focuses on the practices of a Christian faith that offers a sense of completeness. But that does not stop those from a later culture learning from his deep experience of the movements of the Spirit in the everyday. The source of his wisdom resides in the principled pragmatism with which he applies the narrative structure of the Gospel to the needs of particular individuals. The *Exercises* do not provide a 'quick fix' for the confusion of our longings. They offer a pedagogy, a way of learning, that is transformative, not just of the self, but of the way the self engages with the wider world and with 'other selves'.

In the last chapter, I explained how two Ignatian preliminaries work together to build an initial response to 'the story' and 'the place'. Here I turn to a third. I am to 'ask God our Lord for what I wish for and desire' – a petition, says Ignatius, that must be 'adapted to the matter under consideration' [48]. This is not just a formal introduction; it amounts to what, in the fifth annotation that prefaces the *Exercises,* Ignatius calls a 'fundamental disposition':

> It is highly profitable for the exercitant to begin the Exercises in a magnanimous spirit and with great liberality towards their Creator and Lord, and to offer him all their powers of desire and all their liberty, so that the Divine Majesty may avail himself of their person and all they possess, according to his most holy will [5].

It feels at first as if a very Christian 'Divine Majesty' is commanding an asceticism in which all personal autonomy is to be handed over to another power. Underneath the style, however, lies something more subtle. Ignatius knows that human desires are conditioned or directed by their object, whether that object is concretely available or a more elusive source of hope. When we approach questions of ultimacy, we literally do not know what is right and best for us, because we do not *know* the ultimate meaning of things. Even at the level of the most basic of appetites, for survival, we do not know what *in the longer term* may turn out to be undesirable, even destructive. Ignatius's awareness of the ambiguities of the movements of the human spirit alerts him to the complex ways in which the very best in us can become subject to the 'enemy' who can appear as an 'angel of light'. The language may seem quaint, but it hides a profound truth: that we are often undone not by our weaknesses but by our undiscerned strengths. That, of course, is the tragedy of all human living, a tragedy with which Ignatius was familiar.

What has to be fashioned is a properly holistic attitude to life that is at once grounded yet purposeful. That is why Ignatius asks us to stay rooted in the particular constrictions of time and place, the concrete circumstances of living – and why I began this chapter with the celebration of Palm Sunday in an Indian village, moving from the joyful moments that unite to the sobering truth of death that separates. Consolation and desolation appear at times like twin poles that define the dilemmas of human living, the search for lasting truth in the midst of the experience of loss and failure. More exactly, they interact or, as the Buddhists might put it, *co-inhere* with each other.

### A Middle Way of Co-inherence

Earlier I used the metaphor of journey to speak of the spiritual life. Here I want to offer an alternative, one that is suggested by the dialogue with Buddhism. Many years ago, I wrote a brief comparative study of Zen and the *Spiritual Exercises*, which began with the speculative thought that spirituality is the 'right channelling of desire'. Whether we think of the first disciples seeking out Jesus at the end of the first chapter of John's Gospel, or of the many questioners who came to the Buddha to have their doubts settled, spirituality begins with a movement of searching. To that extent it consists of an asceticism, a methodical structure of practices against which progress can be measured, and a clear vision of the ideal to which it is orientated. The problem is always to get a balance of the two. Discipline alone can kill the spirit, while the best of intentions, if unchecked, can be vapid or perhaps positively destructive. My claim, as I put it somewhat portentously at the beginning of that article, is that both traditions approach the problem in the same way: 'Pure asceticism is not enough. Asceticism must lead to a contemplative way.'

Discipline of practice and contemplative vision interact with each other. The Buddhist quality of equanimity that leaves the meditator at the threshold of *Nirvana* complements the attitude of indifference that Ignatius puts before his exercitant at the beginning of the *Exercises* as key to realising the end for which human beings are created. In the body of my earlier article I spent some time comparing the inner dynamics of two spiritual traditions, noting that as Ignatius puts his exercitants in touch with God at the heart of their everyday experience of the world, so the Buddha tells his disciples to be mindful and aware of whatever is presented to their experience, because all things already possess the Buddha-nature. I then concluded that

> the fundamental dynamic of the two traditions is the same: action and contemplation, the ascetical and the mystical, meet and are resolved in an attitude of equanimity and openness to the Divine Mystery which allows God to be God and the rest to be silence.

As far as it goes, I think the main thrust of that article is still correct. And we will come back to this point about indifference and equanimity at the end of the chapter, where I will introduce a thought from one of the great Christian mystics, Meister Eckhart. Is it correct, however, to end with that coy little flourish about leaving the rest to silence? It's a little too open-ended, perhaps, if only because Christianity draws much of its energy from the Jewish prophetic tradition, the Word that precisely *breaks* the silence. Was that not the revelation of that Palm Sunday afternoon?

To ponder further the mysterious 'co-inherence' of Ignatius's spiritual movements of consolation and desolation, let me introduce a brief discussion of the dialogue between Buddhists and

Christians – especially Christians brought up in the Ignatian tradition – with another metaphor for the spiritual life, the one which began my article: the flow or channelling of a river.

At its best, what any spiritual exercise does is shape our searching and orientate us towards our end or the object of our desire. But journeys are always processes of interaction. On the way I will meet, and be met by, the unexpected stranger, and my single-minded desire to make progress will have to adapt to changing circumstances. We met one such stranger at the end of the last chapter. Walter Benjamin is hardly an example of the Jewish prophet. On the other hand, his life and writing remind us how echoes of a half-remembered past interrupt an easy contentment with the narrative of the victors. What about the forgotten victims? What about other readings of the past they make possible? And not just readings of the past, but a present that is built on how past tradition is understood?

This is where the complexity of 'channelling' comes alive. In the era of climate change, the image of a river flowing majestically between solid banks has taken on more ambiguous connotations. The banks are not indestructible; they require maintenance if they are to withstand inevitable shifts in weather patterns. What makes channelling *right* is attention, not just to the given structures of practice, but to those unexpected moments that threaten to make progress impossible. To put it another way, the grand ideas that express our deepest imaginings exist in uneasy relationship with the tragic mistakes that routine repetition of the tradition cannot always prevent. Right channelling is about learning how to respond to a world of consolation *and* desolation, success *and* failure, fulfilment *and* disappointment.

*A Middle Way*
Understood in terms, not of a system and philosophy, but as the spiritual exercise that responds to all sorts of human desires, aspirations, needs and wants, Buddhism and Christianity have much

to learn from each other. *Nirvana*, the most celebrated, and most obscure, of Buddhist concepts, is to be understood literally as the 'blowing out' of the causes of rebirth. In many texts, it is glossed as a blissful state beyond the reach of the march of time and the effects of suffering, ageing and decay. That would seem to make *Nirvana* either a 'way out' or 'release' which brings to an end what most afflicts human beings, or an everlasting extension of the very best one can imagine. There are many schools of Buddhism, from the austere scholasticism of the monastic Theravada to the expansive theistic devotion of Pure Land traditions. Whether *Nirvana* is to be given a negative or more positive gloss, or some version in between, is less important than establishing the context which gives the 'discourse of *Nirvana*' its shape.

Now that is not to say that accounts of the ultimate aim or purposive intent of any religious tradition, whether played out in the language of *Nirvana* or the Beatific Vision, are not religiously or philosophically significant. They are, but that's not the point I want to make here. While the supreme objects of desire are strictly beyond comprehension, they do perform an important *regulative* sense of direction for all sorts of religious practices; the river, to repeat, is a combination of flowing water *and* constraining banks. It's in that context that they need to be understood. At its simplest, Buddhism is a Middle Way between extremes. In the story of the Buddha's enlightenment, the extremes are described in terms of self-indulgence (the life of pleasure) and sheer asceticism (the life of severe self-control). Before his enlightenment, Gotama – the young prince who was to become the Buddha – moves dramatically from one to the other before finding a point of balance. That sounds fairly straightforward. In fact, rather like the story of Ignatius's conversion, it is painfully difficult.

Rather like the *Spiritual Exercises*, the Middle Way promises freedom from all disordered desires. But both raise similar questions: how does one *know* when a desire is disordered or ordered, or in Buddhist terms 'skilful' or 'unskilful'? Let's go back to my earlier point about desires existing as a sort of spectrum from the 'gut-level' of basic urges to more 'head-centred' purposeful aspirations. We might agree that the latter is prior to the former, that a vision of what makes for the good life orders all one's activities and relationships. In practice, nothing is so simple. Ultimate goals – such as the life of the resurrected body that Paul talks about in 1 Corinthians 15 – of their very nature are beyond definition. They are matters of faith and hope rather than fact and experience. And undiscerned faith can be notoriously fallible, as Ignatius with his sensitivity to the malign arts of 'the enemy' knew all too well.

Even the most sincere of believers can get it wrong. St Augustine would remind us, for instance, that if we think we have grasped the mystery of God, it is not God we have grasped. If I paint the issue now in Buddhist terms, it is because Buddhism makes the point with some starkness, even if, at first, it seems teasingly perplexing. The First Noble Truth states that our human condition is shot through with suffering. The Pali word in the Theravada tradition is the wonderfully onomatopaeic *dukkha*, which I always feel should be left untranslated and treated as an exclamation of disgust. In English it usually appears as 'suffering'. Literally it means 'hard to bear'.

The Second Noble Truth gives the cause or 'arising' of suffering as 'that *thirst* which reproduces re-existence and re-becoming, bound up with passionate greed'. This description is subsequently expanded to include ignorance, hatred and delusion, and all manner of disordered feelings and emotions. But in the first place suffering is the result of 'thirst', an insatiable longing, which takes three forms: sensual gratification, a more intellectualist obsession with preserving some eternal essence, and a nihilistic materialism that denies the significance of any purposive future. The three together give us something of St Augustine's point in Buddhist guise. The wonderfully enigmatic saying, 'If you meet the Buddha on the road kill him', is perhaps making the point that, if you think you have met the Buddha, it isn't the Buddha you have met. Buddhism may not be a theistic tradition in the Christian sense, but it does ponder the implications for human living of a lack of sensitivity to a disordered desire that does no more than construct its own meaning.

At first it might seem that all forms of 'thirst' or desire, cognitive intending and affective yearning are subject to the same strictures. The fixation typical of the early Theravadin school – that even the most blissful of states, such as peace and joy, are open to corruption – runs through many later forms of Buddhism. Zen, for example, is famously full of instructive stories about the dangers of misdirected zeal for enlightenment. 'How long will it take?' asks the eager pupil. 'Maybe ten years', says the master. 'But if I work really hard?' asks the pupil. 'Then it will probably take twenty years', comes the acid reply. It sounds like the cynicism of the disdainful ascetic who has escaped from 'the world' in order to cultivate some form of egocentric inner isolation. That's where the historical context of the 'discourse of *Nirvana*' comes in. What we hear is the advice, not of a distant philosopher, but of the wise and experienced physician who gives an accurate diagnosis of the sickness that afflicts the human condition, and who prescribes the appropriate medicine, the practices that make up the Middle Way, the Noble Eightfold Path.

These eight stages consist not just of 'right intention', a clarity of vision, but 'right effort', which covers all manner of well-directed ways of thinking and acting, and 'right mindfulness', a sensitivity to what enters into and passes out of consciousness. They all need to be kept together as a graduated and interdependent set of steps that reinforce each other. The word translated 'right' sounds like 'fullest' or 'highest' – what is most in line with the noblest aspirations of human living. In fact, it is more pragmatic than teleological. It is what is 'right' or 'correct', what *works*, what keeps in check the human tendency to deal with our sense of incompleteness by projecting some remedy into an undefined (and for the Buddhist undefinable) future.

As with any form of energy or surge of power, which is what that obscure concept of desire is like, it can only be shaped or directed by a discernment that grows from meditative exercise and ethical practice. The question is not, therefore, 'Can one desire *Nirvana?*' One can, because one does. The question is *how?* How is intention to be 'right', effort to be 'right', *desire* to be 'right'? Whatever we mean by desire, whatever the 'mode' of its intention or focus, it cannot be obliterated, ignored or eradicated. It can only be *channelled*.

## Following the Path

There are some important resonances here with the Ignatian tradition. Ignatius, of course, had no contact with Buddhism. With Francis Xavier it was different. Like Ignatius, he was dominated by the conviction that everything in his life, all he did and all he endured, was orientated towards the praise and service of the 'Divine Majesty'. Yet this was no abstract Absolute hovering at the end of a great long journey into the unknown. What took him off to the distant East was a God who, in an important sense, travelled with him *in companionship* on the journey. As we know, Francis intended his personal journey of faith to take him to China where, he was convinced, lay the key to understanding the sophisticated Buddhist teachings he had encountered in Japan. Circumstances (one hesitates to say 'fate') dictated otherwise. The ideal, the guiding vision remained, but he had to adjust and learn the limits of enthusiasm and control.

When he arrived in Goa his theology of salvation was straightforward and uncompromising: all people are created in the image of God but sin tarnishes that resemblance, thus making them less human. Baptism is what restores that image. Undoubtedly this was the main motivation for his mission; at times he seems almost overwhelmed by the prospect of the damnation of so many. Yet, as he got to know this alien world into which he had been catapulted, some of his sharper opinions began to mellow. In 1545, a few years

*Statue of St Francis Xavier in Bom Jesus*

after arriving in Goa, he could still state that the mission among the 'gentiles' did not require much training. Five years later he became more aware of the wisdom of Buddhist scholars in Japan. He tells the story in letters to Ignatius which record, not just information about the progress of the mission, but what in the *Exercises* is called an 'examen', a personal reflection on the movements of the Spirit. A couple of quotations will suffice to give something of the flavour of what was urging him forward.

In Goa, in March 1548, he was arranging the work of the wider mission and making plans to go even further afield. It was a chance meeting with a young convert, a reformed Japanese murderer called Anjiro, which convinced him of his ultimate destiny.

> If all the Japanese are as eager to know as is Anjiro, it seems to me that this race is the most curious of all the peoples that have been discovered ... I asked Anjiro if the people of Japan would become Christians if I went with him to his country. He replied that those of his country would not immediately become Christians but would first ask many questions and would see how I answered them and what I believed and, above all, if I lived in accordance with what I said.

A year and a half later, accompanied by another Jesuit and Anjiro, he landed at Anjiro's home-town of Kagoshima in southern Japan. In a letter to the Jesuits back in Goa he speaks favourably of the dignity and sense of honour of the people he met.

> They have something which I do not think is to be found among any Christian lands, namely, that the nobles, no matter how poor they may be, and the commoners, no matter how much wealth they possess, have as much esteem for a very poor noble as they would have for him if he were very rich ... They are very courteous in dealing with each other ... A large proportion of the people can read and write, which is a great help in learning prayers and the things of God in a short time ... They are a people of great good will, very sociable and eager to know.

Francis is intrigued to find himself dealing with difficult questions arising from an intellectual engagement with a religious tradition that set great store by the exercise of reason. He never engaged in a sophisticated dialogue with Confucian mandarins like Matteo Ricci in China; he did not spend years living the life of an Indian sannyasi like Roberto de Nobili in Madurai; he did not travel across the Himalaya to Lhasa and write a history of Tibet like Ippolito Desideri. Yet without the example of Francis – his readiness to enter into another conceptual framework, to face new questions and open up new horizons for the Church – these extraordinary scholars of later generations might never have had the inspiration to follow.

I touched on the theme of missionary accommodation to other religious ideas or 'inculturation' in the opening chapter and will have more to say about it later. The practice of translation from one language to another is, of course, as old as the Church itself; St Paul's attempt in Athens to shift from Hebrew concepts to Greek is only the first and most celebrated of exercises which came to define the Church as a community for mission. The early Jesuit missionaries made it more than an exercise; it became a way of life, a way of expressing their companionship with Christ. The culture of Renaissance humanism acted as a major formative influence on the early Society, shaping a response not just to dialogue with 'the religions' but to scholarly and intellectual ministry as a whole, both in the humanities and the sciences, from archaeology and linguistics to astronomy and mathematics. In this light, what is often regarded as a 'Catholic missionary paradigm' more exactly represents an approach to mission based explicitly on a radical theology of Incarnation: the Paschal Mystery of the Death and Resurrection of Christ has transformed the whole of creation, and therefore is already at work transforming human culture as well.

Such a paradigm expresses not just the activity of the Church but its *very being*, the conviction that the Holy Spirit is at work bringing to fruition that transformation of culture which has been initiated through God's act of creation. For the Society of Jesus, and those formed by the Ignatian charism, the sensitive, thoughtful humanist in Francis is its founding exemplar – but not because he worked out a 'strategy'. He was a thoughtful tactician, adjusting like the Buddha to what worked. To go back to the river metaphor, he found himself 'channelled', no longer commanding the way forward, but subject to the constraints of the everyday, and learning how and when to yield control to the powerful guidance of the Holy Spirit.

*The Interdependence of all Things*

The number of contemporary Jesuits who have been similarly 'channelled' at a serious and sustained level by their engagement with Buddhism, and especially with Zen, is quite remarkable. The Irishman William Johnston is only the best-known. He taught at Sophia University in Tokyo for most of his active life as a Jesuit, gaining a reputation as one of the most prolific and accessible writers on the contemporary 'shift to interiority'. In his set of instructions on Christian prayer, *Being in Love*, he comments on a dialogue between Thomas Merton and the great Zen Buddhist scholar, Daisetz Suzuki:

> They find parallels between the stories of the Zen masters and those of the desert fathers; they find parallels between the poverty of the Christians and the emptiness of the Buddhists, between the wisdom of Christianity and the *prajña* of Buddhism, and they discuss such terms as purity of heart, innocence, suchness and knowledge. What is most interesting is their discovery that the Zen monk who went in search of enlightenment and the Christian monk who went in search of holiness – the Christian returning to the state of original justice and the Zen monk searching for his original face – were on very similar paths and had much in common.

Johnston would be the first to admit that what sensitised him to important resonances between Christian prayer and Buddhist meditative practice was his experience of the *Spiritual Exercises*. But are we simply talking about the contingency of context, the sort of thing I discovered in India when I had to refract my accustomed mode of prayer through a different local culture? Or do the resonances point to something more profound, even an 'inner affinity', between Zen and Ignatian spirituality?

At first a positive response to the latter question seems unlikely. Christianity and Buddhism inhabit very different cultural spaces, the one a strongly personal form of theism in which God reveals something of Godself through the incarnation of the Word in the person of Jesus, the other a non-theistic tradition that eschews all talk of ultimates, whether in terms of the human person or the final state to which human beings are somehow oriented. And yet, when the philosophical and theological differences are set to one side, and the focus is put on spirituality or religious experience – what people *do* as opposed to what they say about what they do – significant links and even commonalities begin to appear. The Ignatian 'way of proceeding', as already noted, is concerned with bringing order into a disordered existence by aligning the individual with the pattern of living taught in the life, death and resurrection of Jesus Christ. In the cross is symbolised Christ's capacity to reveal the *Godlike* quality of love, the giving away of self while remaining truly self. The ethical-meditative Buddhist Middle Way builds up an intuitive awareness, a sensitive response to the suffering of human beings that brings 'Buddhahood', enlightenment or 'awakening' to the way things are.

The Dalai Lama – a supremely awakened man, if ever there was one – is supposed to have remarked that there are no absolutes in Buddhism, but, if there were one, it would be compassion. That typically Buddhist quality of wise compassion or compassionate wisdom as the source of motivation for human living comes from a shift of consciousness – in Christian terms, a conversion – that embraces the whole world, rejoicing with those who rejoice, and suffering with those in pain. That takes me back to my opening 'composition of place' in this chapter: Palm Sunday in an Indian village where I went from one end of Holy Week to the other in a very few minutes. Joy is the beginning of freedom, an initial sense of well-being that is to be celebrated; but it is only one dimension of the complex story of how human beings mature into full understanding of the way things are, as the Buddhist would put it. While the 'Divine Majesty' of Ignatius always remains veiled in mystery and the Buddhist will refuse to speak of *Nirvana*, the language of spiritual growth is well-developed in both traditions.

*Detachment and Equanimity*

Buddhists talk about the quality of 'equanimity', born out of joy and peace, with connotations of a simple silence that 'looks on' all things, takes note of what is presented to the senses and is not disturbed by what it beholds and touches. To put it in less negative terms, a life of ethical and meditative practice builds a heightened awareness which is still very much 'in touch' with the everyday. For the Christian meditator, following the Ignatian path to true freedom of spirit, the initial 'Principle and Foundation' becomes an intuitive response, embedded in the heart and forming a virtue of 'indifference'. Neither equanimity nor indifference is a meek subjection to whatever happens but a generous openness which, far from commending a ruthless self-effacement, is marked by what I like to call an 'active waiting'. That is, of course, a description of an Ignatian pilgrimage rather than Buddhist 'right striving', since waiting implies an expected object and only in Christianity is it correct to say one waits upon something or, more exactly, *someone,* the Word of God that is spoken in the world. For the Buddhist, the alert stillness that learns to see things as they are, and to *accept* things as they really are, is almost an end in itself.

This takes me back to that remark about the 'rest being silence'. That Christianity adds an extra dimension to Buddhist equanimity – the careful attention to the Word which we will talk about in later chapters – should not take away from this quality of Buddhist acceptance. It is no hopeless passivity, even if, as my Buddhist teacher used to repeat with great firmness, 'hope is not a Buddhist virtue'. If I understand him, equanimity is what holds the two sides of that enigmatic double-virtue of compassionate wisdom together. Perhaps this is one way of talking about the supreme truth of what Buddhists call *Pratityasamutpada,* the 'nexus of conditioned origination'. All phenomena, and all sentient beings, arise and continue in dependence on others; they 'co-inhere' in each other.

That was something I learned that Palm Sunday. At the time, I can remember like a good Jesuit thinking that the morning was full of consolation, peace and joy, while the afternoon was an experience of desolation, a moment of sober dark reality. Undoubtedly it did have its dark side; even the happiest of deaths leaves a sense of loss, a reminder that death awaits us all. But it would be a move into 'annihilationism' of a very negative kind to find nothing positive, nothing consoling, in any experience of human interaction. The fact that that moment has stayed with me all these years later witnesses to its significance as some sort of revelation.

Christians tend to think that revelation comes out of the blue, suddenly hitting us and knocking us sideways. That can happen, of course, as Paul discovered on his journey to Damascus. But there is always another side, just as Buddhist experience of enlightenment is made up of both cognitive and affective dimensions. Wisdom grows from a heightened awareness that persists through all activity; compassion sums up the affective dimension of the relations between sentient beings. The 'three trainings' – ethics, concentration and wisdom, which summarise the Noble Eightfold Path – are interdependent. There's something analogous at work in Christian spirituality, a channelling of desire through worship and devotion, study and social action, that seeks a balance – a Middle Way – between action and contemplation.

## One Thing Necessary

I always think the best example comes from one of the most misunderstood stories in the New Testament, that of Martha and Mary. It's not helped by a translation that renders Jesus' words to poor over-worked Martha as 'Mary has chosen the better part' (Lk. 10:41). There's no comparative in the Greek. It should be rendered as 'what is good'. When Jesus says 'only one thing is necessary' he is not setting out some sort of hierarchy of tasks or vocations, as if the work of contemplation is intrinsically more valuable than the active life of teaching, social justice and reconciliation. I find it significant that this story comes immediately after the parable of the Good Samaritan, which ends with Jesus's words to the lawyer, 'Go and do the same yourself'.

Martha plays the part of the hospitable householder, welcoming Jesus into her house. Rather like another host in the book of Genesis – Abraham, who receives the three strangers at the Oaks of Mamre – Mary is getting busily involved in the preparation of the meal. She attends to the needs of her guest, doing what is necessary at that moment, just as the Good Samaritan puts himself out for the man who has fallen among thieves. If there is a fault, it lies with something deeply human, what most of us feel when we end up doing the domestic stuff while someone else is engaged with something that seems more important, more worthy, more interesting. Martha suffered a quite understandable sense of resentment that her sister had ended up with a much more cushy number.

If you link together the parable of the Good Samaritan and the story of Martha and Mary, it becomes clear that what is being proposed is not a juxtaposition of, still less a judgement between, two ways of life. Rather what we are given is a warning about what can happen when we allow ourselves to get caught into binary thinking: if so-and-so has a blessing, then someone else has not. The 'one thing necessary' is a very particular and special virtue; what is commended – albeit using different words and different illustrations – is a quality of calm and confident perseverance that both keeps a sense of direction 'on the way' while being prepared to adjust to whatever one meets.

Desire, I suggested earlier, is like an energy that propels us forward, that enables us to move towards our goal. How do we know we are on the right path, that we are being 'channelled' in the right direction? We don't. We take it on trust that what a tradition of faith has taught is based on the wisdom of experience which we would be foolish to ignore. The river, dodgy banks and all, was there before us. But the direction with which we set out on any purposive journey is only half the story: the 'Mary half', with its focus on the ideal that guides us. There is also the ever-necessary attention to the everyday pressures that come from all sides and can distract us from the goal: the 'Martha half'. The two cannot be separated. Our inner moods and the circumstances around us conspire to take us from one to the other, sometimes with disarming ease. Whatever we call it – Ignatian indifference or Buddhist equanimity – the aim of any disciplined religious life is to learn how to live with, if not resolve, the inevitable tensions of life in 'the middle of things'.

If only to allow that Jesuits and their Ignatian spirituality do not have all the best tunes, let me conclude this chapter with some wisdom from the great Dominican mystic, theologian and preacher, Meister Eckhart, whose teaching of 'detachment' or *Abgescheidenheit* – literally 'cut-offness' – has won him many Buddhist admirers. Eckhart turns the traditional distinction that makes Mary's part 'better' on its head. For Eckhart, Martha is the one who has achieved a detachment from things. She is praised for standing on the 'rim of eternity'.

> Martha knew Mary better than Mary Martha, for Martha had lived long and well; and living gives the most valuable kind of knowledge. Life knows better than pleasure or light what one can get under God in this life, and in some ways life gives us a purer knowledge than what eternal light can bestow.

Eckhart upholds Martha's criticism of Mary. Martha is concerned that Mary risks somehow becoming 'stuck' in her ecstasy, being caught up in an experience of 'desire' that is more about seeking the fullness of God's life rather than leaving God freedom to act in the soul, or – to use that beautiful medieval image – to bring the Word to birth in the soul.

# CHAPTER FIVE

## Inculturation — Aesthetic and Ethical

THERE'S A delightful Latin phrase in the first *Formula of the Institute* which speaks of the Jesuit vocation as *diversa loca peragrare* – 'to travel through diverse places'. This is the figure of the restless searcher who channels his desires, not by turning aside for lengthy periods of contemplation, but by learning *on the way* – or, to be precise, *from* the Way, the Christ who is a constant companion of the pilgrim. Even after the Society took the momentous step to establish colleges and commit itself to the ministry of formal education, it was remarkable how wide was the geographical reach of those sent – or, in the Jesuit jargon, 'missioned' – beyond Europe. By the time Ignatius died in 1556, Jesuits were in India, Japan and Brazil, with more intrepid travellers scattered across various parts of Africa. Not all of these enterprises prospered; the risks were great and the distances enormous. That so many did bear fruit is testament to the ingenuity and perseverance of some extraordinary individuals as well as their faith in the providence of God.

Contrary to the stereotype of the ever-obedient 'soldier of Christ' zealously pursuing the agenda laid down by domineering superiors, what Ignatius wanted was men with clarity of purpose, independence of judgement and the imagination to adjust to particular local situations when they were thousands of miles from 'central office'. This was not the world of instant emails and relentless social media; no possibility of a Zoom conference to work through the action points of the last meeting. Jesuit missionaries to far-flung corners of Asia and South America had to be able to discern what was of God wherever they were sent. If there is such a thing as the typical 'Ignatian pilgrim', it is not the feckless romantic, entranced by exotic other worlds, but the one who is *at home anywhere*, equipped with the personal resources to work *without* the support of familiar institutions and *within* a local culture that is often suspicious and even hostile. This is the inner spirit that gave rise to the Jesuit approach to the Catholic missionary paradigm, what has come to be known as 'inculturation'. This involves entering deep into the culture of a people and communicating with them through the medium of their own religious universe.

The best known of its exponents in India is Roberto de Nobili (1577-1656) who adopted the garb of the Indian *sannyasi* or holy man in order to make himself socially acceptable to members of the Brahmin caste, the scholarly elite of what in modern times we have come to call Hinduism. What de Nobili encountered was no unified 'ism' but a whole family of religious cultures and spiritualities which he first needed to understand if he was to make Christian teaching understood. In Madurai, he learned both classical Sanskrit and Tamil, the local vernacular. He wrote a catechism, several important treatises, and apologias for his missionary method, insisting that learning the language was not in itself enough; one also had to share the life of the people in order to gain their respect. He was inspired by an earlier generation of Jesuits, particularly Matteo Ricci (1552-1610), mathematician, astronomer and theologian, who practised an extraordinary dialogue with the Chinese world. Both men were influenced by the organising genius of Alessandro Valignano {1539-1606), Ricci's novice master, who was responsible for developing the strategy of inculturation in the Society's East Asian missions. Valignano followed Xavier's enthusiasm for the sophistication of the Chinese and Japanese cultures.

He had a more disdainful regard for what he saw in India, an opinion that de Nobili rejected. While de Nobili's personal dialogue was largely with the classical Sanskritic tradition, he also knew and respected the broader devotional or *bhakti* spirituality of the lower castes. When he arrived in Goa in 1605, it is highly likely that de Nobili met another Jesuit, a contemporary of Ricci's, the extraordinary Thomas Stephens (1549-1619). Stephens was the author of the *Kristapurana*, a retelling of the biblical story in a devotional form which appealed to the heart as well as the head.

Stephens was the first English Jesuit to travel to India, and quite possibly the first Englishman, preceding the adventurers of what was to become the East India Company by a few decades. A recent journal article refers to him as the 'Shakespeare of India'. They were near contemporaries, but Stephens did not set out to be a poet. His first work was a grammar (in Portuguese) of the Konkani language, his second a treatise on Christian faith, written in Konkani. The *Kristapurana*, an epic poem of no mean proportions written in Marathi, was not the result of natural talent alone, or of an education that taught him to value the importance of learning wherever it was found and wherever it took him. It grew out of his experience of a beautiful yet conflicted world which moved him greatly. I have long been fascinated by Stephens and, if I turn to him now as an example of interreligious inculturation, it is not to forget what the great missionary intellectuals achieved, but to add an extra dimension: the use of the aesthetic imagination in the work of communication.

### From Wiltshire to India

What drew a country boy from Wiltshire to join this new religious order and answer a call to travel to a part of the world that none but a handful of his fellow-countrymen had even heard of? No doubt we have here an example of Levinas's relentless spirit of adventure, drawing him away from the need for security. Or maybe it would be more accurate to talk, in Buddhist terms, of the former being *co-inherent* in the latter, growing organically from within. At any rate, the Abrahamic journey of Stephens began, not with any great conversion, but in the midst of very ordinary circumstances, in the tiny hamlet of Bushton, just south of what is now Royal Wootton Bassett in north Wiltshire. Here Stephens was born in 1549, the second son of Thomas and Jane Stephens. His father was a successful merchant who held the lease of Bushton Manor. There is no church in the hamlet; the nearest is about a mile away, in the village of Clyffe Pypard, half-way up the Ridgeway escarpment which commands magnificent views of the bare, gently undulating countryside. It is possible that Stephens was baptised here, though his baptism is more likely to have taken place in the chapel attached to the Manor.

His elder brother, Richard, studied at Oxford, joined the newly founded seminary at Douai, and worked as professor of theology until his death in 1586. Thomas did his schooling at Winchester, after which he traipsed round the country in the company of a larger-than-life character called Thomas Pounde, a sometime courtier of Queen Elizabeth, whose main purpose in life seems to have been introducing suitable young men (and himself) to the Society of Jesus. Pounde and Stephens were much taken by the radical commitment expected of recruits to the new Society, as well as by the letters written by far-flung missionaries that were circulating round Europe at the time. They resolved to go to Rome together but, on the eve of their departure, Pounde was betrayed and arrested. Stephens escaped and travelled to Rome alone, where he joined the Society of Jesus along with six other Englishmen, among them the Oxford-educated Henry Garnet, William Weston and Robert Persons.

In 1577, Edmund Campion wrote to Persons from Prague: 'You are seven; I congratulate you; I wish you were seventy times seven. Considering the goodness of the cause, the number is small.' Campion was, of course, referring to the needs of the English mission. And given that it was such a priority for English Jesuits at that precise moment, it might seem strange that Stephens had other ideas. That would be to underestimate the power of the founding vision of Ignatius and the demand it made for a personal commitment to following of Christ the King. By the time Stephens set out from Lisbon on 4 April 1579, the Society had shifted its missionary focus from the radical dispersal which Ignatius originally envisaged to the routine of educational institutions, the work for which the Society would soon become famous. Even without the powerful attraction of the letters of Francis Xavier and other early missionaries, he would have been well aware of the expectations of the *Formula* which already in its third paragraph speaks about members of the Society being ready to go wherever the Supreme Pontiff sees fit, 'whether he sends us to the Turks or other infidels, even to the land they call India'. Stephens clung to the original ideal, no more taken by the prospect of the settled life of the schoolteacher than he felt committed to resisting persecution back in his native land.

## *The Humanism of a Strange New World*

Stephens landed in Goa on 24 October 1579, one of forty-three Jesuits to arrive that year. He vividly describes this epic journey, with its privations and dangers, in a long letter to his father. His communications, whether to his family or to members of the Society, reveal something of his character. He comes across as keenly observant, blessed with an enquiring mind and a natural curiosity, thoughtful and clear-sighted in his judgements, yet also fascinated by the strange and unexpected. He is, for instance, struck by the exotic flora of this new world. The letter to his father finishes, 'Hitherto I have not seen trees here whose like I have seen in·Europe, the vine excepted, which, nevertheless here is to no purpose, so that all the wines are brought out from Portugal'. And his growing interest in language and translation comes through in a letter to his brother Richard, written in late 1583:

> Many are the languages of these places. Their pronunciation is not disagreeable, and their structure is

allied to Greek and Latin. The phrases and constructions are of a wonderful kind.

At the Roman College, Stephens had been schooled both in Thomistic thought and in the humanist values of the Renaissance. What held them together was no theory of intercultural dynamics, but a language – Latin – that opened up access to literature of all kinds and, perhaps as significant, modes of *using* language of all kinds, from syllogistic reasoning to the tropes of classical rhetoric and poetry. Stephens knew that Sanskrit was connected to Marathi and Konkani as Latin was to Italian; the one was the linguistic and cultural key to the other. The typically Jesuit approach to Christian mission came out of this humanist education. As noted earlier, Ignatius expected his Jesuits to be learned, but also to be able to communicate their learning. The two are interdependent, two sides of the one coin, a dialogue that begins with the desire to understand and finds itself rooted in the heart.

As with all the religious who came to Goa, the Jesuits received a stipend from the Portuguese. Without financial support they could not have operated at all, yet there was always a risk that their freedom of movement would be subject to imperial diktat. Stephens, like de Nobili, appears to have experienced a degree of ambivalence towards colonial power and the dilemmas it raised for the missionary. But whereas de Nobili quickly moved outside the area subject to the Padroado, Stephens spent the rest of his life in an area which was of particular concern for the Portuguese in their efforts to establish control of the Goa hinterland. He responded naturally to the concern of Ignatius that, wherever necessary, Jesuits should learn to address people in the local vernacular. Yet he also knew that something more was at stake than mere ease of communication.

Today we would have little difficulty in recognising other religious cultures as places where the Spirit is already at work in the world. In modern pluralist societies, familiarity with other religious worlds has encouraged a more generous outlook on what is 'other'.

For Stephens, like Xavier before him and de Nobili afterwards, the truth and superiority of Christian faith were taken for granted. Nevertheless, the combination of Thomistic theological framework and the great Ignatian vision of 'finding God in all things' was enough to open up his own natural curiosity and fertile imagination. It required only the impact of a particularly traumatic event to make him see that the fabric of human culture is always fragile and sometimes needs to be protected from unthinking violence.

## The Trauma of Violence

The Salcete mission, situated on the very edge of the Portuguese enclave and always subject to internal conflicts and shifting loyalties, was never easy. According to Georg Schurhammer, the population of Salcete, scattered over fifty-five villages, amounted to about 80,000; scores of temples were dedicated to Santery, the cobra-goddess, a form of the fearsome Durga. In 1560 there were about 100 Christians. By the end of the decade there were over a thousand – a remarkable growth, but one that was achieved in no small measure by force, with the destruction of Hindu temples. Almost inevitably there was a violent reaction, and in 1583 four Jesuits, including Rudolph Acquaviva as superior and forty-eight native Christians, were attacked and violently hacked to death at a small outpost called Cuncolim. Today the site of the massacre is covered by an innocuous little chapel. Another chapel, a couple of hundred yards away, covers the 'well' – more a damp pit – where the dismembered bodies were dumped. Stephens, recently installed in the 'college' or Jesuit community in Rachol, was caught in the aftermath. It fell to him to recover the bodies – one of them a fellow novice from Roman days – and then go about the painful business of rebuilding the community's work.

When I visited the spot with a group of Jesuits, I was struck by the simplicity of the site. There was no great monument proclaiming what had happened. I did, however, notice a more recent memorial to another massacre set up in a garden on the other

*Jesuit Church of Rachol, Salcete, Goa*

side of the dividing wall. It made for sober reading.

> This memorial is dedicated to the bravery and valour of the chieftains of Cuncolim who stood against the Portuguese and were treacherously massacred when attending peace talks at the Assolna fort in July 1583.

Some dozen names are listed, a tangible reminder of the 'other side' of history. Acquaviva had come to Cuncolim with his companions to mediate in a bitter conflict that had broken out over the desecration of the local temple. Instead they were violently killed, and their deaths led subsequently to a further terrible act of vengeance. The memorial acts as a reminder that it wasn't just Catholics who suffered violence at that time. Religious difference is never the whole story in inter-communal conflict. The economic and political consequences of disruption of the cultural status quo are often equally significant. Hence a pertinent comment from the Jesuit historian, Teotónio de Souza. He criticises recourse to binary thinking, such as the assumption that the 'pagans' were implicated in 'the work of the devil' while those who supported the missionaries were doing

'God's work'. The truth is always more complex. This was something Stephens came to know through painful experience.

However this tragic episode is to be dissected, it was, says Schurhammer, a 'major disaster'. By strange chance, two months later came a letter from Stephens's brother Richard, telling him of the martyrdom of Edmund Campion and his companions at Tyburn on 1 December 1581. In his reply, written on 24 October 1583, just four years after his arrival in India, Stephens gives a graphic description of what happened in Cuncolim. He then passes on a happier story about the strength of faith of a Brahmin boy who was imprisoned by his family yet resisted all attempts to make him give up his Christian faith. The story is not a pious aside, intended to counter the traumas of Tyburn and Cuncolim. Stephens is touched by the movements of divine Providence in the middle of terrible experiences of suffering. The world the brothers share is going through a period of darkness, but Thomas consoles Richard with an example of patient goodness. The process of conversion takes time and its own form of heroic perseverance; unnecessary pressure leads only to obstinacy, and risks further violence.

Another historian, Ananya Chakravarti, author of an insightful analysis of Stephens's life and mission, draws attention to his 'willingness to impute reasonable motivations and sentiments to the people of his adopted land'. His awareness of the seeds of violence, she says, built up in him not resentment but a remarkable capacity for empathy which enabled him to identify with the local culture and its people. There had to be a better way, a less violent way, to witness to the Gospel message of peace and reconciliation.

## Pastoral Care and Catechesis

Stephens spent most of his forty years on the Indian mission in Salcete. The first half was dedicated to pastoral work, for the 'salvation of souls', as Ignatius decreed in the first *Formula*. Stephens was clearly a wise and sensitive priest. The labour of administration came less easily to him. He was conscious that simply keeping

*The Chapel at Cuncolim built over the site of the massacre*

control of the mission would lead to an encounter with the people that was superficial and took little account of his people's loyalty to their customs and patterns of behaviour. He was aware that Brahmin converts were concerned that their newfound faith lacked the cultural and liturgical structures they had been so used to. So he began to think in terms of an accompaniment to the catechism, a story to be recited and prayed, raising questions and opening up elucidations of the truth of the Gospel. The *Kristapurana* was the fruit of long years of prayerful study, preaching and pastoral work. Once he had mastered Sanskrit and produced his grammar of

Konkani, Stephens was more and more captivated by the language of the Marathi saints which, according to a modern history of Marathi literature, he described as 'a jewel among pebbles, like a sapphire among jewels, like the jasmine among blossoms and the musk among all perfumes, the peacock among birds'. He became convinced that no better language could be imagined for communicating the truth of the Gospel. What was Stephens seeking to convey through this great text? And does it have anything to teach a modern audience, some four hundred years later?

In a letter to the Superior General, from 1601, Stephens writes about 'the little chapels which Fr Provincial ordered to be erected in remote villages. Here the children can gather to study their catechism and the people can stop to pray when passing by'. By focusing his efforts on the instruction of children he hoped to found a new type of community, far removed from the old rivalries which had proved so destructive. Not that the text is a purely liturgical accompaniment, a vehicle for devotional assimilation of Christian truth. Cut into the story are occasional questions from an enquiring Brahmin or 'an intelligent person' which enable the teacher to develop further the meaning of what has been recounted in the narrative.

There is, in other words, more to the *Kristapurana* than an imaginative retelling of the biblical narrative. Apart from the obvious influence of the *Spiritual Exercises,* we should not forget the one text that Ignatius allows his retreatant, *The Imitation of Christ.* Stephens's novice master, Fabio de Fabi, refers in his Directory to the 'hidden power' of the *Exercises,* 'grounded as they are in the teaching of the saints, the truth of scripture, and long experience'. In good Ignatian fashion, the *Kristapurana* seeks to bring the powers of the soul and *all the senses* into a single whole-hearted response to the love of God poured out for humankind in Christ. This is no nod in the direction of 'popular religion'; it is a sophisticated and highly effective catechesis.

## The Puranic Style

If the content is very much the Gospel story, the form or style in which it is recounted comes from the cultural world of Stephens's Brahmin converts. The word *purana,* literally 'old' or 'ancient', may be translated as 'account of past history'. It refers to a genre of Hindu literature which in its classical form is held to deal with topics such as creation, destruction and re-creation, the genealogy of gods and ancient sages, and the rule of kings and heroes. *Puranas* are lengthy stories associated with various theistic forms, *avatars* – literally 'descents' – or manifestations of *Bhagavan,* the 'Blessed Lord'. Compared with the ancient Vedic hymns and the philosophical texts of the Upanisads, these are the most tangible expressions of the great movement of *bhakti* religion, with its seminal literary form in the *Bhagavad Gita,* the 'Song of the Lord', the best-known and most beloved of Hindu scriptures.

*Bhakti* means 'participation' and may be loosely translated as 'loyalty', with connotations of the divine grace that inspires all forms of heartfelt love. In their written form the *puranas* represent the imaginative ordering of exemplary stories. Their origins, however, lie not with the artifice of a writer but with the *sutas* or bards who were responsible for the oral recitation that gathered a community together. The form of semi-liturgical performance is still to be found all over India as the familiar stories are sung and recited in villages, temples and more formal settings.

Stephens used the form to exhort his audience to lead good and honest lives in imitation of Jesus Christ. But it would not have escaped his attention that the ritual, which is inseparable from myths and legends, has a certain political or social dimension. Friedhelm Hardy links the formation of *puranic* texts with the growing emergence of autonomous kingdoms which needed somehow to identify and preserve a 'common history'. Bards were often employed at court to celebrate ancient lineages and trace royal descent by linking the deeds of ancestors and heroes to the world of the gods. Some stories, says Hardy, became so popular that they turned themselves into 'separate repertoire pieces'. In terms of form, the *Kristapurana* has such a religious and political purpose: the validation of the religious pedigree of the Christian community. The story proclaims who these people are.

### The Demands of Justice

The first part of the text – about a third of the whole – is less the story of Israel than a single lengthy meditation on the coming of Christ as Saviour into a world darkened by sin. It is remarkably full, beginning with the rebellion of the angels and ending with predictions of the coming of Christ from Jewish prophets and Roman sybils alike. The second part, the Gospel narrative, begins with an invocation to God to inspire the teacher to speak worthily of the mystery of divine revelation before moving on to what Ignatius would call the 'history' of the Incarnation and the birth of Jesus. I offer here just a couple of examples which may give something of the flavour of Stephens's story-telling while at the same time pointing in the direction of one of the major theological themes that emerges from this type of '*puranic* catechesis'.

When the three 'rulers, kings of the East' turn up (no mere wise men here), they are accompanied by elephants and chariots, massive umbrellas, flags and banners, war drums and the sound of trumpets. No wonder Herod was put out.

> As if struck by a whip, or as the moon loses lustre, the king lost his demeanour and his lotus face faded. As if turned to a stone statue he could not utter a single word.

The three travellers meanwhile, with their pomp and magnificent array, find their way to Bethlehem and the poor cowshed where the child lies on his mother's lap. The encounter is movingly described, and what they see of the humble surroundings of this king provokes something of a conversion, as they remember how they have just promised Herod to report back on the whereabouts of the child. The next day they talk to each other about the dream they have had. They praise and worship the child and take their leave, sending the army back to their own country by 'another way' while they themselves disappear wordlessly off the scene.

It's as if they have never been there. The streets of the city are silent, and Herod blusters on about their finding nothing and having to return home 'full of shame'. Inwardly, of course, he is consumed with envy, hatred and a desire for vengeance. He realises he has been deceived and eventually his anger bursts out:

> Great flames rose into his insides [and] his brows were knit with knots. He shouted wildly and loudly in the palace and walked about like a mad man.

The slaughter of the innocents is told in graphic detail. Jeremiah's prophecy – 'in Rama a voice is heard; Rachel weeping for her children' – is quoted, but it is impossible not to imagine something of the dreadful events of Cuncolim playing on the mind of Stephens. There is, however, a sequel. Having given a brief account of Herod's further crimes, and having pondered on the sins of those who think they can ignore God's justice, Stephens, the narrator of the story, is interrupted by a Brahmin:

> Strange indeed is the story of that king. You have told a narrative of great moral value. So what punishment to such a king was given, to that unfortunate one by God? Tell us that, then we will understand.

The disease that afflicts Herod is then described in gory detail, and is not for faint European hearts. But it would have been pretty normal fare for an audience familiar with the grisly fate meted out to malign monsters.

This takes us back to the comment by the Jesuit historian, Teotónio de Souza. If there is one theme that underlies all Indian religion it is that of cosmic justice: the dilemmas of pursuing *dharma,* the cause of right, in a less than perfect world. In the Epic and *Puranic* literature, this theme is played out as an endless battle between the personalised forces of good and evil. Very often it is the god-figure appearing in human or animal form who uses his superior powers, often gained through acts of asceticism, to overcome the wiles of the demon. This is the basic framework with which Stephens works. But he does more than set up a binary opposition, as becomes clear when he turns to a magnificent rendering of the Temptations of Jesus:

> Inside the hollow dome of the sky, the servants of Lucifer were talking. 'Who is that dwelling, dressed like an ascetic, in the forest? ... He is definitely the enemy. Now let us alert our king.'
>
> While they were talking, the messengers said to Lucifer, 'O King, why are you still sitting quietly? ... We have seen a wonderful thing, a man has come suddenly leaping from the town of Nazareth.
>
> 'We have seen him from far off but we dared not go close to him. His name alone is terror for all the devils.'
>
> Upon hearing this, Lucifer trembled with great anger, as if fire was stirred up by sprinkling ghee on it.
>
> Or like a cobra when it is put in a bamboo box ... great wrath provoked him; from his nose, mouth, ears and out of all the organs, fireballs rushed and showered forth.
>
> As a fierce rocket, when it is burst, it shakes a lot and looks as if there is no end to its fire ... in the same way the fierce tormentor was greatly wrathful. At the place of hell, on the throne of fire he raged upon the chains as he shouted.

This Lucifer dominates the minor demons and they follow him because of their 'pride and vanity'; but when he comes close to Jesus he covers up his 'ghastly appearance' and takes the form of an old man. This is Stephens's version, not of classical Hinduism, but of a very Ignatian theme.

## Discerning the Dark

As we have noted earlier, Ignatius knew that 'the enemy of our
human nature' is a master of disguise. As Stephens tells the story
of the Temptations, it is Jesus who beats the devil at his own game,
allowing himself to get close to the demon in order to destroy him
'stealthily'. This gives Stephens the opportunity to introduce a familiar patristic image:

> As a fisherman puts bait of flesh in the mouth of fish,
> and when the hook is seized, he draws it up and takes
> his life, so the Lord whose wisdom is deep, allowed his
> human form to be carried, to vanquish the wicked one by
> the power of his Divine Nature.

The theological motif of the Divine entering deep into a world ter-
rorised by the demonic runs through much of Stephens's narrative.
What he describes so vividly is the redeeming action of the Trinitarian God who, in Ignatius's contemplation on the Incarnation,
looks down 'over the vast extent and circuit of the earth with its
many and various races'. Stephens himself would have contemplated the rituals and devotions of the people of Salcete, as well as its
recent history, and found there many resonances that would build
up his form of '*puranic* exegesis'. That is not to say, however, that
he would have failed to spot areas of discord, where his Christian
faith jarred with what he found in the local religious culture.

There's a dispassionate side to Stephens's flights of fancy
which always come back to the insights of Ignatius into our flawed
human nature. It would be surprising if Stephens were not haunted
throughout his life by what happened at Cuncolim, and yet this
extraordinary text is characterised by a lack of polemic. There are
plenty of enemies and they get their comeuppance, but they are
simply more or less culpable versions of Satan – and it is the un-
masking of Satan, naming evil for what it is in all its shifty grey-
ness, that most concerns Stephens. The *puranic* world view is by
no means clear of binary thinking; forces of power and violence

are forever coming up against qualities of love and wisdom. The question, to repeat what was argued in the last chapter, is how they work together – and the answer Stephens gives lies unsurprisingly with the person of Christ. Schooled in the *Spiritual Exercises* and familiar with Ignatius's great meditations on Christ the King and the Two Standards, Stephens offers, not a translation of Christian faith into Hindu terms, still less a Christian-Hindu synthesis, but something more direct: an imaginative retelling of the Jesus narrative. In the hands of a master storyteller like Stephens, Scripture is not a *script* to be read and dissected, but the place where God's Word and the promptings of the Spirit are to be discerned. Scripture creates a religious world, and by entering into that world, with all its colour, symbolism, beauty and aesthetic power, one acquires a language which structures and interprets that world.

The story stands on its own merits; its truth does not have to be proved by subtle arguments which exist apart from that story. It speaks for itself, with the occasional addition of well-reasoned commentary on the questions raised by the 'intelligent person' (one of his Rachol Brahmin converts perhaps?). This is what Stephens says by way of self-justification in his introduction:

> No efforts whatsoever have been made in this Purana to prove that their sacred book is untrue and false, and our sacred book is true and real. The difference and the distinctness between the two automatically becomes evident to all. The sacred book of the Christians emerges as beautiful of its own accord ... If you read or listen to this sacred book, it would be enough. It will promote proper understanding of everything.

*Inculturation as Incarnation*
I have tried to tell the story of Thomas Stephens as an example of the missionary practice of inculturation. There is a direct line from Xavier, teaching the fisherfolk of southern India to learn the way of Christ through prayer, to Stephens's *Kristapurana*, with its en-

thralling recreation of the Gospel through a traditional Indian medium. This is not evangelisation as such, but catechesis, taking the truth of the Gospel and embedding its affective power in the heart. When Pedro Arrupe, the former Superior General, wrote to the Society of Jesus in 1978 about the practice of inculturation, it was not the example of Stephens that was uppermost in his mind. Yet the lone Englishman who, with his concern to ensure the spreading of Christian faith did not do violence to local culture, perfectly illustrates Arrupe's definition of inculturation as

> the incarnation of Christian life and of the Christian message in a particular cultural context, in such a way that this experience not only finds expression through elements proper to the culture in question, but becomes a principle that animates, directs and unifies the culture, transforming it and remaking it so as to bring about 'a new creation'.

As expression *and* principle, artistic image *and* the act of artistic creation, the *Kristapurana* is best understood as a sort of sixteenth-century *ressourcement,* by which I mean, not a retrieval of something lost or forgotten, but a deeply meditative engagement with familiar texts that need to be repeated and retold for new audiences and different situations. Much as medieval wall paintings on village churches all over England used to convey a graphic sense of the inner truths of the Gospel, their vivid depiction of a religious world complementing the action of the liturgy, so Stephens based his catechesis on the cultivation of a familiar art form to translate the truth of Christian faith into an Indian symbolic world.

To produce such work is a never-ending exercise which takes time, patience and careful study. Moreover, as Valignano recognised, the acquisition of local languages is not enough; the missionary has to learn a new way of self-presentation to local people, with attention to clothing, diet and housing, as well as the etiquette of speech and conversation. I sometimes wonder whether it was purely accidental that the most prominent figures in the first movement of 'inculturation' owed no allegiance to the Portuguese colonial power. Ricci, De Nobili and Stephens – and many other remarkable individuals – worked deliberately on the fringes, where the innate truth of the Gospel could not be corrupted by political vested interests. There they enjoyed the freedom to develop the personal resources and linguistic and cultural skills that enabled them to communicate at a more than superficial level.

A superficial reading of the *Kristapurana* patronises it as a charming romance, an exercise in devotional rhetoric. It is easy to forget how difficult and dangerous the religious and political world Stephens inhabited really was. The voice of the 'intelligent brahmin' which he injects into his narrative seems pleasantly compliant, a device to get the story moving rather than an objection that needs to be treated with care and circumspection. The memory of the massacre of Rudolf Acquaviva and his companions was never that far away. Stephens does not give us some nuanced theological strategy for coping with today's experience of religious pluralism. That is not why his story is worth telling. It is, more exactly, a witness to the innate power of the Word to speak through all manner of words – a power in which human beings are called to participate.

# CHAPTER SIX

## Translating Memory

IN THE last chapter I offered a historical example of the typically Jesuit practice of inculturation, finishing with some remarks about how sacred texts such as the New Testament create a religious world. This style of accommodation is usually understood as a matter of presenting the truth of the Paschal Mystery of the Death and Resurrection of Jesus through the familiar form of the local vernacular. Careful translation is always necessary, but too strong a focus on 'method' risks missing the critical point. Pedro Arrupe's celebrated definition of inculturation shifts attention away from what is often interpreted in instrumentalist terms – the local language as a dispensable garb in which the Gospel is clothed – towards the theological mystery of the Incarnation itself. This, as noted before, comes from a powerful insight in the *Exercises* based on the conviction of Ignatius that the world is held in the compassionate hands of the Trinitarian God. To repeat Arrupe's point, the mystery of the Incarnation offers a principle which 'animates, directs and unifies the culture, transforming it and remaking it so as to bring about "a new creation".'

Stephens was as much a man of his time as Ricci, de Nobili and the other great Jesuit apostles of inculturation. Their Christian faith was not to be put on the same level as other religious traditions. Nevertheless, they knew instinctively that what the early Fathers of the Church spoke of as 'seeds of the Word' were growing all around them. For Stephens, something more was at stake than the mere colonising of a local art form. The life I sought to recount was that of a pastoral priest living in a Hindu environment. His support of the people entrusted to his care required a narration of the Old and New Testaments which was faithful to the Gospel message yet did not do violence to their everyday culture. If there is a pragmatic principle behind Stephens's practice and Arrupe's incarnational theology, it has to be expressed in terms of a dialectic between the *use* of culture and its protection against *abuse*. In adapting the message to local needs, the Christian missionary faces, not just a pragmatic question about how to make the Gospel heard and understood, but an ethical question about the respect that is owed to the integrity of local culture.

So much by way of repetition. Today such a sensitivity to the 'otherness' that is present in every walk of life is taken for granted, however limited actual responses may be. Alongside a deeply felt confidence in the Word of God lives the humility of the pilgrim, the sense of being drawn by the Spirit of Christ. In this chapter I want to turn to a contemporary interreligious practice that is typically Jesuit in its provenance and principles, a worthy successor to the wisdom practised by the first pioneers. What is called comparative theology – a cross-religious reading of texts from different traditions – is one of the most important fruits of the revolution begun by the Second Vatican Council's *Nostra Aetate*. Much of what I offer in this book is based on this form of theological engagement, even if I offer a rather broader sense of what a 'text' is and how one goes about 'reading' another religious world. Before focusing on comparative theology, however, let me add a few more words of personal experience. This, I hope, will serve to bring the theological questions that attend all forms of interreligious dialogue into a correlation with some of the ethical – and political – issues that attend life in our contemporary globalised multicultural world.

*Life on the Margins*

Let me introduce a religious world very different from Salcete, yet also curiously similar – and not because the verdant undulating landscape to the south of Goa is startlingly reminiscent of the Wiltshire hills that were so familiar to Thomas Stephens. Southall in West London is one of the most diverse multi-religious parts of the UK, with large communities of Sikhs, Muslims and Hindus, a small number of Buddhists, and Christians from a variety of denominations: Catholic, Anglican and Pentecostalist. I first got to know Southall in the 1980s through my contact with Daniel Faivre, that wonderfully eccentric French Brother of St Gabriel whom I have already mentioned. While running Westminster Interfaith, the diocesan agency with responsibility for relations with other communities of faith, Daniel lived in Southall. I struck up a close working relationship with him, and would often visit what he called the 'Holy City' to introduce students to places of worship, to talk with local worthies and to participate in meetings of various kinds.

A year or so before the millennium I moved there myself, establishing a Jesuit community with responsibility for the Catholic parish of St Anselm and a small dialogue centre which we called De Nobili House. I will postpone saying anything more about the town of Southall and its reputation as a model for interreligious dialogue until a later chapter. Here I stay with the work of the Jesuit community as the context that formed the peculiar hybrid of comparative theology I seek to espouse.

Dialogue with local faith communities was the main focus of the new community, but I knew from my previous experience of local interreligious initiatives that there could be problems in not having close links with existing Church structures. So we came up with three key principles to structure our work. Firstly, the *visibility* to other faith communities of St Anselm's would help to strengthen any representative outreach that I did. Secondly, it would gain *credibility* with other Christians, ensuring that our work was seen

*Annual Sikh procession at the Vaisakhi festival, outside
St Anselm's Catholic Church, Southall*

to be part of the single mission of the Church in Southall. To hold those two points together I added a third rationale. What motivates Christians to engage in relations with 'the other' is not just some well-meaning exhortation, but something deeply rooted in Christian faith and practice, and ultimately in the Eucharist, the source of Christian understanding of how the Trinitarian God is at work sending the Word and the Spirit into the world. In other words, it was important to root interreligious activity in the building up of the Eucharistic community that is the Church.

Our patron was Roberto de Nobili who, like Stephens, was appalled by the cultural destructiveness of the Portuguese and the resentment it caused, particularly among the Brahmin elite who quickly came to despise all European customs and religious practices. He quickly came to the conclusion that another way of presenting the Christian faith had to be found. None of our Southall group had any intention of wandering the streets dressed in saffron robes, as de Nobili did. My own twentieth-century inculturation equivalent was encapsulated in a lovely phrase from Daniel which has its own Ignatian credentials: 'listen with all the senses'. In that spirit, I would look for little reasons to visit places of worship and other centres – introducing students, showing friends around, consulting about questions, even reading in libraries – and there was always the Sikh langar (or communal dining room) where a meal was served and conversation ensued. Beyond the pleasantries and good-natured banter was a serious purpose: to discern the guiding presence of the Spirit and become so soaked in a different culture 'as to bring about "a new creation"'.

As a Jesuit community, we took the four forms of dialogue, not just as a pattern for our pastoral and apostolic work, but as the pattern of our life together, with attention to study and reflection, prayer and liturgy, practical engagement with neighbours, and meetings and gatherings of one kind or another. We worked closely with Brother Daniel, always a source of support and critical energy, and I tried to integrate my life and work in Southall with the academic work I was doing at Heythrop in the University of London. I did my best to keep in touch with the endless feasts and festivals that mark the interreligious calendar. One of the most memorable events at de Nobili was an evening of reflection when the Hindu Divali and Muslim Eid happened to coincide. It was an opportunity to see Southall celebrate. After some prayer and discussion in the house, a group of about twenty set out with greetings cards and gifts to various places of worship. This was not high-powered stuff, more a matter of contributing an extra interreligious thread to the extraordinary tapestry of religion in a remarkable melting-pot of faiths. There was no grand strategy, more what Michel de Certeau thinks of as tactical adjustments, as opportunities were taken to raise a question about the danger of leading 'parallel lives'.

*Imaginative Reading*

Let me turn now to a few introductory words on comparative theology: first its provenance and method of approach; secondly a brief reflection on my own contributions and what they owe to life in Southall; and finally a more lengthy example or 'case study' in comparative theology which will pick up on some of our earlier themes.

Comparative theology is more a style of theology than a school, though it has begun to develop a distinctive communal personality of its own in recent years. As a way of reading texts comparatively and theologically, it owes its origins to the genius of an American Jesuit, Francis Clooney, who began to teach theology through this method at Boston College in the 1980's. I didn't – quite – meet Frank in India. I had finished my Jesuit tertianship in a dialogue centre in south Chennai in 1982, when Frank came to complete his PhD a few weeks later. It was another decade before I met the studious New Yorker at Boston College, where he introduced me to his courses in the comparative reading of Christian and Hindu texts. It was a very simple idea for catching the imagination of undergraduates: set a familiar text alongside an unfamiliar one on the same theme and get the two to talk to each other. The process of interpretation – moving between one 'religious world' and another – raises questions about meaning, and one begins to 'do theology'. It demands some study of the texts themselves, but it also asks for critical attention to experience and the wider hinterland of everyday living. As well as being thoroughly grounded in the great Jesuit pedagogical traditions and a classically trained theologian, Frank is an accomplished Indologist, with a knowledge of Sanskrit and Tamil. Now at Harvard University, he has over the years produced a never-ending flow of sometimes dense studies of the interface between Christianity and Hinduism.

Comparative theology is an exercise in teaching and learning, bringing texts into a theological correlation where their insights enlighten each other. Frank describes it as 'a practical response to religious diversity read with our eyes open, interpreting the world in light of our faith and with a willingness to see newly the truths of our own religion in light of another'. In mode of practice it is not dissimilar to Scriptural Reasoning which I mentioned earlier. That began, and is still largely limited to, the exploration of the three Abrahamic traditions. Its more remote origins lie within the tradition of Jewish Talmudic reasoning, and it still maintains a strong prophetic element with the emphasis on sharing of insights raised by cross-religious readings that are done 'for the sake of God' and for the good of wider society. If Scriptural Reasoning is characterised by a distinctive 'reparative reasoning', comparative theology is more an 'exploratory reasoning' which is committed to searching out the full extent of God's providential purposes. It can be traced through the Second Vatican Council to the recovery of the Catholic missiology of de Nobili, Ricci and Stephens, and therefore has about it an important element of inculturation. In a pluralist world saturated with the wisdom of classical texts of all kinds, it represents a response to religious diversity that seeks an authenticity of understanding rooted in sensitive and imaginative reading.

Some time ago, a kindly reviewer described me as an 'eclectic post-Vatican II Catholic theologian' (which did not please me particularly) and the sort of thing I do as comparative theology (with which I was a lot happier). I have, however, come to realise that my version of comparative theology is broader in scope, and definitely less detailed in form, than what Frank produces. He is nothing if not the consummate scholar, dedicated to learning from the Hindu tradition and its great philosophical and theological texts. My writing owes more to practical context, to places like Southall which stimulate attentive listening and a measure of the imaginative contemplation Ignatius commends in the *Exercises*. Both of us – and other practitioners – would agree that comparative theology is born from an abiding curiosity about the different ways human beings speak about themselves and whatever they take to have ultimate value. The question is about the limits of the imagination, how much of what is properly other can legitimately become the focus of Christian reflection. I'll take up that question in a later chapter. Here I want to stay with that point about context or place as the focus of attention.

When moving into another place – such as crossing the threshold of mosque, synagogue, temple or other place of worship, or seeking to negotiate a shared space, such as the politically charged civic world – ethical questions arise from the asymmetry of inter-personal relations. How to make comprehensible what is other without reducing it to something one can control or imposing alien categories on it? I use the title 'Translating Memory' for this chapter, because I think that's what comparative work does at its best. It takes the most formative of memories – what grounds a tradition of faith – and it seeks to move them across borders, to expand their reference.

What follows, therefore, is an example of comparative theology 'at work'. I won't preface it with any explanation about method, except to remark that more is involved than lining up comparable texts. Frank talks about following a certain 'intuition'. He doesn't, as far as I can see, have a set method. Reading is a repetitive exercise, a form of *lectio divina,* in which resonances and echoes begin to sound in the process of reading. But what makes that process of 'translation' possible is the imaginative probing of memory, extending the traces and links that the work of remembering – literally, of course, 'putting back together' – makes possible. My general approach is to begin in the 'middle of things', with Gillian Rose's 'broken middle', where thoughts and ideas and symbolic forms – and people – compete for attention. More exactly, this is the 'middle' of the world contemplated by the Trinity in Ignatius's contemplation on the Incarnation, the site of the action of Word and Spirit, sent for the creation-and-redemption of the world.

## Symbolism to Move the Heart

So let me take you to a particular place in 'the middle'. It is, perhaps more a symbolic middle: a Tibetan cultural exhibition which

*Buddhist monks composing the Mandala of coloured powders*

I attended in the centre of London a few years ago. An invited group witnessed a particular practice called in Tibetan *dul-tson-kyil-khor* – the *'mandala* of coloured powders' – and it is part of a complex ritual of initiation. Over the course of some days, grains of coloured sand and rice are laid with immense care on to a flat surface. What is gradually built up is a *mandala* of quite breath-taking beauty. Fresh, sharp, vibrant, but, of course, all too delicate; a careless movement or a gust of wind could ruin it. As if to illustrate the point, no sooner was it finished and the mantras chanted than it was gathered up with a small scoop and the whole thing deposited in a small bag. I can still remember the horrified in-drawing of breath from the visitors as so spectacular a creation was destroyed in a few seconds. So much effort and so much time, all for little more than a fleeting glimpse of perfection.

A few minutes later, with a dispassion and matter-of-factness which were almost as impressive as the skill with which the *mandala* had been built, a little stream of golden powder was solemnly poured into the dirty old Thames. It was impossible not to appreciate the power of religious symbolism to move the heart. Here was a beautiful artefact which had been deliberately reduced back to its rough, raw material, thus pointing to the fragility of creation – and, in Buddhist terms, the insubstantiality of any human attempt to create lasting meaning. What we were given that afternoon was a glimpse into a religious world, a ritual re-consecration of the Universe in which the world of human experience was freed to return to its origins. That may sound somewhat daunting, but it is only to make explicit what is contained within that form of the Mahayana known as Tantric Buddhism. The word *'tantra'*, from a Sanskrit root meaning 'stretch' or 'extend', can be translated as 'continuum'. Tantric texts can be loosely said to 'expand' the meaning of the *Buddhadharma.*

The possibility of such an 'expansion' or continuum is easily justified. The Mahayana tradition established the principle of an infinite number of omniscient Buddhas teaching through an infinite number of *sutras*. The *tantra* takes the principle further, with an emphasis on the immeasurable number of practices and ways to enlightenment. Thus secret initiations, esoteric teachings and the pursuit of *siddhis* or 'special powers' become intrinsic elements of the path to enlightenment.

While this makes the process of interpretation hazardous, it would be a mistake to separate these elements from the wider context of what can loosely be called the 'tantric ethos'. The key concept, in many ways as old as the Indo-Tibetan tradition itself, is the worship of *śakti*, the essentially feminine life-giving power behind creation. Governing this current of thought is a vision of the whole of reality, 'outer' cosmos and 'inner' human person, as pervaded by a creative (and destructive) energy. Tantric practice seeks to correlate the two, enacting correspondences and analogies between macrocosm and microcosm. Tantric temple ritual is perhaps best understood as a sort of 'grid' which fits the one to the other.

Think of the *mandala* as a map of the spiritual universe which acts in meditation as a guide for an inner pilgrimage. 'Reading' the map, impressing it on the heart, the pilgrim returns to the centre of the world, a centre which becomes the innermost heart of the initiate. In other words, a practice of 'centring' brings about an integration of the different levels or aspects of one's personal existence around the cosmic centre. The three outer rings, for example, represent successive barriers – the circle of fire, which stands for purification and wisdom, the 'Vajra-circle' which symbolises initiation, and the gentle lotus-circle which speaks of a newly acquired transformation. Beyond these three initial barriers, however, there arises what is in effect a divine mansion, a four-sided structure which, like real architecture, is richly decorated with intricate walls and gateways. The initiate must be prepared to go through a number of different stages, overcome different obstacles, and engage in a variety of practices in order to achieve that reintegration and deliverance from bondage which is *Nirvana*.

Of all the yogic practices which make this possible perhaps the most important is the art of visualisation. At the same time as one makes the inner pilgrimage one is entering into an imaginative meeting with the Buddhas. Each Buddha can be understood as expressing one of the major qualities or virtues which are necessary for enlightenment – not just wisdom, but compassion and generosity, beauty and energy. *Mandalas* very often centre upon one major Buddha, but the most common of Tantric practices is based on a classic group of five: Akshobhya, Ratnasambhava, Amitabha, Amoghasiddhi and Vairocana. These figures each have their own rich mythology and inspire devotional as much as directly meditative practice. As 'Buddha-families' (each has an attendant goddess or consort and a number of attendant bodhisattva figures) they are also linked with various other sets of five – gestures, colours, directions, mantras – as well as more specifically Buddhist concepts, such as the 'aggregates' (aspects of the human person) and 'taints' or poisons which inhibit enlightenment.

*Reading the Mandala*

How is the non-Buddhist, the comparative theologian, to 'read' such an extraordinary practice? It is important in the first place to know enough about 'the other' tradition. Tantric Buddhism is often regarded as the preserve of a few privileged initiates, an obscure antinomianism in which the adept deliberately confronts the sources of ritual impurity. It is easy to miss the continuity with the wider tradition. As an artefact, the *mandala* illustrates Buddhist teaching, especially the Four Noble Truths: suffering, the causes of suffering, the cessation of suffering, and the way to achieve the cessation of suffering. As a visualisation technique, it can be linked to the familiar *kasina* devices (coloured discs which focus attention) of the Theravada *samatha* form of meditation and the more discursive meditations on the qualities of the three jewels, the Buddha, the Buddha's teaching and the community of disciples of the Buddha. This, with an added whiff of the esoteric, is mainstream Buddhism, one of so many versions of what is depicted in the early

Theravada texts in terms of a movement from the lesser to the greater 'fruits of being a recluse'.

At the same time, it is impossible to ignore aspects both of theory and practice which move us away from Buddhist particularities towards something more cross-religious and universal. Jung, of course, thought he had discovered a deep psychological significance in all forms of the *mandala*, from the stylised Tibetan variety to other examples of religious art and architecture which were designed to catch and integrate the attention through various versions of a 'harmony of opposites'. A *mandala*, he says, 'may be described as a symbol of the self seen in cross-section' and the process of integration which it promotes 'an identification with the totality of the personality, with the self'. How helpful this is I do not know, but I note this comment from Vessantara, a modern Buddhist interpreter:

> If you explore your own imaginative responses to the Buddha's Awakening, without the structure and continuity of content that practising a traditional *sadhana* gives, my hunch is that the images, sounds or feelings that come up will tend to be much more fluid and labile than the figures in our current *sadhanas.* So we may find that many people are in effect practising Jungian 'active imagination'. This has its own value, but may not go as deep as a more focused practice. People practising in this way will need to consider balancing things out, by doing some meditation with a focus that they don't change.

That word of warning is nothing if not a reminder that Buddhism is intensely suspicious of language which isolates some sort of soul-principle or self. It is perfectly possible to 'read' the *mandala* as an aid to Jungian individuation. But that does not mean that you will enter fully into its peculiarly Buddhist wisdom. Vessantara reminds us that a 'comparison' which contents itself with extracting some putatively common structure or pattern, and doesn't respect the depths of possible meaning which a religious practice is designed to provoke, risks a premature 'colonising' of what is properly other – the ethical issue I was drawing attention to at the beginning of the chapter.

The temptation is to remain content with observing the *mandala* rather than entering fully into the questions which it may unlock. If nothing else, that acts as a reminder that there are always limits to what the outsider can 'comprehend' of another tradition. But it does not follow that there is nothing to learn – if not about the 'other' tradition, then about the 'home' tradition, particularly about how that tradition is to be assimilated and taught. I go back to that point about initiation. Before the *mandala* is an artefact it is a ritual: a graduated practice of entry, communion and departure, shaping a never-ending journey, a movement or evolution which can never be finished until all things, and all sentient beings, have found their due place in relation to each other. Paradoxically, that is what the construction and destruction of the '*mandala* of coloured powders' is meant to show. To use a familiar Buddhist parable, it is like the boat which one discards after crossing the river. Like all rituals it does not point to a meaning elsewhere. Its meaning is its purpose, to act as a pedagogy which attends to the truth of what is given in the present moment. A Buddhist truth certainly. The very fragility of all we put together is demonstrated as tiny expanses of coloured sand are reduced to one rather dirty pile, all too reminiscent of the messiness of human living – a point to which all people of faith can relate.

*Reading and Interpretation of Scripture*

We have been responding to being dumped unceremoniously in the 'middle of things'. We observe what is going on, reacting to the stimulus, bringing our own memories to bear upon what is new, casting around for analogies. There is a discipline involved, and sometimes it involves a lot of hard work to soak oneself in another thought-world. Unlike Scriptural Reasoning, where there is always an interpreter present and the object is to listen attentively to the way the text is being explained, comparative theology is a more personal process. As with Scriptural Reasoning, however, the aim is not to impose some meaning on the other tradition, but to come away from the work of comparison with a deeper sense of one's own 'home' tradition. That is why I find the method of *lectio divina* a useful way of structuring the process, if only because a prayerful discipline is involved.

What is at stake is a discernment of interior movements as one follows what is nothing less than a conversion towards God. A Buddhist would not use such theistic language, of course. Nevertheless, as a mode of spiritual understanding, comparative theology comes close to the Buddhist practice of inner transformation. Both are guided by an unspoken but all-dominating question: *how does memory take hold of and translate truth?* If I go back for a moment to the meetings we held at de Nobili House, I am always struck by how quickly people from across the religious spectrum soon learned how to develop a sort of intuitive imagination. The groups that went out that autumn evening when many people in Southall were celebrating Eid and Divali were opening up a form of theological hospitality; their messages started a simple and very practical dialogue. And the welcome they received came back to the house in the form of little insights, further questions and, most importantly, the felt consolation that Ignatius talks about as an 'increase in faith, hope and love'. Once a taste for learning *about* the other has given way to a learning *from* the other, a mutuality of regard begins to build. And that in itself is transformative of the self.

So far I have not done much comparing. Let me turn, therefore, to one of the great teachers of the Christian tradition and the practical question of how in any religious tradition teaching and learning are to be carried on. I refer to what Augustine at the beginning of *De Doctrina Christiana* calls 'Rules for Interpreting the Scriptures'. He is talking here, not about 'Christian doctrine' as a set of organised beliefs, but 'Christian teaching' as an activity of teaching and being taught by the Word of God. He is concerned with the qualities of the teacher – what the teacher needs to be, as well as to know – in order to communicate the truth of the Gospel. Augustine insists the teacher has an important and necessary role. God speaks the Word through human agency, just as, for instance, Cornelius put himself 'under the tuition of Peter'. But it does not follow that the only task of the teacher is to read the text and expound its meaning. More exactly, it is to teach the basics of *how to read*:

> So the person who knows how to read, on finding a book, does not require another person to tell him what is written in it; and in the same way the person who has assimilated the rules that I am trying to teach, when he finds a difficulty in the text, will not need another interpreter to reveal what is obscure, because he comprehends certain rules ... By following up various clues he can unerringly arrive at the hidden meaning for himself or at least avoid falling into incongruous misconceptions.

Already what is clear here is that Augustine does not see learning as some sort of 'by rote' recitation. In the first place one needs the tools to do the job, what nowadays no doubt we would refer to as 'transferable skills' which can be picked up from some 'staff development session'. The jargon was mercifully absent from the Hippo of Augustine's time, but the idea was not. Augustine was interested in encouraging learners in the task of *inventio* – not 'invention' but *discovery*.

Here is where I find a significant link with the *mandala* exercise. In *De Doctrina Christiana* Augustine is talking about how the reading of scripture can set us on the spiritual path. The first stage is to reflect on 'our mortality and future death, and by nailing our flesh to the wood of the cross, as it were, to crucify all our presumptuous impulses'. Then, he says, we must become accustomed to reading Scripture: to 'ponder and believe that what is written there, even if obscure, is better and truer than any insights that we can gain by our own efforts'. Having described these first two stages he goes on to talk about five more, from the knowledge of the love of God which challenges the 'love of this present age', through fortitude, a capacity to extricate oneself from 'all the fatal charms of transient things', to the 'seventh and last stage enjoyed by those who are calm and peaceful'. In the spiritual life one confronts different obstacles and is forced to make changes of direction.

The purpose of Augustine's inner journey is the life of union with God. In Tantric Buddhism it involves a much more circular return to what is given mysteriously in the present moment. Yet both involve a pedagogy, learning how to start out, how to move forward, how to deal with obstacles, how to learn the virtues necessary for the holy life. In all of this I want to suggest that a crucial role is played by memory – a considered attentiveness to whatever has brought us to this point.

## Memory and Remembering

Memory is, of course, always limited and selective. The Buddha would expect us to be attentive to whatever it is in this present moment that brings memory alive, reminding us of what has been forgotten, ignored or just buried. And Augustine in the *Confessions* speaks of the threefold unifying function of memory: looking to the past, providing an intuition of the present and enabling us to glimpse and even anticipate something of the future. In Book 10 he looks into the contents of his own memory for some clue as to how he may rise towards contemplation of the gracious yet incomprehensible God who made him. Memory, he says, is

> like a great field or a spacious palace, a storehouse for countless images of all kinds which are conveyed to it by the senses. In it are stored away all the thoughts by which we enlarge upon or diminish or modify in any way the perceptions at which we arrive through the senses, and it also contains anything else that has been entrusted to it for

safe keeping, until such time as these things are swallowed up and buried in forgetfulness.

It seems as if memory is like a repository for all the experiences we have ever had, a sort of semi-hidden database in which the whole of our past is contained. But, for Augustine, memory is made up of more than the residual impressions of 'facts'; there are also hopes and fears, dreams and emotions as well as perceptions and sensations.

A little later, he talks more about the active faculty of memory – its capacity, to continue the analogy, to work as the 'software' which can access the data:

> The memory also contains the innumerable principles and laws of numbers and dimensions. None of these have been conveyed to it by means of the bodily senses, because they cannot be seen, heard, smelled, tasted or touched ... I have seen lines drawn by architects, and they are sometimes as fine as the thread spun by spiders. But these principles are different. They are not images of things which the eye of my body has reported to me. We know them simply by recognising them inside ourselves without reference to any material object.

It sounds as if Augustine is working with mental structures which are innate to the mind; learning is just a matter of recalling what has been forgotten. But the context within which he is working is the search for God, the Truth and 'unfailing Light from which I sought counsel upon all these things'. God is not to be identified through any particular image or experience to be discerned in the recesses of the mind. It is, in fact, the very mystery of the 'countless things' opened up by the human mind which sensitises him to the transformative mystery that is God. 'My mind', he says, 'has the freedom of them all. I can glide from one to the other. I can probe deep into them and never find the end of them'. Like the woman in the Lukan parable who searched for what had been lost, he tells us that he is drawn by an image which is set as an obscure memory deep within him.

Just how it may have got there is not a question which Augustine ever satisfactorily answers. But that is not what is important to his quest. He seems much more interested in how memory, as a faculty which forms human beings in their search for Truth, is responsible for tracing together a continuity of experience. This, however, is a fragile activity. He is clear that calling anything to mind requires a regular and repeated effort: things which have been remembered can easily become dispersed and lost; they need once again to be gathered together. Ideas and concepts are not stored as discrete elements in the mind; they are part of an active process of learning and discovery.

In these terms, Augustine is telling us that the work of memory is more structured and more creative than we sometimes allow. This is where the wisdom of a traditional practice of reading, such as *lectio divina,* has something significant to say to a culture which takes it for granted that everything we need to remember is already there in Google. Techniques of regular recitation, whether the rhythms of ritual or formulae which summarise significant texts, are well known in a variety of cultures, Christian and Buddhist. Take, for example, the *Anguttara Nikaya,* one of the five groups of texts which make up the *Suttapitaka* of the Pali Canon. It consists of topics grouped according to number – an encyclopaedic version of all the topics which appear in more narrative form in the *Digha* and *Majjhima Nikayas,* collections of longer and middle-length discourses. The two forms, summary and narrative, work together. Memorisation is enabled by the creation of an interlocking storage system based on nothing more complex than a set of numbers. In this way, further more detailed material is built into a sort of grid, thus making it possible to break down a whole variety of ideas and themes which would otherwise be too unwieldy to hold together. Once having stored away such a set of graded material, it becomes possible to gain access to it by recalling the codes or tags.

Now there is clearly a mechanism here, an aid to memorisation, but it is by no means *mechanical*, as if the sole aim is to develop a prodigious memory which holds together and can quote at will vast amounts of information or proof texts. The object of the exercise is to develop a sensitivity, not to the stored material as such, but to the very *process of storing and using* the material. There is, in other words, a pedagogy involved in the schemes of memorisation, a way of passing on, not just knowledge, but wisdom, a learned capacity to use knowledge well, for its proper purpose.

For the Buddhist, the aim of remembering the various stages of or impediments to enlightenment is precisely to become enlightened; it is to learn how to take the right steps from Right View, the beginning of the Noble Eightfold Path, to the focused Right Concentration which leads to *Nirvana*. The pivotal role is played by Right Mindfulness – a careful attention to whatever appears in the present moment. The word means memory or remembrance and refers, not to a gathering together of disconnected stimuli, but to the ordering of what is present through its relationship to everything that has gone before. This is not far from the Christian ascetical condition of 'recollection', keeping the mind from wandering by attending to the moral purpose of one's life. To that extent, the process of mapping out future possibilities is part and parcel of the constant contemplative return to life-giving memories. For Augustine, it is only through the linking of this present moment to the memory of what has gone before that the hoped-for future can become a reality. Through what he calls the 'distension of the soul' the three dimensions of time are held together; autobiographical confession or address to God in the present moment unifies memory of the past and hope for the future.

### The Inner Pilgrimage

In the next chapter I want to pursue this theme of mindfulness in a little more detail. Here I conclude by tying together these reflections on 'translating memory' by returning to my earlier point

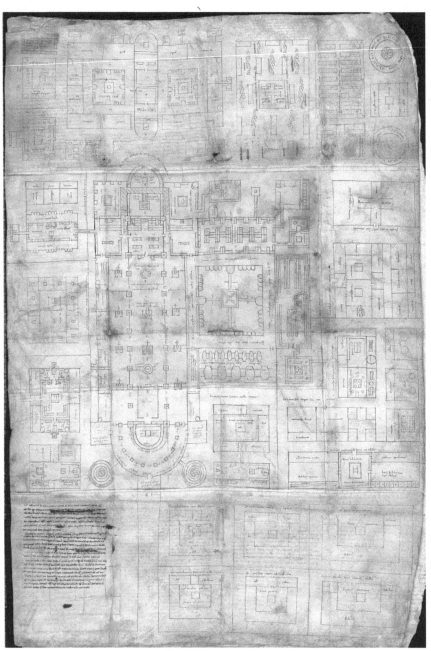

*Plan of the St Gall monastery, Switzerland*

about memory as an active process of re-membering, constantly learning how to integrate what is new and different by re-imagining the terms of what is already given. Ignatius the pilgrim, like Augustine the teacher, walked his way through memory formed by the pages of Scripture and the great texts of the classical tradition. Pilgrimage, as described earlier, is usually regarded as a physical devotion. But, as the *mandala* demonstrates, it is also a practice of interiority, the outer activity of walking forming an inner habitual response to the key points and places of a religious world.

Christians don't use *mandalas*. Or do they? Let me finish with one example: the extraordinary Plan of St. Gall, a ninth-century annotated manuscript which visualises a monastic complex, complete with gardens, brewery and orchard. The purpose and character of this document continue to divide art historians. Was it intended as an actual plan for a monastery or does it represent, perhaps, a vision of how the Benedictine life was to be lived, a work of art in its own right? An intriguing argument is mounted by the medieval historian Mary Carruthers, for whom the plan is a two-dimensional 'meditation machine' on the ideal form of monastic existence. It enables the monk to visualise a place within the religious world which the plan or map represents – to correlate memory and imagination or, to put it another way, to encourage the imagination to make a personal appropriation of what is given in memory.

Carruthers argues that the monastic practice of using architectural plans for meditation derives from the exegesis of buildings in the Old Testament, particularly the vision of the Temple in Ezekiel:

> The man said to me: 'Son of man, look with your eyes, and hear with your ears, and set your mind on all that I shall show you, for you were brought here in order that I might show it to you; declare all that see to the house of Israel' (Ez. 40:4).

It might seem as if the object is to imagine some glorious future which will compensate for the misery of the present. But imagination is not wishful speculation. Meditations on a map of the religious world were never intended, says Carruthers, as a sort of 'tourist's guide to the New Jerusalem'. It is one aspect of what she finds in medieval monasticism: 'the craft of making thoughts about God'; the building of a transformative way out of certain foundational images, the bedrock of an ancient tradition. This seems at first about as far from Tantric Buddhism as could be imagined. But while there may be no historical links, Carruthers notes their 'cognitive similarity, a likeness in use'.

Earlier I raised a question which has guided my work in comparative theology, about how we are to map familiar and non-negotiable 'places' on to analogous places which make up another religious world. Comparative theology entails, not the garnering of insights about the inner workings of another tradition, but a way of thinking theologically which, while it always seeks out some cross-religious focus, is concerned primarily with developing a pedagogy which can 'read' other religious worlds. Human beings are forever learning how to translate and adapt – not to overlay or replace one world with another, but to work within the structures of memory to produce creative variations which can both speak to and learn from particular needs and occasions. Acts of remembrance and imagination go hand in hand as a compositional art, fostering qualities of creativity needed to maintain the inner coherence of the life of faith. It is instructive to recall that image from Augustine, the craftsman's lines 'sometimes as fine as the thread spun by spiders'. Maybe we can think of comparative theology as just such a craft: a contemplative pedagogy which teaches how to build up networks of wisdom within which patterns of thought can be established – more exactly *visualised* – and thus *made memorable*.

# CHAPTER SEVEN

## Signs of the Times

IN THE standard texts of traditional Buddhism, mindfulness is given as the penultimate practice of the Noble Eightfold Path. It is, however, somewhat misleading to talk in such terms, since the Path is more a spiral of repetition than a set of well-regulated cumulative stages. The Buddha saw himself as a practical physician, teaching people in the vernacular, and passing on, not a metaphysical truth about the meaning of things, but a set of practical instructions on what to do in order to overcome suffering. Buddhism is not a monolithic entity handed down pristine from an original process of formation, but a flexible engagement with the needs of particular individuals. In this sense, Buddhism and Christianity share a similar ethos: a universal truth is to be communicated to all 'suffering sentient beings', as Buddhists put it. Rather like Christianity, Buddhism adapts itself to culture, to reinvigorate it and bring something new to birth. So it is that new forms and schools are forever emerging, from Engaged Buddhism in the West to Soka Gakkai and Nipponzan Myohoji in Japan.

Mention the word 'mindfulness' today, however, and most likely you will unearth one of the many models of meditative practice which have been adopted in schools, prisons, hospitals and similar environments. Research studies have shown that mindfulness-based interventions can provide therapeutic benefits for people with psychiatric disorders, contributing positively to the promotion of healthy life-styles and to the management of mental-health problems, as well as countering symptoms of depression, reducing stress levels, and dealing with drug dependency and other addictions. It is not an overstatement to say that mindfulness has become one of the defining features of contemporary culture.

There's nothing wrong with that in itself. But what does such popularity do to the original tradition? As noted earlier, this is the risk any form of inculturation runs. As a form of adaptation, it becomes, more exactly, *acculturation* – the process of assimilation to the dominant culture. Just as, in many parts of Europe, Christianity is little more than a cultural relic of a once all-powerful Christendom, so the well-being industry has plundered the great tradition of the Buddha, rendering it 'Buddhism lite': a spiritualised commodity that can be bought and sold in a variety of marketplaces, but lacking the energising power to do more than bestow a few practical benefits and useful spiritual tips on wider society. Religion, it seems, is always subject to the inexorable power of secularisation.

## Remembrance and Hope

Is that too gloomy an estimate? Is the risk still worth taking? And if so, how can we protect the original spirit of a religious tradition from being subsumed into the spirit of the age? The title of this chapter recalls one of the great clarion calls of the Second Vatican Council. It is not intended as a word of warning; I take it for granted that great aspirations will always fail unless constantly renewed and carefully discerned. Rather, the point I am making is that central to the task of inculturation is the act of remembrance – not recalling a few formative moments from the past, but correlating present 'signs of the times' with hopes for the future. Jesus' preaching of the Kingdom may be regarded as the first actively 'Messianic moment' in the Gospel. The proclamation that 'God reigns' is more than a reminder that the God of Israel continues to guide God's people; rather God is revealing Godself *in this present moment*, in the here and now, demanding a prophetic return to the cause of reconciliation and justice. Whether we are talking about Jesus proclaiming the breaking in of the Messianic Kingdom or the Buddha teaching the *Dharma* of the Four Noble Truths, what is at stake is not a 'spiritual' solution to human ills which takes people out of the everyday, but a remembrance that brings the present alive *in* the ordinary everyday reality of our richly diverse ethical and social interactions.

I want to argue that this is what the secular form of mindfulness tends to miss, what gets lost in the process of *acculturation*. The theme of inculturation, so important to the Ignatian tradition, demands attention to the way language, culture *and* the social context that forms human relations all interact. The challenge is to work out how to communicate something new and life-giving into a moral world that is constantly changing and adapting. Perhaps the most important contribution the Ignatian tradition makes is to insist that *both faith and culture* are significant features of the self-revelation of God in the world. What in the interreligious jargon are known as the dialogues of 'common life' and 'common action' are not just nods in the direction of the practical and political side of life; they are intrinsic to the full unfolding of the Paschal Mystery.

It is this social and political dimension that most concerns me in this chapter. In what follows I will first be offering a few examples of the curious secular-spiritual hybrid that is mindfulness. I cannot hope to give anything more than a glimpse of the vast amount of material that has appeared on this topic, from do-it-yourself therapies to serious academic studies. While much could be said about how the 'turn to the spiritual self' has developed and how it maps on to both traditional religious paths and the more ill-defined religiosity of the 'New Age', I shall not be seeking to account for this development, still less to offer a sustained critique. Rather, I will focus on 'Right Mindfulness' as a Buddhist meditative practice, and specifically the connotations of memory that the early tradition preserves. I have already drawn attention to a certain 'inner affinity' between Buddhism and Ignatian spirituality. With that in mind, I want to argue that an Ignatian reading of Buddhist mindfulness commends attention to the 'now' of the present moment; that now is not some sort of discrete spiritual space that can be safely insulated from what has gone before and comes after, but a moment that casts light into the contemporary crisis of human relations precisely because it names them as *in crisis*.

## Benefits of Mindfulness

Let us first stand back with a few examples from the umpteen websites dedicated to 'applied' mindfulness. In Britain, the NHS website on mindfulness begins by commending attention to one's thoughts and feelings as a way to improve mental well-being. There is nothing religious here, nor overtly spiritual, and certainly nothing esoteric. It's about being *healthy* in the broadest sense. Some meditative practices are mentioned, including Yoga and T'ai Chi; otherwise the website gives various bits of simple and straightforward advice about how to benefit from paying attention to what is *there* in this present moment that is so easily ignored.

Several key points about the basic practice are given:

- Keep it regular: picking a time during which you decide to be aware of the sensations created by the world around you.
- Try something new: sitting in a different seat at meetings, going somewhere new for lunch, can help to notice the world in a new way.
- Watch your thoughts: letting thoughts and worries crowd in and then gently letting them go as if they are buses coming and going through a bus station.
- Name thoughts and feelings: silently voice them for what they are, whether bringing anxiety or peace.
- Free yourself from the past and future: taking time to move away from being trapped in reliving past problems or getting caught by worries about the future.

In some ways, it all seems rather bland and obvious, useful bits of sage advice about how to get some balance into a frantic existence. Yet it is the very simplicity of the basic practice that is so often missed. Professor Mark Williams, an Oxford-based psychiatrist and sometime director of the Oxford Mindfulness Foundation, is a major source of wisdom on the clinical application of mindfulness. He is quoted as saying:

> It's easy to stop noticing the world around us. It's also easy to lose touch with the way our bodies are feeling and to end up living 'in our heads' – caught up in our thoughts without stopping to notice how those thoughts are driving our emotions and behaviour. An important part of mindfulness is reconnecting with our bodies and the sensations they experience. This means waking up to the sights, sounds, smells and tastes of the present moment. That might be something as simple as the feel of a banister as we walk upstairs.

Such simplicity of practice can be adapted to a variety of environments, some of them extremely stressful. I have only worked in a prison setting when called in as Sunday chaplain or to give the occasional talk. I have never found the experience less than challenging. Even getting inside is enough to put one on edge: the clank of keys and the bang of heavy doors creating a sense of menace. The application of mindfulness techniques to rehabilitation programmes is active in a number of prison settings, some of them housing serious long-term offenders.

Perhaps the best known and most impressive of the groups taking meditation and mindfulness into prisons is the Prison Phoenix Trust which started in Oxford in the late 1980s and included as one of its teachers for many years Sr Elaine McInnes, Catholic nun and Zen master. In a conversation with Elaine some years ago I remember coming away deeply impressed by the way she had adapted what by any standards is a fairly elite practice to the needs of some disparate and fairly dodgy characters. One cannot but be touched by this sort of comment coming from someone within a large Category C training and resettlement prison:

> I still find it hard to get in touch with my feelings. My gut tells me sadness is something I have a lot of. Today after my morning sitting I stopped and thought about how I feel about myself. My awareness shot to the memory of me as a little boy, and I felt a cocktail of sadness, feeling sorry, and maybe compassion for this little boy, who I realise is still within me. Sometimes I feel a vast space down inside my body that is so still. Anger can come back like a tidal wave and if I'm quick I observe it and the flames die very quickly and I feel like I've grown or maybe changed. This is so empowering.

Mindfulness, says an Open University on-line course on health and psychology, is a useful and cost-effective way of tackling a variety of mental health difficulties. The adaptation of a religious practice into secular settings seems wholly plausible. But, as the course notes, it does raise ethical issues: 'People are frequently unequally valued within hierarchical structures, often bullied or otherwise abused, and treated as objects to produce outcomes and reach targets rather than as full human beings.'

When we move to the teaching of mindfulness in schools, the ethical issue shifts, but it does not go away. Here we are no longer concerned with mindfulness as clinical application, a therapeutic use for dealing with a variety of pathologies. As part of the educational provision it fits best under Personal, Social and Health Education, a rather general heading intended to cover a wide range of concerns to do with well-being, finance, the law, relationships and the consequences of drug abuse. In these terms, mindfulness is a skill that can be taught, part of a personal toolkit for adapting to the wider world. In schools with a religious ethos, the question is not where such a discipline fits into the general curriculum, but whether – and, if so, how – the Religious Education syllabus should give space for a practice that, in its origins, comes from another religious tradition.

An interesting example of how mindfulness can be practised in schools comes from the Mindfulness in Schools Project (MiSP) which was started in Britain in 2009 as a national, not-for-profit charity, with the aim of improving the lives of young people by making a 'positive difference to their mental health and wellbeing'. One of the founders, Richard Burnett, has written a thought-provoking critique of the whole mindfulness phenomenon. Combining careful study of the Buddhist tradition, especially in its Theravada form, with anecdotal report and data analysis from his experience as a secondary school teacher, he makes some important observations.

On the one hand, he allows for the undoubted benefits of mindfulness in contributing to personal health and well-being. At the same time, he is conscious that the distinction between a secular, therapeutic discipline and the traditional Buddhist path risks missing the point. While it is always possible to see mindfulness as contributing to the necessary 'platform' of calm attentiveness without which more focused psychological interventions cannot be built, what is at stake is something more subtle. A healthy dialogue between the two requires that proper attention be given both to the originating historical context which formed the Buddhist tradition and to the wider contemporary cultural context where that dialogue is taking place. Otherwise we buy into the worst type of uncritical postmodern eclecticism, what is now being wonderfully referred to as McMindfulness.

This is what makes uncritical attention to the 'now' of the present moment problematic. Not that long ago, the neologism 'globalisation' referred to an ambiguous process of interconnectedness – financial, economic, social, political, cultural – which pointed to the emergence of a single global culture. More recently, in the 'post-truth' world, a growing sense of insecurity and threat from a laissez-faire individualism has made us aware that we are not just consumers of globalised commodities but *products ourselves*, subject to the powerful interplay of clever algorithms and vast databases that know our 'likes' and 'preferences' before we ever knew we had them. Massively influential platforms, such as Facebook, Twitter, Apple and Amazon, dominate our lives. I take a room in a cheap hotel for an over-night with my family in Ipswich and, before I know it, I can't get away from the place. Notifications that it is 'time to plan your next trip to East Anglia' soon morph into a cyber-bombardment with enticing ads for exotic holidays in Bali.

What is now being turned into a tradeable commodity is not just our reading, our travel, our eating habits, our every fad and foible, but our *attention*. How do you 'wake up' to the 'feel' of ordinary taken-for-granted objects, let alone persons and events, when the 'present moment' is constantly being shifted this way and that by a thousand pressures? What is the phenomenon given in this present moment, and how does one become conscious of it without turning it into some mental construction or concept? How 'present' is the present moment? Present to whom and what? And who controls 'my' present? Mindfulness might seem like a powerful antidote, a deliberate move to stand back and get a better view of the whole and 'take back control'. And to an extent it does precisely that. But does attention to the present moment open up or obscure that wider field of ethical relations in which our selfhood is set?

The 'McMindfulness' version comes with a cost. As Peter Doran, a lecturer in law at Queen's University Belfast, says, 'Mindfulness practices are too often presented and taught without adequate acknowledgement of the power structures that are themselves an important source of our distress.' It is, therefore, quite understandable how, in particular situations in the secular world, mindfulness as a practice of attention has found an audience. And where there is an audience there soon arises a market. The commodification of any religious artefact, text or practice involves a reduction or simplification of the broad and often quite complex cultural context of relationships where alone it makes sense. With that word of warning in the background, let us turn to the originating context of mindfulness within the early Theravada Buddhist tradition.

## *Buddhist Meditation and the Yogic Tradition*

To repeat the point with which I began this chapter, Buddhism always seeks to engage with culture and transform it. Rather like Christianity, it finds new life not apart from but precisely in encounter and dialogue with what is different and other. This is why I like to think of mindfulness as a sort of Buddhist transcendental, a quality of human living or a moral value that suffuses the whole of existence. That may sound a little solemn. It is important, however, not to reduce mindfulness to some useful spiritual technology. At its best what mindfulness does is provoke *insight into the way things are*. In other words, far more is at stake than relieving headaches, rehabilitating prisoners, educating children or helping stressed-out executives become more productive.

In order to clarify what is, properly speaking, to be understood in the context of the Buddhist Noble Eightfold Path as Right Mindfulness, I first want to consider its origins as a specifically Buddhist concept within the yogic traditions of early Vedic India. Let me personalise the point with a little more autobiography. Back in the mid-70s I was studying Indian religions and working my way into a comparative study of the theme of yoga in two texts which I took to be roughly contemporary: the *Moksadharmaparvan*, a section of the *Mahabharata*, the Great Epic of India, and a text on meditative practice that repeats itself in a number of the Buddhist texts that make up the *Digha* and *Majjhima Nikayas*, the 'long' and 'middle length' collections.

It was the time of the Thirty-Second General Congregation of the Society of Jesus, a great gathering in Rome, attended by delegates from all over the world and a number of others who acted as interpreters. One of those attending was from my community, and when the Congregation finished he came back bringing with him a set of typed pages. These were, he said, brief guided meditations which an Indian Jesuit ran at the beginning of each working day. I looked at them and immediately recognised the central meditative practice which held the whole lot together. Unmistakably, this was the Buddhist mindfulness I was studying in the ancient Pali texts. It was based on attentiveness to sensory perceptions, building up an intense awareness of what is seen, touched, heard and tasted.

The Jesuit's name was Anthony de Mello, and the typed sheets were subsequently turned into book form and published as *Sadhana*, his brilliantly successful introduction to meditation. Tony was an extraordinarily charismatic individual who died suddenly on a visit to New York at the age of 56. He acted as a psychotherapist and spiritual director, and facilitated a number of retreats based on his methods of prayer. I shall never forget the one I followed. He had an extraordinary conversational style and a knack of re-membering people's names; within a single session of one hour he knew everyone. He was able to run through all sorts of ideas and variations on this single theme of attention to the God revealed in everyday experience. He touched people deeply. One old priest, not exactly renowned for spiritual ebullience, made a little speech at the last session of the retreat I attended, confessing humbly that this had been the most important spiritual event of his long life. He died ten days later.

During that retreat, I walked with Tony one day in the garden and asked him where he got his key idea from. He told me that some years before he had done a retreat with a Buddhist layman, the Burmese S. N. Goenka. Although I had never met Goenka, I knew his reputation as an inspiring teacher. What he taught was the authentic form of Theravada Buddhist meditation, *Vipassana*, or insight. His courses are based on observation of the natural – not controlled – rhythms of breathing, what in the Therava-da tradition is called *Anapanasati*. Observation of bodily sensa-tions builds up an equanimity as one becomes progressively more aware of the inter-relationship of all contingent phenomena. We'll come back to this rather abstract point shortly. The techniques of practice are described in my thesis, but I'll spare you the details. My starting point was within the yogic ascetical practices of early India, a sort of religious alternative or counter to the Vedic sacrificial tradition. Yoga is best translated as 'spiritual exercise', with connotations of effort and striving to tame unruly emotions, getting them under control as a farmer yokes bullocks to the plough. Before yoga became a philosophical school within classical Hinduism, it was a generic title which covered practices ranging from focus on the breath to forms of physical self-control.

It was the early tradition that interested me. I argued that, in principle, a distinction can be made between practice and purpose, the 'bank' of spiritual exercises and their aim or intent, whether cashed out in metaphysical terms or not. In what is often called the 'renouncer culture' of early Indian religion, yogic spiritual exercises led in due course to the establishment of a variety of sectarian traditions with their particular vision of the end of the way. Thus it is possible to distinguish various forms of Hindu yoga, or Jain yoga, or Buddhist yoga. In terms of belief-structure they are all very different; in terms of practical approach they partake of the same simple ascetical structures. The question then arises as to whether there cannot, by extension, be a *Christian* yoga. Yoga as spiritual exercise is the necessary *preparation* that disposes the practitioner to set out on that journey towards the goal.

*Mindfulness as Attention to the Present*

That was my starting point. The substance was the textual tradition, and what I was interested in was the difference between the yoga recorded in the *Mahabharata* and what was to be found in the early texts of the Theravada Buddhist tradition. To cut a long story very short, it quickly became apparent that, while many differences of detail were to be found, the pattern of approach was much the same: ethical precepts and an appropriate life-style, physical exercises, the cultivation of peaceful space, the focus on one point in order to overcome distractions.

There was, however, a very subtle yet important difference between the texts which it was easy to miss. The yogic tradition includes a practice known as withdrawal of the senses, which is intended to guard against evil influences. It is a practice *within* the time and place of meditation proper. For the Buddhist, however, that guarding of the senses is extended into *all aspects of life*; practices of vigilance and attention are to *accompany all actions*. Thus I found that in the Epic tradition there are times when one should *not* practise meditation. In the Buddhist text, however, one should be attentive and conscious *at all times* – even, it is said, when obeying the calls of nature. To repeat my opening point about the Noble Eightfold Path as a spiral of mutually reinforcing practices, what Right Mindfulness connotes is an attitude of careful attentiveness to all the other stages, the ethical and the ascetical; it pervades and unifies the sum total of human experience. In other words, Right Mindfulness is not one specific practice among many but a gathering attentiveness to all that is presented in every activity of life.

That is the first key point. The second I mentioned in the previous chapter. In the Pali language of the early texts, mindfulness translates the word *sati*. In Sanskrit the word is *smrti*, coming from a root meaning 'remember' – to bring right attentiveness to bear, not just on the present moment, but on *this moment as it relates to what is past and what is still to come*. Walpola Rahula says that practising mindfulness is not a matter of learning a formal method, but of attending to the everyday, and to what is given to consciousness in the present moment:

> This does not mean that you should not think of the past or the future at all. On the contrary, you think of them in relation to the present moment, the present action, when and where it is relevant.

In the narrative texts that describe the progress of the meditator, spelling out what are sometimes called the 'fruits of being a *samana*, a recluse', *sati* is very often coupled with another word *sampajañño* which means something like 'thoughtful', with connotations of constant presence of mind. It is thus that Rahula extends the practice from specific exercises of mindful attention to an interiorised attitude or heightened awareness that takes seriously all intentional acts. The 'ways of meditation', he says, include 'our daily activities, our sorrows and joys, our words and thoughts, our moral and intellectual occupations'.

## An Attitude of Critical Distance

I distinguished above between practice and aim, or intention. Buddhism is, of course, distinctly anti-metaphysical. There is no *summum bonum;* one may start out on the way with particular ideas and constructs about the end, but the purpose of the way is to become free from these, in order to achieve an equanimity or detachment. I am tempted to suggest, therefore, that in Buddhism *the practice has become the purpose*, an end in itself. To become mindful of all that is given to consciousness, one begins with an initial concentration on one point. The aim, however, is to *avoid* absorption into the focus; it is important to refrain from identifying with the object. More positively, the technique is to observe the object, whether it lacks any specific cognitive or affective 'content' or is familiar and meaningful and evokes a particular response. In practice, the meditator does not seek one focus to the exclusion of others, but by simply observing one point manages to become sensitised to the presence and influence of other points.

In the yogic examples I took from the Great Epic, the focus often has an arresting quality (for example, it might be an artefact or, as in the *Bhagavad Gita*, the person of Krishna). But in the Buddhist texts, the immediate focus of attention usually has a much more dynamic quality, something which moves or changes as it is observed; for example, the breathing, a sound, a feeling, or a relationship with another person. Unlike the yogic method of 'breath-*control*', therefore, the Buddhist simply watches and notes what happens, allowing the present moment to take its own form and open up a series of relations.

To practise mindfulness is a matter of learning how to transcend forms of desire, whether this is expressed in cognitive or affective terms. Only through clarity of attention can progress on the path be achieved. In a thoroughly paradoxical sense, what is entailed is a focus not on ends but on the building of a gradual attunement to the treading of the path itself. Buddhist Right Mindfulness teaches a growing awareness of everything which has brought the searcher from an initial relationship of trust in the Middle Way (and its teacher) to a deeper sense of self-reliance and clarity of purpose. The searcher is always on the way, and thus each and every stage has a value in itself.

### Mindfulness – Secular or Religious?

Let me return now to the relationship between religious and secular mindfulness – or, more exactly, that element of overlap between the two. Strictly speaking, to achieve enlightenment all that is needed is to raise the quality of mindfulness to the point of insight. Mindfulness becomes 'Right' when one sees things as they really are. In practice, however, one needs to build up and strengthen an initial mindful attention by practising one of many focusing exercises. In the Theravada tradition there are two 'schools' of meditation: *samatha* or 'calming', and 'insight', *vipassana,* the school taught to Tony de Mello by Goenka. But this is largely a matter of emphasis. While it seems plausible to argue that the religious form of mindfulness is bound up with the *samatha* school while the secular therapeutic variety is limited to the *vipassana,* my point is that mindfulness is concerned with the observation of the *whole* of human experience. The two schools are inextricably linked because both are needed if the otherwise laudable aim of attending to the present moment is not to be subverted by cutting out whole swathes of human experience, however awkward and inconvenient these may be.

I finished my thesis with a couple of texts designed to show how the earliest tradition sought to marry insight with personal experience, a rooting of wisdom in the depths of an affective understanding. I quote one of these texts here: the end of a conversation in which two monks talk about the experience of enlightenment. One insists that, while he has seen the truth and understood it, he is not truly enlightened because he has not made 'bodily contact' with it.

> It is just as if there were in the jungle-path a well, and neither rope nor drawer of water. And a man should come by, exhausted by the heat, far gone with the heat, weary, trembling, thirsty. He looks down into the well. Truly in him would be the knowledge – water! – yet he would not be in a position to touch it. Even so, I have well seen by right insight as it really is that the ceasing of becoming is Nirvana, and yet I am not an enlightened one for whom all the hindrances to enlightenment have perished.

There is, in other words, a distinction between *knowing* the truth (the purely intellectual view or understanding of what the Buddha taught) and the deep *experiencing* of that truth which counters the usual motley crew of human pathologies – doubt, worry, impatience, laziness. Enlightenment may occur at any moment or stage of the path but it does not take us off the path into some blissful state away from the journey. It embeds us in the daily practice, enhancing an initial mindful attention to the present moment with a lively awareness of the rich complexity of human living and the interconnectedness of things.

Now the various forms of 'secular' mindfulness I have tried to describe are scarcely concerned with the mechanics of enlightenment. Mindfulness in this accommodated sense is of value *in its own right*. Where the Buddhist text begins with the intellectual and moves to the affective, the secular form begins in the middle of the affective and moves to the cognitive as the still point around which the messiness of the everyday can somehow be fixed. But in doing this it risks turning the present moment into a construct, an abstraction from the flux of life. What I understand the Theravada tradition to be saying is that the present moment is not an isolated single point which arrests emotional distraction, but the *centre of unity around which a network of relations revolves.*

The question Buddhism seeks to address is severely practical: how to be released from entanglement in the confusion of desire? And the response is always to seek a Middle Way, to achieve a personal equilibrium that avoids an inner division between the cognitive or analytic and the broadly affective dimensions of human nature. To overcome the potential for such a personal 'violence', it is necessary to develop a mode of perception that has both an aesthetic *and* an ethical dimension. On the one hand, mindfulness builds a sensibility that responds to the way in which phenomena are apprehended in and through *all* the senses, not just sight or hearing. On the other hand, it roots that sensibility in an awareness of how all things, and all sentient beings, already coexist in a network of relationships of power and dependence.

It is that final point which takes us back to my opening remarks about the politics of remembrance and hope. The translation of the Sanskrit *smrti* or Pali *sati* by 'mindfulness' turns out to be a tad misleading. It loses the important connotations of memory or remembrance, an act of holding together those traces of the past that continue to haunt the present of our imaginations. The less subtle forms of secular mindfulness practice are little more than variations on the fundamental yogic practice of 'one-pointedness', narrowing down the attention to one point. The aim, as explained earlier, is to overcome the tendency of the mind to wander, to become distracted – as the opening words of the classical *Yogasutra* puts it, the 'eradication of the movements of the mind'.

But what if the 'distractions' are significant, even in some way 'revelatory', not mental events that take away from the single-minded focus on the present, but invitations precisely to enter more deeply into it? As I understand the Buddhist practice – and I have not had space to discuss it any detail here – the object is not to become absorbed in any particular centre of attention but to observe whatever appears, whatever is 'given' to consciousness, and thus to hold together a number of points of attention, building up a skein or network of relations which, of its very nature, crosses not just spatial but temporal boundaries.

*A Messianic Future*

This is where the 'inner affinity' of Buddhist meditation and Ignatian spirituality turns out to have ethical and political dimensions. With its radical commitment to the 'doctrine of no-self', Buddhism shifts attention away from any egocentric obsession with inner states of consciousness to a vision of the 'interconnectedness' of things, opening the 'selfless self' towards the suffering of all sentient beings. Similarly, in the Gospel narrative are preserved, not just memories of the people of Israel and the life and teaching of Jesus of Nazareth, but a pattern of living and dying that incorporates so many disparate individuals into a single vision of a redeemed or Messianic future. Yet in neither tradition is enlightenment, to use the Buddhist term, or conversion, which I take as an acceptable Christian equivalent, achieved by an effort of the will. All schools of Buddhism commend, not just the virtue of wisdom (seeing things as they really are), but compassion (a commitment to the welfare of all). Our Jesuit Zen masters would, of course, interpret the experience differently; they are waiting on God's action in the world. Yet both are touched by that theme of remembrance that brings what is past into the present, allowing its mysterious trace to unfold something new and even unexpected. By retrieving the wider perspectives of mindful attention to the present moment, a sense of crisis challenges the all-too-human tendency to forget or smooth out the awkward edges of history. That in an important sense is true of both traditions.

In the next chapter I will ponder further on the political questions raised by life-in-community, by recounting my own Ignatian response to the four forms of interreligious dialogue in a particular context – what I call 'dialogue in the dust'. Here I want to end these reflections on mindfulness as a contemplative practice by focusing briefly on the intrinsically political dimension of 'the now' – what in the New Testament is referred to as *Kairos,* the 'acceptable time'. This is not the end-time which gathers everything together in God, but *this* moment in time which offers itself up for conversion, calling for a decision that reflects the radical seriousness of the Messianic community. Eschatological time is different from, but only accessible to us through, this *kairological* time. The question is not how the flow of time is somehow to be stopped, so that the end can briefly be glimpsed far off somewhere in the distance (though the end of the Bible, the last great visions of the book of Revelation, seems to do precisely that) but, more exactly, how Christians are called to live in the present moment *as if it is the last.*

The Church is a political entity; it is, whether we like it or not, a human institution with a visible existence within the wider field of human relations. But it is, of course, much more than that. Because it claims to have witnessed the Messiah and therefore to participate in the *Missio Dei* – the mystery of Word and Spirit sent by the Trinitarian God into the world – it points beyond itself to a completion that is *already* and *not yet,* begun yet never final. Put like that, the time appropriate to the Messianic community feels distinctly uncomfortable – the time, not of a settled people complete with their versions of the State apparatus, but of the pilgrim or sojourner, the one on the fringes of society, yet utterly dependent on it for support. And, if that is correct, then the political action appropriate to the Church is not that which would seek to mirror or parallel institutions and structures elsewhere but, on the contrary, to question and critique their settled status. Just as secularised forms of mindfulness risk losing touch with the originating religious insight that gave it such creative power in the first place, so any ecclesiology or political theology that runs too close to the established status quo runs the danger of compromising its own authority.

Reading – and acting upon – the 'signs of the times' requires more than attention to the shape of the political weather (the original context of Jesus' words in Mt. 16:4, of course). It demands a much more hard-headed act of remembrance that is not limited to commemorating success, but actively seeks to unearth and correct the injustices that vested interests always tend to ignore. An inculturation that names and faces down the brash populisms and callow nationalisms of the current political culture would be one worth having. I shall have something to say on that theme in the last chapter of this book. Let me anticipate, however, with a brief quotation from the Italian political philosopher Giorgio Agamben. At the end of a measured yet sharply focused lecture on 'The Church and the Kingdom', given in Paris and published in 2012, he concludes:

> [T]he question I came here today to ask you, without any other authority than an obstinate habit of reading the signs of the times, is this: Will the Church finally grasp the historical occasion and recover its messianic vocation? If it does not, the risk is clear enough: it will be swept away by the disaster menacing every government and institution on earth.

# CHAPTER EIGHT

## Dialogue in the Dust

THE SCRIPTURES and symbols, artefacts and images that form Christian life act as the externals of faith which, like sacraments, point to an inner truth. But it is not until they engage with a particular context, the secular reality of 'the world' or another living culture of belief, that the Word of God to which they point comes properly alive. It is within the texture, the earthy bedrock, of human living and everyday interaction that the Holy Spirit unlocks in human beings a capacity to hear the Word. Such for a Christian is the mystery of the Incarnation. Earlier I drew attention to Ignatius's meditation on the Trinity in which the three-person God looks down upon the world with a compassionate gaze and decides that the Second Person will become incarnate for the salvation of humankind. What Ignatius calls the 'history' does not impress itself on human consciousness until this touchingly naive piece of theologising connects with a very different scene, the intimate encounter between a young woman and a strange visitor.

The Annunciation has been immortalised by the greatest of classical artists, with very different implicit theologies. Fra Angelico's fresco in San Marco in Florence depicts a moment of extreme clarity as the Word of God seems to hover unnoticed between the two figures, Gabriel gently interrupting Mary's prayerful reading of the Bible. The architecture of the cell frames both the familiar encounter and a more mysterious space of meeting, symbolised by the intriguing window-passage which beckons the viewer elsewhere. Botticelli's almost overpowering fresco, covering an entire wall of the Uffizi, depicts something more like an explosion of the Spirit. At one end Gabriel appears to crash into the central space, all energy and enthusiasm; at the other Mary recoils as if caught in a gale, with the Bible she is reading flying out of her hands. The iconographic image they share is so familiar, but it has given rise to thousands of imaginative versions. Technical skill and a creative affectivity combine to celebrate an extraordinary moment in a single life that becomes archetypal of every moment of hospitality in which the heart is opened to the unexpected other – and in which *God*'s otherness is encountered.

## Aesthetic and Political

This chapter is about as far away from the subtle aesthetics of representational art as can be imagined, and yet there is an important connection that needs to be explored. Earlier I gave the briefest of introductions to life in the London suburb of Southall. This is the context in which I lived and worked for many years, following out what I have always thought of as a 'dialogue in the dust'. Very few of the dozens of places of worship in Southall would score high for architectural merit or beautiful artefacts. Even the imposing Śri Guru Singh Sabha Gurdwara, which is the most prominent landmark instantly recognisable from the flightpath into Heathrow, is a worthy but dull melding of concrete abstraction and traditional Sikh form. Most of the other places are humble adaptations of existing buildings that have a strictly utilitarian purpose.

To expect artistic excellence, however, is to miss the point. Establishing a place of worship, for prayer and social life, gives people a sense of ownership and pride. External appearance and internal decoration build a sense of identity. Places make statements about how the space – the 'between' – of the world, is criss-crossed by traces of human interaction. In being 'cultivated', it becomes secure. If there is a 'Southall culture', it is Panjabi. The town is

*Śri Guru Singh Sabha Gurdwara, Southall*

marked by food, decoration, dress and language that put the visitor instantly in touch with the north of India. Which is not to say that other cultures do not contribute to the vibrant mix: Afro-Caribbean, Gujerati and Somali, not to mention the many sub-communities that make up the mini-melting pot that is the Catholic parish of St Anselm.

The more the sheer diversity of cultural markers becomes apparent, the more insistently is the observer confronted with the question of what holds it all together. Telling links and more diffuse connections with the iconography of India and the Middle East are scattered everywhere. For some outsiders, notably the National

Front in the 1970s, this invasion of English space was a provocation; for others in more happily multicultural times, it represents a ferment of creativity to be valued and celebrated. Although Southall has a reputation as a place where visitors and pilgrims of all kinds can meet, the *political* culture – what makes for a people, a *polis* – is much more difficult to define.

To say that it is pluralist and interreligious is a statement of the obvious and not very informative. I well remember the first time I visited Southall. After coming back from India, I began teaching religious studies at Heythrop College, but soon became dissatisfied with treating Hinduism and Buddhism as purely academic subjects. Most of the students were studying theology and philosophy and, quite rightly, were asking questions about meaning. Given that we were all living in a city surrounded by faith communities of all shapes and sizes, I decided to explore possibilities for enhancing my teaching by contact with living traditions, with people who would be able to correct the textbook stereotypes. By chance I came across a poster advertising a lecture and local pilgrimage in Southall. I was immediately hooked as a gaggle of teachers, students, healthcare professionals and local parishioners wandered from one place to another, increasingly dazzled by the sheer 'otherness' of the decoration and the kindness of the welcome. After that, visits to places of worship in Southall became a central feature of my teaching.

The political question of what holds it all together and therefore how difference is to be negotiated 'on the ground' never goes away. Indeed, in the post-9/11 world and its toxic aftermath it has become increasingly fraught. Years after my first incursions into places of worship in Southall, when it became possible to set up a new community there, it was important, not just to get to know the people in the temples, mosques and gurdwaras, but in tramping the streets to ponder the question of what linked them all together. Was it a matter of an almost indiscernible 'cultural glue' which gradually built up social capital, or was it perhaps something more intractable yet more profoundly transformative? My friend Brother

Daniel, speaking with the measured assurance of years of experience, would talk about 'people of faith'. In a place like Southall, where faith is to a great extent 'inter-faith', I wondered what sense could be made of his conviction that what links people together is something as simple, yet as contentious, as 'faith'?

*Central Jamia Masjid, Southall*

### Pastoral activity in the 'middle of things'

I spoke earlier about the basic principles that underpinned the work of the Jesuit community in Southall in the years immediately after the millennium. In terms of mission, what we were trying to achieve was something like a twenty-first-century inculturation. The dedicated dialogue centre and the parish were conceived as a single whole, catering for all manner of human relationships – most importantly the people of the parish, but also those on the fringes of the Church, the poor and marginalised, and those who owed their allegiance to other religious traditions. I was the 'inter-religious specialist', the one charged with that last relationship, but it was never entirely clear how dialogue between persons of faith was to become less a fringe activity and exercise a more central role in the everyday life of the Church. How were we to mediate and build conversations between the two?

When I started teaching at Heythrop, there was no obvious place for me within the institutional structure of a specialist centre for theology and philosophy, so I was consigned to the department of pastoral theology. At first I felt like a fish out of water, alongside topics like ethics, spirituality and ecclesiology. Later I realised it was exactly right. With my Southall contacts, I began to reflect further on the theological implications of the various forms of interreligious conversation I was holding, and then, with the help of colleagues, I began to engage with the theoretical work being done within the discipline of pastoral theology itself.

In most Christian Churches, pastoral or practical theology used to be the preserve of the clergy, and amounted to the profession-al training that followed from systematic study of Scripture and the great philosophical and theological traditions of the Church. Thanks largely to the Second Vatican Council, that has changed dramatically, with attention shifting from a handful of peripheral 'extras' to a theological discipline that has its own intrinsic value, as an integrative reflective activity that works out of a fundamental trust that God's will for human beings is to be discerned, not apart from, but at the very heart of 'the world'. In this sense, all theology is 'pastoral' not because it is concerned with addressing particular needs of the 'Church in the World', but because it is committed to opening up an intelligent and imaginative account of the signs of God's grace as a service both to the Church and wider society. Pastoral theology, in other words, is not the 'applied bit' at the end of the curriculum, but central to the articulation of what the Trinitarian God, exercising that compassionate care for a suffering world, is actually doing in the 'middle of things'.

*Learning how to Read the World*

That was the basic theological framework. As I walked Southall's scruffy streets, I asked myself how I was to apply the reflective practice of pastoral theology, with its holistic or integrative demands, to a world dominated by a plethora of religious imagery *and* a contested pluralist political space. It was in wrestling with the limits of the imagination that I found myself gravitating towards the method that Francis Clooney had developed for comparative theology. Here was a way of bringing together the familiar theological claims of Christian faith, as they were being lived out in the Catholic parish of St Anselm's, and analogous beliefs and forms of life from other religious communities. As noted earlier, however, there was a major difference of approach. Clooney is a textual scholar who works with written texts and commentarial traditions. In my version of comparative theology, 'text' is to be understood as anything that can be *read,* not just scripture or written commentary, but the context or the *texture* of things, whatever gives shape, energy and substance to a religious world.

This takes me back to a point I made at the end of the Introduction. We are used to the idea that reading is an exercise in extracting meaning from a written text. Whether it is a novel or a scientific textbook, we read in order to engage with what the author is seeking to communicate. The idea that reading is an activity worth cultivating *for its own sake* is less familiar but equally important. We do not read just to get to the end of the book, to 'get the message'; we read for the sheer pleasure of appreciating the beauty of the writing, its power to evoke a mood, to open up an aesthetic response, to make us think – and imagine how things might be different.

In this sense, we *read* the world of nature that bears the marks of culture or cultivation. To repeat that earlier point from the Jesuit historian Michel de Certeau, the 'space' of the world is marked by all sorts of signs of human activity which confront us with a *form* that in some sense can be said to 'speak'. It does not have to be a classic text with some sort of canonical status. It can be anything with a history, anything which evokes memories, and which therefore has a *voice*. In this sense, the act of reading is not a matter of picking out and feeding off the nourishing bits but, to shift the metaphor, listening for the *inner* voice that is inspired by the act of reading and *responds* to what is somehow given in the text. I am touched and *changed* by my reading, just as I am moved by confronting, or being confronted by, a great work of art. Understood in this way, there are always two dimensions to the act of reading: the action of my speaking the narrative and the *re*-action of my listening. In the theatre, I enter into the performance of the play as an empty space comes alive with action and movement. In the art gallery, I sit and marvel at how earthy materials – oil, powder, dye and stone – combine in the making and remaking of images that touch the heart. Reading as a metaphor for encounter with the other is never a passive absorption. Two movements work together; to recognise the inner dialogue that accompanies the outer encounter is the beginning of responsibility.

The same point applies to the world of interpersonal relations with all their ethical and political complexities. The life of the city – its places of learning and culture, its centres of commerce and government, the relations between the people who live there and intermingle with each other – can be *read*. Like the text of a book, the life of the city can be described as 'textured', bearing a recognisable cultivated pattern. In seeking to make sense of this world, we look beyond the immediate 'form' to consider what that form represents. The image of the Annunciation, whether in a snapshot Fra Angelico or an epic-scale Botticelli, has the same 'content', tells the same 'history', but makes its impact on the everyday world of the observer through the subtle artifice of a unique configuration. Something similar applies to the unfolding of the 'inner meaning' of events which turn a crowd of disparate individuals into a people.

To repeat a point from an earlier chapter, when Jesus made that familiar observation about the 'signs of the times' (Mt. 16:3), he was not expecting a great revelation somehow to erupt out of the ordinariness of the everyday – 'the political' as apocalyptic. He was commending an attention to the familiar features of our experience – those that are almost taken for granted, such as the signs of fair or threatening weather – without which the ordinary everyday reality of our lives would be evacuated of meaning, reduced to a load of commodities to be rearranged to suit human whim and convenience. 'The times' are not the episodic phenomena of a purely contingent existence; they carry the weight of God's constant care for the world.

## A political dimension

That conviction – the Ignatian vision backed by Brother Daniel's idea about what makes persons '*people* of *faith*' – runs through what follows. I first offer an open-ended look at the public and political arena that is Southall. This is no more than a sketch in which I have presumed to introduce a handful of remarks from various conversations I have held over the years. They show how life in a multicultural world is not without its tensions and problems; yet somehow the intensity of the pressure – the need for some 'common life' and 'common action' – generates its own wisdom. This will raise one of the more intractable political issues of our time: how we can speak to, and work alongside, those we disagree with. While I never thought of myself as a political commentator, the longer I spent in Southall the more I became convinced that my version of pastoral theology, pursued in comparative fashion 'in the dust', demanded a political dimension.

Those early years in Southall coincided with the fallout from 9/11, which shifted the debate about religion in the public arena away from social cohesion to issues of security and control. I remember being invited on at least three occasions to consult with civil servants at the Prime Minister's office in Downing Street so that briefing papers could be prepared for ministers. It was a fascinating experience, brain-storming away about how the undoubted political energy religion releases could be harnessed for the common good. What could it achieve, and what were the pitfalls? It taught me a lot about why politics is called the 'art of the possible'. The best politicians know the limits of what can and cannot be said and done. Not that everyone was happy about our putting religion high up the policy ladder. A grumpy Alastair Campbell once retorted to an inquisitive journo who presumed to ask a question about Tony Blair's prayer life, 'We don't do God'. My visits may have been the remote cause of that remark.

It tends to be taken for granted among the commentariat that in a secular society religion, and more particularly the plurality of religions, has somehow to be subsumed, even constrained, within the wider institutions of the State. Counter to that assumption, one hears the mantra that, if religion is the problem, then religion is the solution. In an important sense I think this quite correct. I want to argue, therefore, that what is needed above all is a humane and respectful conversation between persons of faith in the 'middle of things': a 'dialogue in the dust' which can inform political debate in the wider civic sphere about the role that faith plays in forming communities of common concern.

*Faith in Southall – a 'Chota Panjab'*
Mention the name of Southall and you provoke comments about a 'vibrant' and 'exotic' world of Asian tastes, colours and aromas, or – just possibly – you conjure up an image of a youthful Keira Knightley trying to 'bend it like Beckham' with an ugly gas-holder hovering on the horizon. Yet, like all places, Southall – or the 'south corner', to give the name its Saxon root (as an area of some social deprivation, it does feel as if it's squeezed into a forgotten enclave) – has its own history. The medieval Archbishops of Canterbury owned tracts of land in the area. As noted earlier, the Catholic church is dedicated to St Anselm, and I like to imagine the great man riding out there on his day off for some peace and quiet when he was puzzling out the ontological argument.

Today Southall is an immigrant centre. Ever since Brunel established a fuel and water depot for the GWR in the mid-nineteenth century, Southall has acted like a magnet for one wave of prospective workers after another. In the 20s and 30s, Welsh labourers came to escape the poverty of the Great Depression. The first Sikhs came from Panjab in the 1950s, originally to work in a rubber factory. Pakistani and Panjabi Muslims arrived in the 60s and 70s, Somalis in the late 80s and 90s and a community of Sikhs from Afghanistan rather later. A diverse Hindu community includes Panjabi- and Gujerati-speakers; like the Sikhs many came via East Africa in the early 70's. They have joined Afro-Caribbeans – mainly from the islands of Antigua, St Lucia and Grenada – and the longer established Irish community. Since the turn of the millennium, Southall has experienced another wave of immigration: EU nationals from Eastern Europe and Russia. This has given rise to the sardonic comment that the only Caucasians in Southall do indeed come from the Caucasus.

It is perhaps unsurprising that Southall has a troubled history of race relations. I have already alluded to the infamous confrontation with the National Front in April 1979. Those who lived through that dreadful time remember it as a defining moment. While for some it revealed the 'dark side of Britain', for many it marked the beginning of their political commitment. I remember being told early on in my time there that the older generation were deeply formed by the riots and were determined never to be coerced by the far right again. Memories are fresh, and the experience of a successful fight against racism has left a lasting impression. It may be this commitment, a civic pride, that has generated a genuine warmth and affection with which many speak about 'our' Southall.

Apart from a wide variety of Christian churches – Anglican, Baptist, Methodist, Pentecostal – there are some ten Sikh gurdwaras, four mosques, three Hindu temples, and a Buddhist vihara, not to mention many more informal places of worship, within the bounds of the Catholic parish. It's this extraordinary concentration of religion in one relatively small area that has made Southall a byword for interreligious coexistence. How has this come about and why does it work? One of my hunches is that it is precisely the spread of different commitments, the fact that no one community is strong enough to be 'in control', that makes for a certain balance of interests.

That, of course, is just a hunch, and I have never managed to construct a survey that would prove the point. But it has guided my many conversations with friends and neighbours. None of them was structured and most of what I jotted down is anecdotal and allusive. Nevertheless, despite the scruffy nature of the place, its manifest social problems, and tensions between different religious commitments, I have always been struck by an extraordinary willingness to accept the pluralist reality and work within its constraints. One comment, shared by a Sikh family I got to know, was offered spontaneously over a meal, but with the sort of assurance that showed it was not just an off-the-cuff remark. It had been given some thought.

> I have a father and my father has got other children; my brother supports one football team, and I support another. Every now and then we fight and argue – but at the end of the day we come together because we have faith in our father, have all one father. God is like a father, and we are all his children. We all have our little faults. At the end of the day, when we have stopped squabbling, we are all brothers and sisters again.

Gentle affectionate stuff which has its own wisdom, an illustration, perhaps, of a certain learned capacity to deal with – and reflect upon – a less than ideal situation. Is this what goes on in Gillian Rose's 'Broken Middle', when the guarded protection of space has to give way to a more generous hospitality? My conversations – the dialogue of common life – would often begin with sharing some thoughts about how Southall has changed, about how our respective communities have dealt with change, and then move to something more personal, ending – as with that analogy of the squabbling family – with a question about the nature of faith itself. Is there perhaps something here which holds us all together? And if so, has that changed in some way, along with the context in which it is lived?

Most people, it must be said, speak of faith as bound up with 'codes of life', with doing what is right according to traditional norms. Yet it is clear that there are all sorts of tensions within communities and across the generations. For some older folk, Western values and education are viewed with suspicion as undermining tradition. Many younger people are conscious of living between cultures and not wishing to play roles that suit their elders. They seem admirably confident about the future, speaking freely about contentious issues such as caste and discrimination. What is particularly striking is how many freely admit that the presence of people of other faith traditions has made them more open – and better practitioners of their own faith. A few have studied traditions other than their own, and I have had some interesting little conversations in Sikh refectories, sharing *langar,* over parallels between Christianity and Sikh prayer and practice. A common theme is that living alongside neighbours – 'talking and being together' – often acts as a challenge to become a better person. The following little thought may act as a summary of the sort of thing I would constantly come across:

> It's easier to practise the truth that God is in everyone and everyone in God here in Southall because of the amazing variety of people. If I were in just one community I don't think such values would have become so important and played such a role in my life.

I am wary of the danger of romanticising the great melting pot, and indeed, at the best of times, I have to remember that, as a white, male, educated Christian, I am always going to be regarded as an outsider. On the other hand, I have often been touched by moments of genuine trust when I felt I had been granted an insider status. I once took a group to the big gurdwara where they organise tours with dedicated guides. Unusually, on that occasion something had gone wrong with the booking and no one was available. 'You carry on', said the administrator to me in the office. 'You know us; we can trust you.'

Such little moments of genuine hospitality have highlighted for me a quite remarkable humanity and generosity of spirit that spreads out across the religious divisions. I remember another community leader admitting that there had been plenty of tensions with the community next door, but then insisting that overall their faith has 'given us encouragement', convincing him that there was something of value to be learned from what they taught and stand for. 'Each person, each day,' said another to me in a comment I have never forgotten, 'each experience that I have leaves me a different person, a richer person.' The familiar fault-lines, dominated by historical conflict and economic inequalities, sometimes turn out to be more permeable than one imagines.

My focus has been on garnering a sense of a 'local wisdom', touches of genuine practical learning that reflect insight into how human beings act and relate to each other on a daily basis – the sort of instinctive response to the work of the Holy Spirit on which the integrative method of pastoral theology is based. Southall is a town for which the evocative term 'super-diversity' might have been invented. What holds Southallites together is not any clearly articulated idea about what inspires our common humanity, still less some cross-religious 'essence', but the very *process* of seeking ways of living together in a town of surprisingly cohesive minorities. No one community dominates; everyone has had to learn to adjust and accommodate. To repeat: I do not suggest for one moment that this is a comfortable situation or is at all straightforward. On the other hand, I find consolation in the fact that at least a few have discovered – or, perhaps better, *rediscovered* – resources for articulating their identity in vastly changed circumstances. The 'side-by-side' dialogues of common action and common life have encouraged a limited 'face-to-face' exchange about the practice of faith and its motivations. People have learned how to look with integrity to insiders, to their own community, and with generosity to outsiders, to 'the other'.

Brother Daniel would speak of the 'people of faith' in his 'Holy City'. Is this a mind-numbing bit of pluralism in which difference is elided into a well-meaning but diffuse common essence? Or is there a wisdom or a virtue at work in the midst of what, before it becomes inter*religious* encounter, is an inter*personal* encounter, a meeting of persons? Before it gets transformed into the life-giving words with which we address each other, faith is vested in that human capacity to *read* the objects of our encounter – whether the 'strange visitor' who unexpectedly arrives in the middle of our ordered existence, or the 'signs of the times' which prompt a move- ment of the will, the taking of responsibility for the way things are.

When Jesuits talk about the 'faith that does justice', that is what they are referring to: not a set of propositions culled from the Gos- pel or Church tradition, but a movement of the heart that seeks to collaborate with the grace of God discerned at the heart of a suffering world. The entry of the Word into the world with which I began this chapter is a moment in time, an intersection between eternity and everyday human experience of 'the dust'. Something of its uncanny iconic power has been caught by artists down the ages – Word *and* Spirit, form *and* energy, repetition *and* interrup- tion – constantly provoking new ways of human interaction.

### Towards a Political Theology of Religions

New contexts call attention to tried and trusted wisdom and gen- erate new ways of reading and acting. A few years ago, I was in- vited to attend a debate hosted by a newspaper about whether Is- lam had a place in London. The speakers were all articulate and plain-speaking, and much was said that needed to be said. Two young Muslims argued their case with clarity and passion. It was obvious, however, as the conversation argued back and forth that the world out of which they all spoke was very different from the one I had just come from. And it's the disconnect between contexts that is alarming. Almost any debate about Islam in the West raises complex problems about religion itself, and how the great belief systems intersect with ethnicity and culture. The questions repeat themselves with great regularity. How much diversity can any nation tolerate without fragmenting? How can the different communities of interest that make up British society become less polarising and more generous as they talk to each other about matters to do with justice, fairness and equity? More particularly for our topic: what responsibility do persons of faith, sometimes separated by very different religious beliefs, bear for the well-being of civic society?

That term 'super-diversity' acts as a reminder not just that current levels of diversity are significantly higher than a few decades back, but that there is a range of divisions and subdivisions *within* what were once defined in more homogeneous terms. That may say something about the growing sophistication of our discourse about race, religion and culture. But it also acts as a reminder that what were once identified as discrete, semi-homogeneous groupings (the 'religions') are now more likely to claim their own identity than submit to some pre-existing stereotype.

I remember being gently corrected by one of the leaders of the Valmiki Sabha in Southall. My knowledge of their history was limited to what I knew of low-caste insurgency in the Panjab of the late nineteenth century, a period which witnessed the growth of reform movements in both Hinduism and Islam. 'So you are Hindus?' I asked. 'No, we are not Hindus', came the slightly testy reply; 'we are Valmikis'. No doubt in India the prevailing religious ideology would consider them Hindu, albeit relegated to the bottom rungs of the brahmanical hierarchy. But in the UK they are not a sub-set of that great British construct, Hindu-*ism*; they are one more religious group which take its place alongside the prolif-

*Interior of Śri Valmiki Mandir, Southall*

erating religious communities of super-diverse Britain. This is not the 'identity politics' sanctioned by *laissez-faire* multiculturalism, but something more intractable and subtle.

Half a century ago the dominant identifier was race, and to some extent that is still the case. Then came the disenchantment of postmodernity and we started differentiating groups by culture, lots of it. Now I think we are moving into a new phase, the *re-enchantment* of the world of human experience and interaction through the discourse of a politically aware spirituality. It's the sort of thing I noticed among the most thoughtful folk in Southall.

Faith is more than a religious sensibility based on immediate and familiar cultural concerns. Faith in an interreligious context of common concern is more open-ended, attending to a more remote future, with a confidence that life somehow, sometime, can and will make sense. Is this just a vague 'hope-against-hope', or does it have something more robust to teach us?

In the previous chapter I talked about interreligious 'meditators' and the growing practice of mindfulness in so many areas of our communal life – schools, prisons, health service, even the professions. I argued that at its best the practice looks in two directions, linking the present moment with memory of what is past and anticipation of the future. There's more here than a New Age fad. This is 'identity-plus', not a fixation on self to the exclusion of the other, but a much more complex and ambiguous awareness of how my life is inseparable from the other. If there is a logic behind the current upsurge of political populism, it represents the downside of that ambiguity, a politics of grievance that over-identifies the enemy and can sometimes get quite violent. But we should not forget the more positive side: a politics of compassion typified by the environmental movement, solidarity with the oppressed, and hospitality to migrant groups all over the world.

Religious difference is usually regarded as a theological and political *problem*. But the guarding of difference, that specificity of faith which confers a particular identity, is not in itself a problem. The problem arises when religion goes toxic, as it were, when the naturally inward-looking and conservative mindset of any traditional creed is turned outward, demonising some threatening 'other'. The root of all conflicts, as René Girard points out, is not difference as such but *competition*, what he understands in terms of a mimetic rivalry between persons, countries, cultures. If that is correct, then attention needs to be paid to the conditions which create that mood of 'competition' and form – or *mal*form – the public space.

State-sponsored structures – whether relatively benign, such as local faith forums, or more threatening, such as measures intended to counter radicalisation – have their place. The danger, however, is that even the most subtle of external pressures can disturb the delicate fabric which makes up religious traditions. The issue is not how to create structures which allow religious communities to bury differences, but how conditions are to be created within which sometimes very different accounts of the world can go on flourishing together. Only the religious communities themselves can address that issue. It takes energy and effort for people of faith to understand each other, let alone to be critically supportive of each other for the sake of the common good. Historically in the UK a fund of social capital has been provided by the Church of England which, in its parochial structure, still takes responsibility for managing various aspects of social cohesion in local areas – not least in facilitating forums of faith. That responsibility is now more broadly shared.

All faith communities bring their own resources of spiritual wisdom for mobilising people for political action, and many have developed their own resources for achieving social cohesion in their locality. In more general terms, precisely by keeping alive ultimate questions about the nature of humanity and the good life, they act counter to the secular received wisdom about the intrinsic divisiveness of religion, as well as challenging the power of the market and the State. What is needed is more attention to traditional practices of hospitality which can underpin and encourage the different forms of social capital. Learning the simple virtues of forbearance and generosity that allow people sometimes to be the host, responsible for giving a lead, and sometimes to be guest, willing to be led, will create the conditions in which the most searching of questions can be asked. Putting it in terms of a question discussed earlier: what is it to be human in the middle of a world fraught with danger and difference, longing for something we can call 'home' yet also stimulated and made curious by what is 'other'? Maybe that opening image of the young woman confronted with the divine stranger reminds us of something that underpins the act of faith.

*Schools of Faith – Teaching and Learning Together*
In addressing ultimate questions about the meaning of things, persons of faith come to terms with the dilemmas and challenges that haunt our everyday lives. That is why it always makes sense to speak of religions, not as discrete sets of beliefs, but as akin to schools, centres of teaching and learning where a hallowed tradition is forever being brought into a creative correlation with contemporary issues and questions. That is what it means to read and to allow ourselves to *'be read'*.

Let me finish this chapter, not with a 'message', but with another question. How can persons of faith find an integrity in their prayer and practice that does not ignore the surrounding context but actively responds to it? No doubt there are times when persons of faith, as well as persons claiming no allegiance to religion, feel that life would be a lot easier if we all focused on faithful practice and forgot about 'the other'. But in an intrinsically pluralist, globalised, multicultural world, *whether we like it or not,* faithful practice can never be a purely private, personal concern. What I believe is always affected by the world around me, by different accounts of what it means to be human, not to say by the suspicions and prejudices that sometimes make civil society seem very uncivil. Even if my priority is a matter of carving out a space where 'home' provides security, some measure of engagement with the diversity that surrounds me is going to be necessary. The challenge is whether I can be positive about that interaction.

Common life and common action do not provide a political programme. But they do provoke a broader conversation which already has a political shape *if* it allows space for a religious practice that includes 'the other'. We all know how religion can go toxic, how well-meaning efforts to speak about Divine Mystery reveal less the glory and majesty of God than the dark side of human nature. Nevertheless, at their best our schools teach a truth and reveal a beauty that enables all sorts of people to make that tricky journey from the world of 'home' to the world shared with 'the other'. They do this, not just by recounting foundational narratives and edifying stories, but by a continuous round of liturgical recitation and performance – *and,* let's not forget, by the social capital generated by all manner of cultural and political events, moments of hospitality that build civic virtues, the glue that binds wider society together.

Just as responsible government is always looking to address the possible disconnect between aspiration and reality, always aware of the risks to the cohesive functioning of society, so responsible religious communities will always be pondering the wider implications for faith in local situations that are shared with other groups, other accounts of what makes for the common good.

# CHAPTER NINE

## Grey Wisdom

IN THE first chapter, a touch of autobiography focused on my final year of Jesuit training and my encounter with St Francis Xavier, whose influence I found to be very much alive in the villages I visited in south India. I had spent the previous four years as a young priest, teaching two terms of each year in a large Jesuit boarding school and the intermediate term lecturing in Buddhism at the Gregorian University in Rome. An unlikely combination, it is true, but one that kept me happily involved in the work for which the Society is best known. While education may not be what we usually associate with Francis, catechesis of young children had always been a commitment of the first companions, perhaps providing a balance to the focus on study. The founding document of the Society, the 1540 *Formula of the Institute,* with its ringing words about travelling immediately wherever the pope decreed, speaks briefly about the purpose of the Society as

> to strive especially for the progress of souls in Christian life and doctrine and for the propagation of the faith by the ministry of the word, by spiritual exercises and works of charity, and specifically by the education of children and unlettered persons in Christianity.

When the *Formula* was confirmed ten years later, the listed activities were expanded to reflect the experience of a rapidly growing and energetic community. In addition to the ministry of the sacraments, 'public preaching, lectures, and any other ministration whatsoever of the Word of God' are specifically noted. In his history of the early Jesuits, John O'Malley explains at some length how education shifted dramatically from catechesis of children to the settled life of institutions. In part this was due to the increase in the number of young recruits to the Society, but mainly it reflected a response to a growing need the new order was ideally placed to meet. O'Malley adds that this was not a deviation from the originating ideal of freedom to move to wherever the need was greatest. What is unchanged in the *Formula* is the fundamental identity of the body as an order of priests involved in pastoral ministry towards all manner of people, including 'the stranger' and 'those found in prisons and hospitals', for the 'glory of God and the common good'. The spirit that governed Jesuit education was focused around a pastoral concern for the moral and spiritual welfare of the whole person. Serving the Word of God and following the guidance of the Spirit was then – and still is – central to the Jesuit 'way of proceeding'.

## Conversation as Ministry

Where are the roots of dialogue, and specifically interreligious dialogue, in all of this? Dialogue is a very modern concept, even if the theological truth behind it is as old as the Old Testament. O'Malley talks about one typically Jesuit activity as 'devout conversation': a certain practical ability to raise ordinary interpersonal encounters to an intellectually more serious and edifying level. He recalls an evocative image: to 'go fishing'. Likely individuals would be sought out in the marketplaces, engaged in conversation, and then drawn back to the Jesuit church where a more demanding exposition of Catholic faith awaited. This, says O'Malley, was 'devout conversation, commando style'. Put bluntly like that, it has the calculating feel, not of a religious order, but of a sect, conjuring up pictures of zealous young men obsessively picking out recruits who can maintain the purity of the founder's secret wisdom. But that would be to interpret one missionary practice of the Word from too modern a perspective.

Devout conversation has its origins within the deliberations of the first companions, a way of life which built up the inner coherence of the group, but at the same time encouraged a wider engagement with everyday human experience, confident that this is where God is to be found. It illustrates an important principle of Jesuit pedagogy: to begin where the pupil is, responding to their questions rather than seeking to impose a set of packaged answers. Today's Jesuits cannot presume upon some sort of latent or residual Christian faith which simply has to be prompted back into life. And yet, the principle of inculturation, which has acted as a 'deep structure' for this book, has something important to say to our pluralist, secularised culture, just as it did to the sixteenth-century Europe of the Renaissance and Reformation. The *Exercises* continue to form particular skills and virtues which have a rich potential for engaging with persons of good will. How are they to be appropriated in a way which addresses a society where 'faith' and 'culture' seem at times to exist in very different compartments? Maybe 'devout conversation' needs to be seen, less as a tactical adjustment of the more explicit forms of proclamation, and more as a theological value in its own right, a human activity rooted in the activity of God's own Spirit.

My first book was called *Religions in Conversation*. If it still has a value, it lies less with any contribution it made to the growing literature on the theology of religions than with that word 'conversation' in the title. I can remember at the time thinking how its connotations of friendship were so much more helpful than the formality of 'dialogue' that dominated the discourse. If the latter conjured up an image of learned experts at an international conference, the former evoked moments of intense yet relaxed personal exchange in corners of mosques and temples. I was no Roberto de Nobili or Thomas Stephens in learning and linguistic expertise, but I did share with them a typically Jesuit 'nose for the supernatural' in all its forms.

To know how to get a conversation going and to leave the resolution with God, rather than demand a particular outcome, represents an authentic development of the properly Jesuit spirit. Where, in O'Malley's account, the first Jesuits were quite prepared to 'shake the dust off their feet' when they encountered opposition, perhaps contemporary Ignatians are called to exercise a greater patience and a more dogged forbearance, both with themselves and with the other, if only because the mending of the various fractures of postmodernity is an infinitely more complex business than Ignatius and the first Jesuits could ever have imagined.

I have called this chapter 'grey wisdom' in the hope that years of experience add value. My point is not that devout or spiritual conversation as a model for interreligious dialogue is a task appropriate to old age rather than the eager enthusiasm of youth. Indeed, it may be that older folk have the confidence and maturity to settle down to talk to strangers without feeling threatened, but that isn't the point. More exactly, the conversation I am thinking about takes time and cannot be pursued in a hurry. In what follows I will offer a few examples of 'grey wisdom' from the great religions, especially the wisdom learned from coming to terms with ageing and mortality. That, however, is the easy bit. More is at stake than the exchange of clever proverbs or even deep ideas. To repeat an earlier theme, it is in the *process* of exchange itself that true wisdom is learned. Just as reflective religious reading requires repetition, to get to the heart of the matter, so reflective conversation entails more than listening to the words of the other. If the true meaning of the encounter is to sink in, attention needs to be given to the broader context in which they are uttered. But before turning to a brief cross-religious conversation about the 'tasks of ageing', let me stay a little longer with the spiritual and theological value of conversation itself.

*Conversation as Theology*

My dialogue in the Southall dust left me convinced that what I shared with people of faith was not any facile 'common essence', but a desire to initiate and continue conversations, if not bringing them to a completely satisfactory conclusion. Just as a number of individuals confessed to a growing understanding and appreciation of their neighbours' faith, so I experienced a growing awareness of what I was learning *about my own faith*. This was the basis of my approach to comparative theology, becoming sensitised to the 'resonances' that conversation, observation and prayer evoked. Even the most prosaic of encounters – with words from books or gestures in worship – might lead to conversations that made me explore the 'deep structures' of my own spirituality more carefully. For instance, I soon realised that the famous 'presupposition' which precedes the *Exercises* proper is itself based on an implicit 'theology of conversation'. The text is worth quoting:

> So that the giver of the *Exercises* and the exercitant may the better help and benefit the other, it must be presupposed that every good Christian should be readier to justify rather than condemn a neighbour's statement. If no justification can be found, one should ask the other in what sense the statement is to be taken, and if that sense is wrong the other should be corrected with love. Should this not be sufficient, let every appropriate means be sought whereby to have the statement interpreted in a good sense and so to justify it [22].

The implication is that God works directly in the well-disposed individual, that truth is communicated through what is articulated in the relationship established between two persons, the director and the exercitant. That may sound like a naive exhortation to give 'the other' the benefit of the doubt, and in a cut-throat world in which power and ruthless self-confidence count for so much, that may seem like a recipe for disaster. What Ignatius is commending, however, is no more and no less than Jesus' words to his disciples, 'I send you out as sheep in the midst of wolves; so be wise as serpents and innocent as doves' (Mt. 10:16). There are always limits to trust and hospitality. That's why the work of critical discernment is always necessary, why Ignatius is sensitive to the distortions that may be exercised by the 'enemy of our human nature'. But, without taking the risk, without the willingness to entertain at least the *possibility* that God's grace may be active in some mysterious way in the conversation that arises from the meeting of persons, nothing gets going and nothing can change.

Somehow a sort of foundational trust, an act of faith in the *power of conversation* itself, has to be converted into everyday ministry, made more explicit, more consciously recognising that the Spirit of Christ is at work in *all* interpersonal relations where serious discernment takes place. If for the first Jesuits, devout conversation was one more way of persuading the other to see things their way, maybe today the risk of faith is set a stage further back, as it were – trusting in people's God-given capacity to *persuade themselves*. That does not absolve Christians from the need to be clear about who they are and what they stand for; it does, however, mean learning how to be more relaxed with, and hospitable to, those facts, whether set deep in postmodern nostalgia or emanating from the sometimes threatening world of faiths like Islam and Buddhism, which challenge their sense of self-sufficiency. Something similar must apply to other persons of faith: before debate about the meaning of 'a neighbour's statement' comes a loving commitment to the neighbour.

This implicit theology of conversation becomes explicit for anyone following the *Spiritual Exercises* when Ignatius recommends that, at the end of each period of prayer, thoughts and feelings are turned into a 'colloquy'. This, as Michael Ivens says, is a personal and spontaneous prayer responding to the grace of God, and 'never a set task to be performed on set lines'. Occasionally Ignatius is a little more prescriptive, for example with the three conjoined colloquies, or Triple Colloquy – conversations with Mary, Jesus and the

Father. This single sequence, which retraces the movement of the history of salvation, is a 'consciously Trinitarian prayer', says Ivens, 'leading to the Father through the incarnate Word, Son of Mary'. The idea of an ascending movement implies a more formal approach in petitioning for God's grace, but the manner of the prayer is left open and remains personal. Understanding and the feelings it arouses are to be drawn together and articulated with reference to one thing only, the shape or nature of grace as it impinges on the needs of the particular individual.

This is how each period of prayer is to be completed. I present myself before the Divine Majesty, speaking honestly of my deepest desires and seeking only to be conformed to God's own desires for me. Compared with the classical form of the monastic *lectio divina* – Reading, Meditation, Prayer (*oratio*) and Contemplation – Ignatius reverses the last two. Contemplation always leads back into a prayer of discipleship.

It is easy to understand how Ignatian spirituality has become so popular over the course of the last half-century. Once the formative practice of a single religious order, the *Spiritual Exercises* are now recognised as a gift to the whole Church – indeed, in the context of the relational ecclesiology of the Second Vatican Council, a gift to the whole world. But that isn't to say that they promote a theological programme. Like any form of spiritual exercise, they invite individual exercitants to take part in a journey, promising to those prepared to take the risk that they will discover something in this world of everyday experience that speaks of nothing less than God's creative and redeeming action.

I have often thought that this helps to understand the difference between the spiritual charism of the Society of Jesus and that of two other influential active religious orders, the Dominicans and the Franciscans. Dominicans, the Order of Preachers, work within the great theological tradition associated most importantly with the towering figure of St Thomas Aquinas. For Franciscans, the equivalent is probably St Bonaventure. But there is no such equivalent for Jesuits. According to a demanding programme laid down by Ignatius in the *Constitutions*, the curriculum for those in studies is to include philosophy, humane learning, languages and science as well as theology. In the late sixteenth century, Francisco Suarez assumed a dominant position in Jesuit theological circles. His influence, and that of the scholastic method that was in many ways more Thomistic than Thomas himself, lasted into the beginning of the twentieth century. Then, in the wake of the Modernist crisis, a number of influential Jesuits and Dominicans, most importantly Henri de Lubac, Jean Daniélou, Yves Congar and Marie-Dominique Chenu, began the great movement of *ressourcement* that was so influential on the Second Vatican Council.

If there is a typically Jesuit approach to theology, it is eclectic and integrative, gathering a variety of sources, from patristic and scholastic traditions to the likes of Barth, Moltmann, Eberhard Jüngel and Congar. It seems that Jesuits take delight in beginning more or less *anywhere*. Under the guidance of the Spirit, reading, meditation and contemplation initiate a conversation in response to the revealing Word, a personal conversation that is always intensely *theological*. My own writing since that relatively youthful *Religions in Conversation* has tended to make a virtue of that 'anywhere', in order to illustrate a profound truth: the insight of Ignatius that God is to be found 'in all things'. A personal and theological conversation, growing out of a repeated pondering on the deepest truths manifested in the Paschal Mystery, gathers insights of all kinds, from Ignatius himself to Augustine, Anselm and Aquinas, from the Pauline Epistles and the Fourth Gospel to Rahner and Panikkar, Nicholas Lash and Rowan Williams. Repetition is a good Jesuit principle, especially when it leads to what Ignatius calls the 'application of the senses'. In the *Spiritual Exercises* this is all part of the process of simplifying prayer, based on the principle that the most carefully considered meditation on truth has to be interiorly 'relished' and fixed deep in the heart. Otherwise one risks privileging the abstract over the instinctive, what can be clearly articulated over what remains obscure yet still strangely life-giving. There is more to repetition than saying the same thing, maybe with different words, only more loudly. And there is more to 'devout conversation' than gently batting back and forth a handful of pious platitudes.

In this book, I have given examples of how the spirituality that flows from the *Spiritual Exercises* teaches a prayerful interaction with the people of faith for whom traditions of ancient wisdom are life-giving. In so doing I hope to have shown that the *Exercises* motivate an intellectual curiosity about the ways of God with human beings, a curiosity that expects something very different from the negotiation of a consensus. Conversation connects; it provokes the imagination into making intuitive leaps.

If there is no settled Ignatian theological tradition, however, what is it that stops 'theological conversation' becoming, not a celebration of 'God in all things', but little more than an imaginative bricolage? What gives it real integrity? With that question in mind, let us first take up our theme of 'grey wisdom'.

## Resonances of Ageing

Our 'anywhere' is not a temple or synagogue, but the National Gallery of Scotland where hangs an early work by Titian. 'The Three Ages of Man' is an allegory. On the right-hand side two babies lie asleep with a cupid figure prancing mischievously above them. On the left, a young man and his beloved sit entranced, their limbs entwined, their eyes fixed on each other. In the background sits the 'third age': an old man contemplating not one but two skulls. Looming over him is the stunted trunk of a tree. The meaning is obvious: the melancholy truth that the innocence of childhood and the passion of first love both end in death. Yet that isn't the end of the story. In the background, silhouetted against the sky, is a small church: a sign of salvation perhaps, or the source of real life – what outlasts the three ages and provides stability and hope in a changing world.

What is depicted by Titian is a progress that finds a certain resonance in a number of different religious traditions. The founding myth of Buddhism, for example, is just such a *memento mori*. The innocence of the pampered prince, kept secluded from the reality of human suffering, is shattered by the encounter with the 'real world' outside the royal palace: a sick man, a dying man and a corpse. But then he comes across a wandering ascetic and the possibility of a way out, *moksha* or release. Not mediated by a church, but a sign of salvation or enlightenment nonetheless, it makes him see the human condition of suffering in a new light.

There's a stark realism here. Similar ideas are found in classical Hinduism. What in the Law Books are called the 'stages and states of life' map out the various proper pursuits of human living. In the first stage or *brahmacarya* one is initiated by a *guru*, learning the ancient traditions, until one is ready for the second stage or *grhastha*, living as a householder, earning a living, marrying and raising a family. The third stage starts, say the *Laws of Manu*, 'when a householder sees that he is wrinkled and grey'; it is marked by withdrawing from family duties and seeking refuge in the forest, what we would call these days 'retirement'. And then there is an enigmatic fourth stage. 'When he has spent the third part of his lifespan in the forests, he may abandon all attachments and wander as an ascetic for the fourth part of his lifespan'. This is the life of total renunciation, *sannyasa*, the time when one can prepare for the end of life itself, both its termination in death and its true meaning and purpose.

When I started teaching Hinduism at Heythrop I would illustrate the 'four stages' with a little film about an old man thinking about becoming a *sannyasi*. One scene showed him having a fierce row with his daughters over a meal. His wife sat silently in the background, no doubt wondering what might happen to her if this self-obsessed old bore got his way and left her. Alarmed or relieved? Probably both. However, after travelling and consulting learned pandits in various monasteries, the old man decided that becoming a *sannyasi* wasn't for him. Not yet, at any rate. The point of the film was that just asking the question was itself a learning experience. He wanted to take seriously a new possibility, that final last stage. But he still hadn't finished his earlier responsibilities. He remained a husband, a father, a grandfather – and there was still work to be done to justify his existence. One can move on too quickly. Rather than risk premature conclusions, it is often better to be flexible and keep open the possibility that at some point a deeper understanding may emerge, even if not yet.

## Mortality and Old Age

Titian's version of the allegory of the stages of life makes two important points. Firstly, it says something about how we human beings construct narratives to give coherence to our lives. Secondly – and more importantly – it approaches the last stage, not as some triumphant resolution, but with an open-ended humility. However the last stage is conceived in religious or cultural terms, it centres round a qualitative shift from everyday tasks to something more personal and profound. At the same time, we cannot make any sense of that last shift without seeing it in the light of what has gone before.

It is easy to romanticise old age as a time of mellow contentment, during which bright young things sit rapt in admiration as granny muses upon the secrets of human living gleaned over four score years and more. Old age does not exempt anyone from the crises and turbulence of faith. It's as difficult a time as any other. Neat lists of stages and ages, with their accompanying tasks, cannot be understood in straightforward linear terms. Life just isn't like that. And yet it may be that very context of messy intractability that gives us some clue to understanding the crucially important nexus between the third and fourth 'stages'. The image of the church on the hill in Titian's painting is nothing if not a reminder that an account of human life which stops with a 'third stage' is not enough. There's evidence that old people do indeed think about the 'meaning of life'; it would be surprising if they did not. Hence the importance of taking seriously the particular value and power of that – perhaps indefinable – fourth stage.

This stage deserves our attention, not because it brings resolution – very often it doesn't – but because it opens up a contemplative space that cultivates attention, not just to the great sweep of life, but more exactly to the present moment. The move from the third to the fourth stage is never achieved in a hurry. 'Grey wisdom' is not a fullness of anything but, more exactly, the *readiness* to face mortality and the inevitable tragedy of a life which is rarely fulfilled as one dreamed it would be all those years before.

That is where we all begin, not with some discrete 'problem' that faces the wrinklies, but with something that affects us all, young and old alike. Qoheleth the preacher is second to none in musing on the ambivalence of everyday experience. The final chapter of the book of Ecclesiastes ends with those familiar words that all academics, old or young, should take to heart, 'There is no end to the writing of books, and much study is wearisome' (Eccl. 12.12). What saves this book from the charge of cynicism is the underlying theme, noted more explicitly throughout the Hebrew scriptures, that God can and does overturn human expectation by granting the blessing of old age and fullness of years – as, for instance, to Abraham (Gen. 25:7-8). The preacher knows that nothing lasts, everything returns to the dust from which it came. And yet God's spirit somehow goes on enlivening the world.

The same sense of realism, expressed in less obviously theistic form, is to be found in the Upanisads, where learned gurus initiate young people into the great mysteries of life that are so often shrouded by human folly and ignorance. Rarely, however, is wisdom bestowed like a lordly gift from on high. The *Katha Upanisad*, for instance, begins with an angry father lashing out at his son for pestering him with unanswerable questions. 'Oh, go to hell', he says. And the son obediently complies, only to find that the god of the underworld is away on his travels. On his return, the god is embarrassed to find his guest alone and apologises by agreeing to grant three gifts – answers, of course, to the very questions which the father has been unable or unwilling to address. There's a neat ironic twist here: it is the guardian of death who gives away its secret. The serious point is that confrontation with the thing we most fear is often what brings an unexpected depth of understanding. In that light, death is not a grim and all-powerful force that destroys all rationality, but rather one more change – albeit a very substantial one – in a process human beings experience in every moment. A peculiarly Indian 'grey wisdom' gives an insight into how the 'four stages' are to be configured; more exactly, it is about how that tantalisingly obscure virtue of hope helps to knit together and keep going the narrative people hesitantly seek to make sense of their lives.

## Marking the Movement of Time

Speaking in purely descriptive terms, what we find in the Hindu Law Books is the amalgamation of two different types of human religiosity, that proper to the person in the world and that of the pure contemplative or solitary. The first three stages are all dedicated to various aspects of *dharma* – loosely to be translated as 'duty', the work that is appropriate to each stage as life unfolds. The fourth stage is not a duty or a task at all. For the Hindu, it is what comes *after* I have *spent time* justifying my existence to someone else. Now I *take time* to reflect on what has been and where it is all leading. In Hindu terms this leads to *moksha* or release from the cycle of birth and rebirth.

Perhaps the point can be illustrated by brief reference to a far less well-known example of Indian contemplative religiosity. The Jains, contemporaries of early Buddhism, stand within a lineage of 'ford-makers' or *tirthankaras,* sages who are adept in passing over the river that separates this life from the next. A while ago I had the opportunity to speak at a meeting of Catholics and Jains at an interreligious gathering in north London. Not that far off the crazed

*Jain temple, Oshwal Centre, Potters Bar, Hertfordshire UK*

traffic jam that masquerades as the M25 stands a beautiful Jain temple, built into a tiny valley in the middle of a luxuriant park, all rose stonework and delicate tracery. Merely to gaze upon this magnificent 'anywhere' is to be reminded that the human imagination and capacity for aesthetic celebration knows no bounds.

The most familiar teaching of Jainism is the value of *ahimsa* which so influenced Mahatma Gandhi. The word is usually translated as 'non-violence'. We can, however, so emphasise the 'non' that it attracts connotations of passivity, of avoiding any action which might destroy, disturb or upset. That is unhelpful. The form of the word in Sanskrit has a desiderative or intentional force. The root is *han*, to kill; literally it means 'wishing not to kill' or, better perhaps, 'wishing well' to someone, that they may enjoy a life which is free of all forms of violence. The practice of *ahimsa* runs through the whole of Jain culture, giving rise to the equally important principle of *anekanta*. Meaning something like the 'many-sidedness' of things, *anekanta* is a deliberate refusal to retreat into some sort of dogmatic system. It sounds at first like a naive relativism, suggesting that no account of absolute truth can be given. But this is a way of thinking which capitalises on the 'grey wisdom' of those who are closer to the end of life. At the meeting, words were quoted from one of the most important Jain scriptures, the *Acaranga Sutra,* which insists that no sentient creatures should be killed or abused or treated with violence. The text then continues:

> This is the pure, eternal, unchangeable law ... seen (by the omniscient ones), heard (by the believers), acknowledged (by the faithful), and thoroughly understood by them.

What is described is a chain of reception, a living tradition based on the experience of the wise which therefore has an open-ended, never-finished quality. It is, of course, an ideal. Were the grey elders of the Jain community who entertained us to a splendid lunch 'omniscient', fully versed in the 'eternal, unchangeable law'? I very much doubt it. Yet they were treated as if they were, as if long years alone granted wisdom. And maybe that's the point. Jainism shares much with Buddhism. In both, the fourth stage of *sannyasa* is not a particular choice appropriate for a few, but the crown of religious life which informs every other stage. Being alone, being allowed to take time, no longer having to justify oneself to others: this is not just the privilege of old age but a gift to the young, a reminder of how the regular commitment to *dharma,* duty and responsibility, has its own purpose and reward. This is what the grey and wrinkly dare to offer to the youthful and fresh-faced.

## *Harmony of Youth and Old Age*
At the risk of indulging myself in what I promised not to do – produce a compendium of 'religious wisdom' – let me move swiftly from the Indian religious traditions back to the prophetic world of the Middle East. The most important precepts would be at home in that Jain assembly. 'Honour your father and mother', says the fourth commandment of the Decalogue. In the Holy Qur'an the point is expanded:

The Lord hath decreed that ye worship none but Him, and that ye be kind to parents. Whether one or both of them attain old age in their life, say not to them a word of contempt, nor repel them, but address them in terms of honour. And out of kindness lower to them the wing of humility, and say: 'My Lord, bestow on them thy mercy even as they cherished me in childhood'.

Jewish and Islamic tradition is concerned less with preserving the particular experience of old age than with commending the harmony of young and old. In the prophet Joel, we find the Lord saying that 'I shall pour out my spirit on all mankind; your sons and daughters will prophesy, your old men will dream dreams and your young men will prophesy' (Jl. 2:28). Zechariah speaks about the restoration of Jerusalem in these terms: 'Once again old men and women will sit in the streets of Jerusalem, each leaning on a stick because of great age; and the streets of the city will be full of boys and girls at play' (Zech. 8:4-5). Prophetic wisdom is always touched by visionary and even romantic ideals of restoration and harmony.

But that again is the easy bit. It's what it costs to become a prophet that opens up for us a more profound 'grey wisdom'. Before ever speaking, says Abraham Joshua Heschel, the prophet is touched by the pathos of God. Running through Old and New Testaments alike is the great theme of the God who speaks a Word, who is indeed *the* Word that brings creation into being, and who enters deep into the suffering heart of that world, and goes on energising, provoking and restoring it. It's in response to that Word that we learn how to become a self – not enclosed and self-sufficient, but intrinsically related to another. Here it is possible to detect something that begins to mend the simplistic divides that we tend to erect, between the theistic Abrahamic traditions and the non-theistic traditions more typical of that great crucible of human religiosity, the religions of India. Again, it may be a mark of a little 'grey wisdom' to question such dichotomies

– even if mending them is more difficult.

Whatever we mean by that elusive 'fourth stage' is bound up with a profound sense of the irreducible otherness of human living. Earnest *brahmacarins* think they understand it all; by the time they have got to retire to the forest they know they do not. We are deeply dialogical creatures, made, as Emmanuel Levinas reminds us, 'in the accusative', always called to respond to an otherness or difference that takes precedence over our desire to dominate. Christians may be committed to *naming* the Word of God in a way that Buddhists simply aren't. But both, in the repetitions and reflections that characterise their respective patterns of holiness, are concerned with what it means and what it takes to face a future that is never predictable and remains always utterly other.

There are two ways of reading the Hindu four stages. The first is in linear terms, one after the other. The idea of a temporal sequence has its place; it's the way we tell our stories, to ourselves and to others. If we are not careful, however, we risk colluding with a narrative of growth and decline. We end up with a series of identifiable tasks to justify our existence, to keep young and old contentedly occupied. Maybe there is another way, what the Buddhists would call mutual co-inherence. Beginnings and endings are interdependent, things coming to be and falling away in the same moment. The glory and the tragedy of human beings is to participate in both, to welcome and to let go, to enjoy and to set aside. To put what is the same point in more familiar theistic terms, I recall a phrase of Emil Fackenheim. Revelation, he says, is an 'event of Divine Presence'. In Christian terms, that can be translated as the action of the self-communicating God, a cosmic drama initiated and sustained by the divine 'other', the Holy Spirit. But to be aware of that drama, let alone become caught up in it, means building into both our beginnings and our endings some measure of receptivity, a confidence in the sheer 'rightness' of things and the goodness of human beings.

Again this means taking a risk, and yet being wise and discerning. And it is this complexity that makes it a task for young and old alike, for young and old *together*. At their best our religious traditions subvert our expectations and challenge the ease with which we collude with personally appropriated 'answers'. There's always a different way of looking at the tried and familiar. We don't have to make a choice between contemplating the futility of it all and overcoming meaninglessness with hefty rhetorical force. There's also that generosity of embrace which takes delight in what the Fathers called the seeds of Word, while at the same time finding life in the depth of the unfathomable mystery which underpins all things.

*Receiving Hope*

This theme of the stages of life may give some hint of how people of faith, both youthful and grey, go about engaging in the conversation of religions. Something resonates across the 'texts' – whatever can be *read* – provoking the imagination to make connections and see things differently. Which takes us back to the question raised earlier: what gives a wide-ranging conversation integrity and coherence?

Ignatius would most probably answer that question by pointing us, not to any theological principle (though he does have quite a few scattered throughout the text of the *Spiritual Exercises*), but to the last meditation of the *Exercises*: the Contemplation to Attain Love. Strictly speaking, this is outside the four-week structure itself. This brilliant schematic rendering of the entire trajectory of the *Exercises* is preceded by two typically Ignatian introductory notes: love is expressed in deeds rather than words, he writes; and love consists in 'mutual communication' [230-1]. It's almost as if Ignatius is aware that, by appearing to reinstate the traditional ending of *Lectio Divina,* he is compromising his earlier insistence that contemplation always issues in action, a commitment to mission in company with Christ. If so, he is quick to correct this impression in the two preliminaries that follow: a 'composition of place', where I stand before God, surrounded by angels and saints pleading in my behalf [232], and the petition to receive

> interior knowledge of all the good I have received, so that acknowledging this with gratitude, I may be able to love and serve his Divine Majesty in everything [233].

Love and service is the aim, but it cannot be separated from 'interior knowledge'. This is what sums up all the gifts that have been received throughout the pilgrimage with Christ, learning intimately from the love of God that is manifested in Christ how to share that love for the well-being of others and the common good. 'Love of God' always has a double meaning – a bit of Christian 'mutual co-inherence', perhaps. The subjective genitive, the *love* of God, God's absolute and unconditional love for human beings, builds up the objective, the love of *God* that is manifested in the world, God's gift of himself in the work of creation-and-redemption, where, in Ignatius's terms, God 'labours and works on my behalf' [236]. The Contemplation takes the foundational trust of the Presupposition noted at the beginning of this chapter and transforms it into faith in the compassionate God who is to be found 'in all things'. Everything is gift because nothing is outside the creative and redemptive power of God. That is not to underestimate the need for discernment, for all the reasons that have appeared in earlier chapters of this book. Rather, it reminds us that discernment is itself a theological activity, not the weighing of advantages and disadvantages, but a collaboration with the Spirit of Christ who reminds us where God has been at work and leads us into 'all the truth' (Jn. 16:13).

I have made the point that true interreligious or intercultural wisdom is to be found, not in culling bright ideas from other faith traditions, but in the process of conversation itself. In the next chapter I will return to the theme of prophetic action, the Ignatian 'faith that does justice'. Let me finish this one by going back to the National Gallery in Edinburgh and engaging again with Titian's painting, or perhaps by returning to those two great frescoes of the Annunciation I referred to in an earlier chapter. My theme has been 'Reading Love's Mystery', and the implication of what I have been saying is that the phases of the *Lectio Divina* can be applied to all manner of 'texts', objects that are open to reading and prayerful contemplation.

There is a learned skill involved in viewing a picture or an artefact, wherever it is displayed. Even apart from all the data and archival material available to help the viewer learn more about the style and history of the artwork itself, cognitive and affective responses can be taught, enhancing the naturally curious gaze. The longer one spends in front of a favourite painting, especially in the company of someone who knows their art history, the easier it becomes to respond beyond the surface impression to its radical mystery. Viewing pictures in an art gallery is no more a passive act of reception than going to the theatre or listening to an opera. In an important sense the audience co-creates the 'conversation' of the drama, the 'third text' between the artwork and the viewer. We do so in silence, entering into the imaginative world created by the writer or artist, and attending to a carefully wrought combination of colour, sound, narrative and space. Without an audience to respond to, actors would be addressing a vacuum. There's a paradox here, for we tend to think of silence as absence, a lack of noise. More positively it connotes receptivity and attentiveness, not just that profound moment of unvoiced truth at the end, but the moment of hope – for it is that – which precedes any work of art and out of which it is born.

Theology is conversation, a dialogical activity which seeks to respond to whatever is voiced out of the human drama. It's what a community of faith does as it engages prayerfully with whatever dimensions of the Spirit's action in the world command attention. In that sense what I have written about in this chapter has inaugurated nothing new. It has only sought to act as a critical catalyst for a more generous if risky welcome to what *God* may be doing in the world, in the 'signs of the times'. The danger is that the words, the many voices, take over – and ordering them becomes an end in itself, a sort of ecclesial quality-control mechanism. If I end by privileging silence, it is not to deny that further conversation is always necessary, that there can be no arbitrary end to the *Lectio*. On the contrary, it is to focus on the hope – often strangely if inadequately realised – that the mystery of God's Word is manifested somehow in the midst of our poor wordiness.

# CHAPTER TEN

## The Power of the Word

THIS BOOK has been peppered with little bits of autobiography. The background story is the great Jesuit tradition of encountering and responding to 'the other', from which I have drawn a number of historical examples, from St Francis Xavier and Thomas Stephens to Francis Clooney and William Johnston. I have presumed to bring in my own experience because the various preliminaries with which St Ignatius prefaces each consideration or meditation in the *Spiritual Exercises* call for a personal response. Ignatian spirituality encourages a remembrance of where God has been active in one's life, attention to 'place' and 'story' within which one seeks to encounter God, and a prayerful openness to the desires which God awakens in the individual. The prayer this encourages is often called imaginative contemplation, a setting of oneself in the scene suggested by a reading of the Gospel narrative. But this exercise of self-engagement with the text cannot be separated from the type of prayer which, in more formal or structural terms, underpins the dynamic of the *Exercises*, namely the Examen.

What is 'examined' – more exactly contemplated – is a growing sensitivity to the movements of God's Spirit. The graces Ignatius expects us to ask for at the beginning of each meditation are always very personal. If they are to intersect with wider concerns for the Church and the world, they have to be to be embedded in the heart, so that what develops is an intuitive religious instinct that is best described in that most evocative of Ignatian phrases, 'finding God in all things'. God's Word meets ordinary frail human beings in their everyday lives, sanctifying them in the flesh, in 'the dust', not abstracting them into some safely 'transcendent' realm. There can be no doubt that such a spirituality, with its deeply affective focus on the person of Christ, commends itself to anyone dedicated to an active apostolic life 'in the world'. But how does this 'mysticism of the everyday' turn out to be so attractive to anyone working in interreligious relations? While witness to what is known of the God revealed in Christ is central to the life of all Christians, it is not obvious how that applies when one enters into a relationship with those who have their own witness to make, their own 'Good News'.

## A School of Contemplative Prayer

I am sometimes asked how a Jesuit priest came to specialise in Indian religions. I am tempted to answer 'by mistake', because the study of another religious tradition was never my original intention. That would, however, be a little disingenuous. In my early years in the Society, everything was changing. Popular culture was being transformed by Eastern wisdom brought back from the hippy trails, while the Church after the Second Vatican Council was awash with small prayer groups and experiments with the meditative practices of Yoga, Zen and T'ai Chi. A number of charismatic figures were experimenting with new types of dialogue, most obviously Thomas Merton, whose tragic death in 1968 only served to intensify his appeal. He was one of a number of monastics who were raising serious questions about how their Christian prayer, rooted in the liturgy, *Lectio Divina* and the tradition of the Christian mystics, might open up a dialogue with similar forms of practice in other religious traditions.

That Jesuits might be part of this movement seemed unlikely in the era of liberation theology and the mission for social justice. St Ignatius the pilgrim wanted his Jesuits committed, not to monastic stability, but to a radical spirituality of constant attention to how the Holy Spirit is always at work in the world. I have already drawn attention to the influence of St Francis Xavier and spoken about the extraordinary work of Thomas Stephens. Yet, if the traditional emphasis of Ignatian spirituality has always been on 'contemplation in action' – with the emphasis on the action – there have always been Jesuits fully committed to contemplative prayer as itself a witness to the Gospel. And that strand is there in the *Exercises* which bear, not just an ascetical interpretation (preparing individuals for mission of some kind), but one that is more mystical (a *school of prayer* which sensitises people to the reality of God in their midst). The two are not mutually exclusive and must be held together as a single logical sequence, not a series of isolated meditations. Two emphases, perhaps, within a single commitment to the following of Christ in his own witness to the Father.

The emphasis with which I was more happy came from the school-of-prayer strand. This was not because I felt no great call to volunteer for what were still in my early years as a Jesuit known as 'the missions', but because it addressed the shift towards interiority that was a feature of the flaky world of the 60s and 70s. I never used the term, but I was becoming interested in how the Gospel could be inculturated into the language of secular, pluralist, indeed atheist Britain. It would be tedious to map out my experiments in religious studies and interreligious dialogue. Instead let me fast forward to an example of the sort of thing I was doing some thirty years later.

An earlier chapter on 'Dialogue in the Dust' was something of a broad landscape sketch, involving the work of a Jesuit community in a multicultural area. By way of contrast I offer now a more straightforward 'micro-study' which represents one Christian's attempt to make sense of some 'other' texts. My initial premise is that these examples of medieval Tamil texts perform an analogous function in Tamil Hinduism to the Gospel; they are to be respected and valued as part of the 'story' and 'place' that Christians who seek to live out their witness interreligiously are expected to examine. While it has touches of Clooney's style of comparative theology, what follows is more exposition than straight comparison; I want to allow the texts themselves to speak, albeit that I present them within an implicit Christian cultural framework

## *The Origins of Poetry*

The great Sanskrit Epic, the *Ramayana*, begins with an incident which has inspired the writer Valmiki. When the sage Narada comes to his hermitage, Valmiki offers him hospitality and asks him a question: who is the ideal hero? The reply comes in a rehearsal of the story of the hero Rama, the foundation of what was to become the Epic. Immersed in the mystery of what he has just heard, Valmiki goes down to the river. There he visualizes the purity of Rama's mind reflected in the placid waters. He muses upon themes of duty and honour, suffering and loss, and goes off to collect wood for the sacrificial fire. In a tree, he spots a pair of birds singing away and clearly taking delight in each other's company. He stands and watches.

Suddenly one of the birds is shot by a hunter and falls bloodied to the ground; its mate lets out a shriek of agony and flies off in pain and confusion. Valmiki finds himself overwhelmed with pity for a suffering creature. His first instinct is to curse the heartless hunter for his act of wanton violence, but to his amazement what comes out of his mouth is a perfectly metrical composition, the first śloka, which is the classical verse form of Sanskrit poetry. Valmiki himself comments, 'that which emanated from me who was smitten with grief was measured, musical poetry'.

This little story, buried away at the beginning of a tale of mighty battles and stirring deeds done in the cause of *dharma*, says something important about the creative process. Poetry, it seems, is the expression of an experience of overwhelming emotion. No doubt that is true. It's easy, however, to miss the complex mixture of emotions ignited by Valmiki's experience – peace, pity, grief, wonder, amazement. It's also easy to miss the subtlety with which the 'inner words' of his musings upon an ancient story are transformed into the 'outer words' of his poetry. It may be the case that religious faith opens up a contemplative space for language, but that is only to beg an important question about the relationship between 'inner experience' and the culture from which it springs – let alone the new cultural expressions to which it gives rise.

## Obedience and Transformation

Notice two salient points in the story. The first is that Valmiki's version of the *Ramayana* springs from an act of obedience, as one teacher initiates another and passes on a timeless message. In that sense his 'contemplative space' is formed by what has gone before. Hinduism and Buddhism are essentially commentarial traditions; that is to say that the language of tradition has a major role in forming consciousness. Secondly, however, the experience of the poet is personally transformative; it is not that anger and grief are overcome but that they awake a different way of seeing things. The carefully crafted verse form with which Valmiki responds seems at first like an effort to overcome or transcend the encounter with the painfully particular. I suspect, however, that it is really the opposite – not a withdrawal from, but a deeper entry into the constraints imposed by everyday phenomena.

Indian religious traditions are often regarded as 'mystical', as opposed to the noisy 'prophetic' religions which arose in the Middle East. This is a line I resist. There is a vast amount of religious writing in India – from the Vedic hymns to Buddhist and Hindus philosophies and the devotional poetry of *sants* and *acaryas* – in which, to use that Buddhist phrase, silence and word are 'mutually co-inherent'. Silence is itself particular; not an absolute quality or value set apart from language, but a way of relating to the world which is itself shaped and reshaped by the myriad forms of human utterance. The question is, not how language can be silenced, but how silence impels speech.

To address that question, I first need to say something about the Indian fascination with the 'power of the word'. More exactly, that should be the power of the sound or 'sounded word', for it is an oral tradition with which we are concerned; the written language is a secondary record. Then I will focus on one particular poet from one tradition, not the Vaishnavism of the *Ramayana* but the Śaivism of South India. Finally, I will contrast – or maybe complement – the ecstatic language of devotional poetry with a tradition which has appeared at various points in this book. Zen Buddhism is more than usually impatient with language – oral or written – but still manages to press the creative limits of the religious imagination.

## The Divine Word

Let me begin with the point that it is only when spoken that language comes fully alive. Paradoxically, it is in the particular moment of speaking that the universal nature of what in the Vedas is called *Vac*, 'Word', is manifested. A truth enunciated in the *Rg Veda* – that there are as many words as there are manifestations of the divine *Brahman* – underlines the sacred revelatory function of language itself. Revelation is *śruti*, what is heard. According to Śri Aurobindo, the language of the Veda is 'rhythm not composed by the intellect but heard, a divine Word that came vibrating out of the Infinite to the inner audience of the man who had previously made himself fit for the impersonal knowledge'.

This is why the Indian philosophers and grammarians insist that language is more than a medium of communication. It has metaphysical as well as phenomenal dimensions, an eternal quality in which human beings are caught up. Sanskrit – the very word means 'elegantly or well made' – contains its own mystique and remains, strictly speaking, the preserve of the Brahmins and the 'twice-born' castes. The grammarians who were responsible for formulating its classical pattern were less concerned with standardising an instrument of communication than with elaborating the nature of language in its relationship to *Brahman*. It is not that the *rsis* – the Indian poet-seers of the Veda – create something new out of their own imagination, but that they relate what has been heard back to the origin of all things; *brh,* the Sanskrit root behind *Brahman,* has connotations of something expanding, growing.

The ways we use language, the ways we open ourselves to the 'power of the word', the ways we struggle to find the right words to give shape to our experience while yet keeping their original integrity of purpose, all this generates its own wisdom. To be learned in the Vedas is not a matter of knowing the contents or understanding the ideas, but being able to speak the texts correctly, with proper attention to accent and metre, so that one becomes habituated to their inner world.

That may sound fundamentalist to modern ears, as if the purity of the Word has to be preserved at all costs. More exactly, the Word is a performative utterance, and what is at stake is the true performance of the Word: how to speak its objective meaning or *artha,* 'purpose', through the medium of particular phrases and words or *dhvani,* 'sound'. It's this relationship which is spelled out in what is called the *Sphota* theory of language. The word itself – from a Sanskrit root meaning 'burst forth' – refers to the 'unit of meaning' which is first heard and voiced in the consciousness of the poet, and is then spoken and becomes embedded in the consciousness of the listener. In many ways, it is a theory of revelation, but is perhaps best understood as a dynamic process of learning.

What is spoken and given form is already there, unmanifest, and is never exhausted by any form of expression. Yet it is always being made manifest through sudden moments of insight or enlightenment which result from the mental activity of the enlightened sage, piecing together a whole series of discrete words and sounds. The grammarians debate at great length the relationship between the transcendent *Vac* and the meaning-giving units of language which 'burst forth' and are communicated to an audience. Poets look to exercise a certain double responsibility, on the one hand to the tradition in which they are set, and, on the other, to the living community which they seek to inspire.

Put like that – a theory of communication, in which some original shared truth is mediated through words inspired by poetic insight – it sounds straightforward enough, albeit a trifle mechanical. In practice, of course, the process by which *Vac* is differentiated into discrete sounds, spoken in such a way that meaning is heard and communicated, yet all the time remains *Vac*, maintaining an essential unity, is always extremely complex. So let me introduce, again all too briefly, another bit of Indian literary theory.

*Aesthetic Moods and Resonances*
Communication involves more than passing on the 'unit of meaning'; it involves cultivating certain emotional 'resonances' or 'moods' which can be said to 'carry' meaning or, to be more precise, to provoke a response which is more affective than purely cognitive. This is what the Sanskrit theorists know as *rasa*, a word which originally means 'flavour' and comes to refer to an aesthetically cultivated experience. Eight *rasas* are usually listed: the erotic, the comic, the compassionate, the furious, the heroic, the fearful, the loathsome, and the marvellous; to these a more purely religious *rasa* is added sometimes: *śanti* or the peaceful. In the first place the aesthetic response depends on the skill of the poet, a quality of the imagination, a capacity to move the listener in a particular way. But to match the work of the poet, a reciprocal quality is needed in the listener, an appreciation of the conventions, the allusions and the symbols with which the poem is constructed.

Norman Cutler calls *rasa* theory a 'psychology of the audience'. 'A work of literature', he says, 'is deemed to be successful if and only if its audience achieves an experience of *rasa*.' The object of the exercise is to achieve an intimacy of communion between poet and audience. Ordinary everyday distracted awareness, what we experience of ourselves most of the time, is overcome not by some effort of withdrawal – setting up some yogic 'one-pointedness' of concentration – but by the mutual focusing on a set of emotions through which, to return to the *Sphota* metaphor, one is 'jolted' into a sense of the whole. It does, however, take time and training to acquire the skill of attentive listening. 'Cultivated spontaneity' sounds like an oxymoron, but it may go some way towards identifying an experience of grace and freedom which is yet dependent on building up a quality of contemplative attention to the well-worked artifice.

Now, the theory of language sketched out here gets fearfully complex and, in its various elaborations, never quite manages to shake off an elitist tinge. It is easy to miss the central point. Learning takes place through the piecing together of discrete units of meaning, like Valmiki's verse, which build together towards an ultimate unity. As each unit 'bursts forth', it communicates something of its inner meaning, by touching emotions and sounding resonances. Theory becomes a little more accessible when we switch from Sanskrit to one of the local vernaculars. Hinduism is a wonderfully anarchic amalgam of what anthropologists call the 'Great' or brahmanical tradition and the 'Little' or local traditions found in village and temple throughout India. No straightforward account of how the proliferating forms of *bhakti* sectarianism can be made to fit easily into the authoritative Vedic tradition is possible. Nevertheless, certain principles and themes run through all the sects and schools of Hinduism and inform the implicit, if not explicit, ways of reading, praying and performing sacred texts. All I want to show in what follows is something of how the broad instincts and ideas behind the poetic culture of *rasa* work themselves through one of the most popular *bhakti* movements, that associated with the god Śiva in the Tamil land of south India.

### The Aesthetic Conventions of Devotion

We have come across *bhakti* several times in this book. The word comes from a Sanskrit root *bhaj*, 'to divide, apportion, share'. In the most important of all *bhakti* texts, the *Bhagavad Gita*, written sometime in the last centuries of the first millennium BCE, the relationship in question is that between the young charioteer Arjuna and the god Krishna. Early on Krishna says, 'In whatever way men take refuge in me, in that same way do I participate (*bhajami*) in them' (4:11). At the very end he delivers his most important message about the nature of God: 'Give ear to this my highest word, of all the most mysterious: "I love you well" ... so will you come to me, I promise you truly, for you are dear to me' (18:64-65). The relationship between devotee and god-figure varies from one tradition to another, sometimes being expressed as loyalty to friends, sometimes as tender care for dependents, sometimes as an emotional, even crazed desire for the beloved. However expressed, this is God's initiative, to establish a circle of desire which draws devotees out of the world towards the transcendent, and then returns them back into the world, their emotions transformed and heightened.

The two great 'schools' of Tamil *bhakti* are formed around the Vaishnava Alvars and Śaivite Nayanars. Both are referred to as 'saints'; more exactly they are creative poets. The Alvars are 'immersed' in devotion to Vishnu and are usually listed as twelve in number. The Nayanars or 'leaders' are a more fluid category; more than sixty are listed, of whom four predominate. Strictly speaking, the fourth is not one of the designated group. In practice he is the most popular, however, and it is for this reason I have chosen to focus on him. Manikkavacakar, writing probably in the ninth century CE, is responsible for the *Tiruvacakam* – the 'sacred or holy word', a collection of fifty-one poems varying in length from a few verses of ecstatic praise to much longer and more complex lyrics which chart the progress of the soul through ever more intense stages of religious experience. The poems are still read, or more exactly sung, throughout the land of Tamil Nadu, in house and temple alike.

According to the tradition, Manikkavacakar was born in a village near Madurai and in his youth served as minister to the king. On a mission to the port of Peruntarai, he encounters a guru who turns out to be the god Śiva. He pleads to be accepted as a pupil, and then gives over to the guru the treasure which has been entrusted to him by the king for the purpose of buying horses. Unsurprisingly the king is not impressed and demands restitution from his erstwhile minister. All is resolved in due course when Manikkavacakar's pleas to the guru/Śiva are heard and the enraged king is mollified. Our hero dedicates himself to the service of Śiva and begins a wandering career, in which he confronts and defeats Buddhist teachers in debate, and dedicates himself to composing hymns in praise of the god. Towards the end of his life a nice bit of mythologising speaks of how Śiva himself comes once again in disguise to the poet and manages to write down the entirety of Manikkavacakar's hymns and poems. Śiva then retrieves his divine form and himself sings them to the delight of the assembled gods.

The background story is not all pious legend and hagiography; it is easy to ignore the personal, even autobiographical, dimension of Manikkavacakar's poems. Rather like the story told in the *Bhagavad Gita*, where Krishna teaches Arjuna the importance of fulfilling his caste duties by taking Krishna as an example of 'detached action', so in the story of Manikkavacakar the desire for an ecstatic union with Śiva is tempered by social responsibilities. The god insists that he work to teach the truth of Śaivism.

There is a personal and a public side to Manikkavacakar's poetry. On the one hand, he seeks to be transformed by the overwhelming power of the god; on the other, he is committed to a Śaivite vision of the perfect society of devotees. Given that he was a Brahmin, educated and with a good knowledge of Sanskrit, it is perhaps surprising that in the *Tiruvacakam* he always seems to prefer to stick with Tamil vocabulary, even when Sanskrit terminology is available. It is almost as if he seeks deliberately to stay within the Tamil tradition. And perhaps that is the point, that he can only express what he wants to say through the form of writing which is unique to the Tamil poetic tradition.

Manikkavacakar operates in a very specific cultural milieu. Thanks in some measure to the patronage of the Pandyan kings, an autonomous tradition of lyrical poetry grew up in the Tamil country in the early centuries of the Christian era. Its single most distinctive feature is a set of aesthetic conventions which enable the writer to convey a variety of human emotions and desires – not dissimilar to the Sanskritic *rasa* theory. The basic distinction which rules the poetic form is that between the category of 'inside', *akam*, and 'outside', *puram*; those in the former category are primarily love poems in which the female role is usually centre-stage, while those in the latter are about life and action in the wider world, celebrating the glory of kings, the heroism of warriors, the tragedy of life unfulfilled.

What develops is an elaborate system of symbolism, in which aspects of the natural environment are correlated with human experiences and feelings. *Akam* poetry, for instance, divides the landscape into five regions, associating each with a stage of love. Thus poems set in the mountains treat of the first attraction of the lovers to each other; pastureland is associated with patient waiting; agricultural land symbolises unfaithfulness; the seashore is the setting for doubt and loss; the desert speaks of the more painful experience of lengthy separation from the beloved. When combined with allusions to other features of the natural world – flora and fauna, seasons and times of day, guardian spirits and gods – the poet is able to produce subtle variations on particular themes. Like the *rasa* theory, the combination of certain features sets off a chain of semantic associations, conjuring up a rich world formed by mutually implicating allusions.

### Love in the Ordinary

As an illustration, let me quote a couple of poems from an *akam* anthology, dating from the third century CE, and then one from Manikkavacakar's *Tirukkovaiyar*, a series of love poems in the *akam* mould which are to be interpreted as an allegory of the relationship between Śiva and the soul.

> Bigger than earth, certainly,
> higher than the sky
> more unfathomable than the waters
> is this love for this man
> of the mountain slopes
> where bees make rich honey
> from the flowers of the *kuriñci*
> that has such black stalks.

> The woman I longed for
> and stayed with
> has hair that bees
> swoop down on;
> it is well-arranged and wavy,
> like fine, black sand
> in ripples on the long beach
> of the prospering Cola's
> Urantai town;
> it is cool and fragrant.

The image of the mountain in the first poem speaks of the first attraction of lovers. The bees collecting honey from the flower evoke their growing relationship. Something of the same imagery is used in the second poem, where the lover is delighting in the beauty of the hair of the beloved. Here she is compared to the great city, a move typical of Tamil poetry which is pervaded by a profound sense of a sacred power at the heart of the land, and particularly in human relations of all kinds.

Manikkavacakar uses the conventions of classical poetry to speak of something more overtly religious, his own love-affair with the god:

O bee,
in your vast fields
are the lilies as sweet
as the mouth of this girl
whose waist is so frail
it suffers like people who don't sing
of Tillai and its Ambalam,
home of the lord adorned with a snake
who melts the bones of his devotees
who worship him with hands joined in prayer?

Cutler notes that the 'skeleton' of Manikkavacakar's poem builds on its classical predecessor, but takes it in another direction. The allusion to 'fields' makes the point that what the poet endures is a period of patient waiting which follows after the immediacy of first falling in love. The very complexity and ambivalence of human experience is what Manikkavacakar seeks to communicate. The phenomena of nature are what they are, sweet yet frail, like the play of emotions. What the poet then does is use these highly stylised conventions to explore the many dimensions of his own experience as a *bhakta*, and to commend to his audience something of his own life of participation in the divine mystery. If this is a dialogue with God, it has a very public or rhetorical dimension. Thus he builds into the *akam* or 'interiority' form of the poem something of the *puram* or exteriority. '[U]nderlying this dualistic function', says Cutler, 'is yet a deeper level, where these two fundamental realms of experience are unified.'

This is where the person of Śiva, together with the mythology associated with the one who embodies both the ascetic ideal of the detached *yogi* and the erotic image of divine fecundity, becomes significant. In the more explicitly religious poetry of the *Tiruvacakam*, Manikkavacakar maps out the interior landscape of the heart *and*, in more heroically ecstatic mode, expresses his utter dependence on Śiva. He takes pride in knowing that this god, hidden from all other gods, has appeared to him:

> O Lord Śiva, who severed my births,
> you dwell tight here in southern Peruntarai
> where the celestial ones can't know you.
> Our Lord,
> on that day when you looked at me
> you enslaved me,
> in grace entered me
> and out of love melted my mind.

The poet seeks to comprehend this mystery of a grace which 'enslaves' and 'melts' the creature through constant reference back to the phenomenal world. The elaborate system of literary conventions from early Tamil anthologies may be muted as it is turned towards a more overtly religious purpose, but Manikkavacakar still uses natural description to heighten the sense of the god who enters deeply into creation. Thus we find the imagery of the clouds and rain of the monsoon pressed into service to express the majesty of the equally awesome transformation which the god effects in the heart of the devotee:

> That ancient Sea of highest bliss
> appeared as a great black cloud
> ascending the hill of beautiful holy Peruntarai,
> with sacred lightning gleaming,
> unfolding in every direction,
> so that the bright snake, the bondage of the five senses,
> slithered away in retreat,
> so that the cruel afflicting intense heat of summer
> goes into hiding,
> so that the thriving beautiful *tonri* flower
> shines in gleaming splendour ...

Into a great celestial river the deluge gushed
rose up and whirled in great eddies of joy.
It thundered, beat, and dashed
against the high bank of our bondage,
rose up and uprooted the great tree of our twofold deeds
which had flourished with fruit for birth after birth.

Guiding this water of beautiful grace
to a juncture in the high hills
a dam was built
forming a tank full of fragrant flowers
dripping honey
on whose banks the bees mingle
With a great cloud of *akil* smoke.

Rejoicing,
watching the water rise higher and higher in the tank,
the devoted ploughmen
sowed seeds of love in the paddy-field of worship.

Hail the cloud
who is hard to reach on the earth,
who gave his ploughmen full satisfaction.

Thus far, everything I have described comes out of the spirituality of devotion, *bhaktimarga*. Manikkavacakar puts his own very personal stamp on the Tamil *bhakti* tradition by pouring out his emotions as he contemplates his sense of being rescued by the god. Like a lover experiencing the emotions that are inseparable from an intimacy which is yet distant, he struggles to respond to the call of the beloved. His religious world has been disarranged, turned upside down. And so he makes use of the only words he has, the words of his Tamil culture, in order to put back together again the dharmic order of *Brahman*. What he writes is not pure measured soliloquy, a personal musing within which he can guard and nurture his contemplative space. It has a purpose – and an audience. Even the most intimate moments are there to inspire an audience; the poet is speaking to the god about his own innermost reactions but, in sharing his feelings, he is also addressing his fellow-devotees. They too are part of the single skein of relations in which god, poet and the wider audience, both initiated and uninitiated, are all caught up.

Such an ecstatic style of poetry may seem light years removed from the careful analysis of *Sphota* theory. But in one regard at least they inhabit the same cultural space. The sound which 'bursts forth' through the agency of the poet has its own form, but is intended to form the same meaning or purpose within the consciousness of the hearer. *Bhakti* devotional poetry builds a certain rhetoric of participation. To go back to that instructive tale about Valmiki's inspiration: what is heard from the tradition within the inner contemplative space comes to expression through the very particularity of ordinary everyday experience, in all its pain and poignancy.

It is through paying attention to the irreducible particularities of everyday reality that we can be jolted out of our limited perception of it. It is true, of course, that much *bhakti* poetry focuses on the more exalted aspects of the divine-human relationship; the aim is to elevate the audience above mundane trivia. The relationship with Śiva goes the other way. Manikkavacakar focuses on the less refined side of human nature, a sort of pre-socialised, almost infantile, spontaneity. By plumbing the depths of the crazed infatuation of lovers he seeks to expose the most arresting paradox, that only in the most particular and prosaic can we experience real universality.

### Power of the Word and the Artifice of Language

Now there's something very Buddhist here: what I spoke about in an earlier chapter as mindful attention to the present moment, in all its messy ambivalence. What the poet does is 'freeze' such moments in time, as it were, giving them shape and resonance which attend as much to ugliness and ignorance as to beauty and magnificence. Like the Buddhist meditating on the Four Noble Truths – suffering, the cause of suffering, *Nirvana* or the end of suffering, and the way to achieve that ending, the Noble Eightfold Path – Valmiki is sensitised to the pathos of the wanton destruction of life. The poet draws attention to the universal significance of the particular, not by refusing every attempt at articulation, but by engaging in the artifice of language.

The Buddhist, of course, is suspicious of the sheer *power* of the word – how even the most venerable of words can become 'mere' rhetoric, an uncritical and unscrupulous manipulation of the minds and hearts of the audience. But that is precisely *not* to set them apart. Silence and word, I said earlier, are mutually co-inherent. There is thus another side to the silent sage which correlates with the *artha*, the purposive intent, of the poet.

The fully enlightened one is the compassionate teacher with the 'skill in means' to communicate the *Buddhadharma* to a variety of hearers. The key meditative quality of mindfulness entails more than a careful guarding of one's inner contemplative space. At its best, it gathers the strangeness of encounters and meetings with the other into an inner equanimity *and* manages to communicate that truth for the benefit of other suffering sentient beings. By way of a brief coda to these exploratory remarks about how artifice cultivates inner feelings, let me ponder the example of a Buddhist poet who has learned to use words, and poetry, as a way to enlightenment.

Zoketsu Norman Fischer is an American Zen roshi in the Shunryu Suzuki lineage. Born into a Jewish family in 1946, Fischer teaches at the San Francisco Zen Center and has been a keen contributor to interreligious relations for many years. *Opening to You*, published in 2002, is a collection of translations – he calls them 'versions' – of the Psalms which were inspired by time spent at Gethsemani Abbey, the Cistercian monastery in Kentucky where, of course, Thomas Merton lived. He had grown up chanting the Psalms, but only in the monastic choir did he pay attention to what the texts were actually saying.

He says he was struck by the 'violence, passion and bitterness' they expressed. To some extent the collection is a way of coming to terms with his own religious background – an exploration of the inner affinities of two very different traditions. But it is also an acknowledgement that Buddhism is constantly adapting and changing as its deepest message seeks to find a home in different cultures. Words from an ancient tradition which still has a hold over his religious sensibility go on resonating and touching something deeply human, evoking, perhaps, a set of typically Judaeo-Christian *rasa* which yet have a universal reach.

Human beings, Fischer says, are often touched by emotions of loss and longing and loneliness, for which mindfulness meditation and the carefully constructed contemplative asceticism of the Middle Way are no remedy. 'We find there is still sometimes a need to call out, to sing, to shout, to be heard, to be answered. These passions deeply persist even though our hearts are settled. All this is the territory of the Psalms.' Fischer's point is not that traditional Buddhism is too other-worldly for Westerners and therefore needs a bit of earthy Jewishness, but that there are ideas and categories in other cultures and religions which can positively enrich Buddhist practice. Even such an un-Zen practice as prayer and an un-Zen concept like God may have something to teach the Zen practitioner. What is most striking about these 'versions' of the Psalms is the focus they put on relationality. Rather than use the traditional titles like 'Lord' and 'King', Fischer reverts to 'the one English word that best evokes the feeling of relationship, the word you'.

### Opening to the You in the Other

In the introduction to his book, Fischer refers briefly to two Jewish writers. The first – unsurprisingly – is Martin Buber. For Buber, as he reminds us, 'there is no God, no absolute, no present moment outside the profound relationship that takes place between the I and the you, between the self and the other'. The other is Paul Celan, a Holocaust survivor who suffered the agony of a German-speaking Jewish poet: how to speak of the unspeakable in a language already tainted by violence? The 'you' who speaks does not have to be the overwhelming crazed lover who so much takes over Manikkavacakar. Nor does our poetry have to be expressed in outbursts of pain and joy which perfectly catch a moment. When Fischer voices the 'you' he seems to be talking about a much more spare conversation which goes on *within*. It's not that he is reducing the emotional excesses of the texts to a more acceptable Buddhist level, but precisely the opposite: recognising, and seeking to savour, the depths of feeling from which they come. Mindfulness, to repeat my earlier point, is not a withdrawal into the 'contemplative space', nor is it a sort of empiricism which stands silently apart from a series of fleeting phenomena. Rather like *bhakti* devotionalism, but in its own way, it describes a 'movement of connection', drawing together a network of relations. By linking together every discrete experience, every manifestation of 'you', even the most unpleasant and unwanted, one learns to overcome the self-referential 'I'.

This particular Buddhist comes from a Jewish world. His life is soaked in the thought-forms of one particular ancient tradition and comes alive through its contact with another. To that extent he is unusual. On the other hand, the overlaying of cultures, words which resonate across religious worlds, is by no means limited to a few spiritual eccentrics. There is no such thing as a pure, unsullied 'contemplative space'; it is always formed by prior words and ideas, and it goes on being disturbed by other words and other ideas. In this sense silence is not a possibility; human beings are born into the middle of words. It is the address of the other, calling 'you', which interrupts, disarranges and – by being spoken and named – painfully rearranges the flow of language.

Let me finish with one poem from Fischer's collection. When

the sound 'you' is voiced, the Jew or Christian will hear a stark yet powerful rendition of a familiar dialogue with the God who calls. For the Buddhist, these are strange words which appear to trespass into the unfamiliar world of 'theism'. They do, however, betray a very Buddhist austerity, a cutting away of whatever is unnecessary to the expression of an inner dialogue in which is mirrored the interrelatedness of all things. Just as there cannot be an 'I' without a 'you' in which 'we' are formed, so in the interior journey towards enlightenment – or, in Judaeo-Christian terms, conversion – 'I' have to come to terms with what is 'other than I' if the 'mutually co-inherence' of all things is to be glimpsed and savoured. What *co*-exists at the deepest of affective levels needs to be befriended as 'you'.

> Out of the depths I call to you
> Listen to my voice
> Be attentive to my supplicating voice.
>
> If you tallied errors
> Who would survive the count?
> But you forgive, you forebear everything
> And this is the wonder and the dread.
>
> You are my heart's hope, my daily hope
> And my ears long to hear your words
> My heart waits quiet in hope for you
> More than they who watch for sunrise
> Hope for a new morning.
>
> Let those who question and struggle
> Wait quiet like this for you
> For with you there is durable kindness
> And wholeness in abundance
> And you will loose all our bindings
> Surely.

# CHAPTER ELEVEN

## The Craft of Theology

THEOLOGY of religions hardly existed when I began my theological studies. The 'problem of non-Christian religions' was handled under what was archly referred to as 'disputed questions'. Is there salvation outside the Church? The question is still around; it has its own venerable pedigree, and commands a whole swathe of magisterial pronouncements. But it's long been sidelined by what I call the 'post-everything culture'. Whether we like it or not, the days when canons of reason presumed to order every aspect of human activity have disappeared. As a wise old parish priest I knew used to say, 'Systems don't work. People work systems'.

Today no one would dream of herding Hindus, Jews and Muslims into some generic category which refers to them as what they are not, let alone as somehow intrinsically 'problematic'. Problems there may be, but they are to do with the dynamics of history and differences of culture, not with preconceived patterns of thinking by 'us' about 'them'. Christians live surrounded by neighbours who profess, sometimes quite loudly, other ways of thinking and acting. They cannot be filed away as remote concerns on the edge of a well-defended enclave.

One of the things Christians have learned from having to think beyond the enclave is that the classical themes of Christian theology – faith and revelation, Church and Mission, the person of Christ and the mystery of God – do not make up a 'Christian system'.

They generate a way of life which stems from the Paschal Mystery recorded in the Gospel narrative and celebrated by communities of faithful Christians for generations. And it is between ways of life, not systems of thought, that the encounter of religions takes place. Once the 'problem of the non-Christian' moves from the periphery of an ordered curriculum and is re-imagined at the heart of Christian living, a complex but important question begins to open up. When other cultures and ways of life seep across the borders, when ancient enmities and resentments give way to collaboration, when hosts morph into guests and guests into friends, what happens to the 'home' tradition, no more an ordered system, but a tangled skein of rituals and symbols, convictions and hopes, that sustain a way of life? What happens to faith when it becomes 'inter-faith'?

This is a question I have often asked myself. It's not just a political and ethical question about the civic space, about how different religious traditions can contribute to the common good. It is also – and more profoundly – an existential and pastoral question, about how everyday experience raises questions about meaning and identity, about how the memories that have formed communities of faith can be awoken imaginatively to life in a new context. Such is the story I have sought to tell in this book. Inculturation, as noted earlier, sounds like a bit of missionary jargon. I have tried to show that it is rooted in the vision of the compassionate God working at the heart of the mucky world of human experience. Inculturation is not a mechanical missionary strategy, clothing one tradition in the garb of another, but a never-ending conversation in which familiar resonances are explored anew and the risk of seeing something differently is taken for the sake of mutual understanding. Christian theology begins, not with abstract concepts about Ultimate Reality, but with the Word made flesh in the person of Jesus of Nazareth. To speak about that truth means engaging with history and culture, with social relations and forms of life through which human beings speak of that which concerns them most deeply.

## The Christological Question

When I first moved to Southall, I remember being approached by a young Hindu who wanted to know more about the *Spiritual Exercises*. 'Is there any way I can use your ideas for my prayer?' he asked me. For a few weeks, we made our way together through the dynamic of the First Week, with a focus on sin, freedom and the human condition. Beyond that, progress was more tricky. The *Exercises* are not just Christian but strongly Christocentric, and this man's particular brand of Hindu spirituality did not open up much space for dialogue. Nevertheless, the experience taught me enough to realise that, at the level of prayer and spirituality in 'the middle of things', it was possible to build up a personal rapport with other persons of faith.

Such experiences of interreligious conversation have run through this book, and they act as not-so-remote background to the first part of this chapter, where I will sketch out the terms of theology of religions as it has emerged in the last few decades. This will necessarily be brief, not for reasons of space, but because the 'map' of the area resists ease of summary, let alone definition. Rather than spend more than a few words in critical review, I will move swiftly to one of the 'big themes' mentioned above, namely Christology, and the implications of Jesus' Christological question – 'Who do you say that I am?' – for Christian living in a world of many faiths. I do so, not in order to provide another 'undisputed answer' to a 'disputed question', but to re-imagine how the traditional symbolism and imagery of Word and Messiah, Lord and Son of God, create a framework within which significant conversations can take place. What I am proposing is a shift of 'levels', away from binary perspectives and more focused on the values and virtues shared within the practice of different traditions.

Having spent all my life with the framework of Ignatian spirituality as an entry point into the Paschal Mystery, I have become increasingly impressed by how so many of its fundamental themes and ideas have an appeal that crosses religious barriers. If that young Hindu took away anything from our conversations, it was that there is a profound correlation between the 'desireless action' that is such a significant idea in the *Bhagavad Gita* and the freedom and detachment before Jesus' call to 'come and see' that marks the Gospel. My argument is that Ignatian spirituality, with its focus on the God whose grace is to be discerned at the heart of the world, gives voice to both practical initiatives and theological reflection that can bring a deeper learning about Christian faith – and about 'the other'.

## Three Paradigms

Let me turn immediately to the 'threefold paradigm' typology in the theology of religions. This is usually ascribed to Alan Race, especially his influential *Christians and Religious Pluralism* which was first published in 1983. How do Christians position themselves theologically vis-à-vis other communities of faith? The first two positions, 'exclusivism' and 'inclusivism', are more or less 'Christianity-centred' accounts of the plurality of religions. In the first instance, 'others' are deliberately placed outside the boundaries of a Christian world, drawing very strict lines of demarcation and excluding them from the mystery of salvation which is proclaimed in Christ. In the second case, 'others' are given a secondary place within that world: by recognising 'aspects' of Christian identity in another conceptual world, boundaries are treated less as barriers than as points of access. The former position is taken up by the evangelical tradition which is centred on the proclamation of the Word; the latter tends to be found in the Catholic tradition which is more explicitly Church-centred. Where evangelical Christians tend to speak of 'Scripture Alone', Catholics speak of a single yet complex source of revelation in Scripture-and-Tradition. From an evangelical perspective, God's act of self-revelation is only known in the Christian mystery; for the Catholic position, it is important to allow that grace may also present in an implicit or 'anonymous' way, to use Karl Rahner's celebrated thesis.

The third pattern takes its stand on very different premises. Christianity is one religion among many, not the norm by which all others are to be judged. 'Pluralism', following the thesis of John Hick, states that there is no *fundamental* difference between religions; all are simply descriptions of a more or less common core or religious experience. Whereas the first two positions are primarily concerned with elucidating Christian claims to truth, this third position emphasises what is common, with the differences viewed as secondary cultural manifestations. For a variety of reasons – from the manifest problems caused by religious chauvinism to the phenomenological similarities between Christianity and other religions – it seems only reasonable, in this view, to shift away from an insistence on the superiority of one tradition, and to cross a 'theological Rubicon'. Building a highly plausible case for embracing the full plurality of religious phenomena, Race follows Hick in arguing that it is arbitrary to go on insisting that the Christ-event is the unique source of salvation. In a manifestly multi-religious context, no one religious symbol or narrative holds a privileged position over all others.

I remember being very grateful for Race's elegant summary of these theological positions. I was not the only one. Within a very few years a number of surveys had been produced, each working within the threefold scheme. I even produced one myself. My first full-length book, *Religions in Conversation*, piggy-backed on the literature while attempting to break out of it with what I called a 'Spirit-based' theology of religions. One reviewer argued that this was a move not beyond but rather *within* inclusivism – a fair point. Another praised it for its intelligence – I quite liked that – but suggested that, having introduced my reader to the important theological issues, I had no idea how to get out again. At first I was not impressed. Later, however, it occurred to me that that slightly dismissive assessment was in fact close to my intentions. Getting into 'the problem', motivating people to engage with the plurality of religions, seemed to me more important than promising some theoretical solution from above which would guarantee a safe exit, and promise 'control' of an awkward conceptual complexity.

That is one reason why the 'paradigm approach' in the theology of religions has become part of the story, not its explanation. The 'map' of the area is no longer adequate for the theological journey, and particularly for addressing my question about what happens when faith becomes 'inter-faith'. The issue is not how 'they' fit into 'our' world but what theological sense is to be made of religious plurality itself. Even the pluralist approach, espousing a radical break with all that has gone before, seems curiously dated. Like the stereotypical 'Christianity-centred' positions it dumps so unceremoniously, it owes more to the thinking of secular modernity than to any principles that emerge from the religious traditions themselves, and therefore from *within* their engagement. The current era of postmodernity may have its problems, but relating – while not relativising – religious traditions to their sources and 'deep structures' is not one of them. Perceptions have changed; different questions are being asked.

The Islamicist Wilfred Cantwell Smith makes the point sharply. Christians, he says, have a doctrine of creation to explain why the Milky Way is there, but no way of accounting for why the *Bhagavad Gita* is there. Is it just one more embodiment of spiritual wisdom, a particular and purely contingent feature of human existence, along with the Hindu temples at Khajuraho, the massive Buddha-figures at Polonnaruwa and the lavishly decorated commentaries on the Holy Qu'ran? Or does their status as classics of human culture point to something purposive about the human orientation towards the Divine? And what are we to say about the power and value of the ways of life which such artefacts form and support – not the abstract constructions known as Hinduism or Islam or Buddhism, but living communities of persons? Why are they there and do they have anything to say by way of witness to a wider world?

*Theology and the Edges of Reason*

As a basic framework for holding together different approaches to religious pluralism, the Threefold Paradigm has proved remarkably resilient. Differences certainly exist. There is no confusing the evangelical principles that inform Reformed theology with the philosophical instincts that underpin the Catholic tradition. On the other hand, the days are long past when theology could be forced into pre-ordained patterns, dictated by the feuds caused by the Reformation and with scant attention offered to the liturgical spirituality of Orthodoxy or the Spirit-based creative force that is contemporary Pentecostalism. So far from one overarching perspective ordering an untidy collection of alternative positions, what is emerging from the 'new ecumenism' is a great deal of richness and nuance as different insights make themselves felt.

The problem with the 'top-down' theology of religions espoused by the Threefold Paradigm is that it flattens out the mix, running three positions together as increasingly plausible responses to a contemporary phenomenon. An unreasonable Exclusivism gives way to a more reasonable Inclusivism which eventually surrenders to Pluralism as the only truly reasonable position. But the distinction between reason and tradition is a false dichotomy; the one is implicated in the other. The Gospel is Good News which forms persons in community, giving rise to a complex historical process which transforms Resurrection faith into credal statements, conciliar definitions and theological schools. Summary paradigms are part of that process. They are misunderstood if they are turned into autonomous exercises of reason that are not related organically to the inner and outer life of the Church.

How, then, are they to be understood? Rather than risk turning Exclusivism into a monolithic ideology, would it not make more sense to think in terms of a 'style' of speaking and writing that takes its stand on a foundational remembrance: faith in God's covenantal promise? Similarly, rather than lump all Catholic theology together as if it represents an unqualified form of theological imperialism, would it not be more correct to recognise the many nuances that characterise a way of thinking that looks forward in hope towards an eschatological completion in God? And would it not be more generous to understand pluralism, not as a third position that trumps the other two in a game of theological one-upmanship, but as a witness to the virtue of love, taking with utmost seriousness the call to offer a hospitable welcome to all persons of faith? These three *theological* virtues are not the property of any one charism, style or school; they inspire all manner of responses to God's Word, crossing interreligious as much as denominational boundaries.

To pick up the model suggested in the title of this chapter, there is more to theology than an intellectual exercise that orders the Church's faith into coherent patterns. I want to argue that theology, and specifically theology of religions, is more like a *craft*, a work of the intellect certainly, but closer to the skill of the artisan who shapes the raw material than the responsibility of the overseer who judges the quality of the finished article. To pursue that metaphor briefly, when Paul likens his Corinthian community to 'God's Temple' where dwells the Holy Spirit (1 Cor. 3:16), he is not just concerned with a bit of early inculturation, reminding a Greek audience of their Hebrew origins; more subtly he is encouraging them to take responsibility for their material and communal living, a life that requires effort and dedication in the same way as a craftsman must attend to the skills of his craft.

In many ways, the Ignatian instinct I have described throughout this book is closer to the first century than the sixteenth, beginning *anywhere,* in the 'middle of things', reflecting a freedom to be led by the Spirit already at work shaping the raw material that is the Church, the pilgrim people of God. This is in marked contrast to a theological construction that begins by foregrounding intra-Christian differences, whether between distinctive Christian charisms and spiritual styles or the contemporary 'schools' of a Barth or a Rahner. If theology is the craft of shaping the people of God into the 'work of art' that God intends the Church to become 'in Christ Jesus' (Eph. 2:10), then attention first needs to be given, not to some schematic solution to a problematic difference, but to the 'tools' that tend and cultivate human living and thus make transformation into the divine image possible. This is not to deny that analogous forms of religious practice exist in all traditions of faith – prayer and meditation, study and witness. On the contrary, it is to become aware that, resonating beneath the particularities of language and symbol that separate human beings, are echoes of mood, style, gesture and the sheer *feel* of things that connect us in our earthy otherness.

*Coming Together to Pray*

It is this sense of connection with the everyday world that often gives shape to the virtues of faith, hope and love wherever people from different religious traditions gather for an act of witness. When Pope St John Paul II invited leaders of various religious communities throughout the world to a momentous meeting at Assisi on 26 October 1986, he was at pains to distinguish between 'praying together' and 'coming together to pray'. The former implied a shared common formula; the latter a shared acknowledgement of the significance of prayer itself. During the day, different groups met in venues scattered through the town. An animist lit a ritual fire; a tribal chief invited spirits into a bowl of water; a Native American brought down a blessing with a movement of his eagle feathers. For a brief span, Assisi was a media paradise, filled with smoke and smells, reverberating to the sound of drums and tambourines, and peopled with exotic holy men in multicoloured robes.

The sight of Catholic and Orthodox Christians, Muslims and Hindus, Sikhs and Buddhists, all standing in a semicircle with the Pope in the basilica dedicated to St Francis caught the imagination. That central event was notable, not for any common act of worship, but for the profound silence of the moment: people of faith, differing enormously in their understanding of the nature of divine reality and human flourishing, yet joined together by their common humanity and concern for the peace of the world.

There was an excess of symbolism, almost too much to take in. Small wonder that some critics were left with the impression that religious differences were being scrambled together indiscriminately. Were not Catholic claims to teach the truth about God revealed in Christ being compromised by an event which appeared to place all religions and cultures on the same level? Twenty-five years later, on 27 October 2011, Pope Benedict XVI called another such gathering, which was advertised as a day of reflection, dialogue and prayer for peace and justice. With the theme, 'Pilgrims of truth, pilgrims of peace', and including Catholics, Christians from different ecclesial communities and representatives of other religious traditions, it took the form of a common journey, starting out from Rome and spending the day in the home of St Francis, the great apostle of peace. The message was simple: every human being is a pilgrim in search of truth and goodness.

The theme of pilgrimage has appeared at various points in this book. A pilgrimage, I noted earlier, is a practice, an activity that gathers people together and makes them, for a short time at least, a more or less coherent body. The first Assisi event inspired many other pilgrimages, those that involved physical journeys and those more interior movements of the Spirit that accompany interreligious encounters everywhere. I have already described one of the Westminster Interfaith pilgrimages I organised with Brother Daniel, the unforgettable 'rally' that snaked from North London through the sedate countryside of Hertfordshire. Others were simpler and more intimate, meditations on a theme of ultimate significance set around a common symbol or image. There were also more formal events, 'interior pilgrimages', most memorably two presided over by Cardinal Basil Hume in a packed Westminster Cathedral. One was held on 17 March 1991 to pray for peace and healing in the wake of the Gulf War, and the other on 17 November 1996, to commemorate the tenth anniversary of Assisi. Both followed the same pattern. When one individual spoke or prayed or performed some gesture of worship, everyone else stood in respectful silence and listened attentively. I always explain this as a reverent act of being present to each other and thus supporting each other in faith.

*Jesus, Symbol of Common Humanity*

Something rather different, more a marker of time than place, was held at the beginning of the millennium at the Jesuit Church of the Immaculate Conception, Farm Street, in central London. *Celebrating Jesus*, as we called the event, had a deliberate Christological focus. Jesus was to be celebrated as a source, not of division, but of unity and understanding. It began with the ritual placing of holy books, carefully wrapped in brocade cloths, on a table at the front of the church. This was followed by a second procession, this time of small carefully crafted pouches containing stones from different places: the bank of the Ganges, the Holy Land, Auschwitz. Together with the books, they spoke of the complexity of revelation, the 'Book of Scripture' and the 'Book of Nature'. But what made this event for the millennium particularly poignant was that we asked people from different communities to read a passage from their tradition that spoke in an appreciative way of the person and influence of Jesus.

The readings, which we put together into a special commemorative volume, vary enormously, yet carry a significant resonance across the traditions. Jesus was a Jew and, even apart from the Jewish prophecies that Christians read as being fulfilled in the Mystery of Christ, there is a growing number of reflections on his significance within a Jewish perspective. In Islam, of course, Jesus plays a more significant role, as a prophet of Islam. Buddhism and Hinduism have their advocates of Jesus as a holy man, avatar and bodhisattva. Śri Ramakrishna had a particular devotion to Jesus as his guru, and the temples that follow his tradition always have a picture of Jesus alongside other religious teachers and founders. Thich Nhat Hanh, the extraordinary Vietnamese Zen teacher of 'inter-being', has written on Jesus, as has the Dalai Lama. But perhaps the most extraordinary text in the collection is by a Sikh statesman, Gopal Singh, who was present at Assisi in 1986. It is a book of poetry, called with deep devotion *The Man Who Never Died,* and intended to catch something of the universal truth that is Christ.

These are a few of his words that were read that evening as the world entered hesitantly into the new millennium:

> This is the story of the Man who never died,
> and who proclaimed
> that he who is born must be reborn,
> and he who is dead must rise from the state of death.
> For it is not in the nature of man to die,
> but to live from no-time to no-time ...
>
> When asked how the world was born,
> he said 'Out of the Word.'
> For, even when the world was not,
> the Word was.
> Men asked him: 'How shall we pray?'
> He answered, 'Does the seed ask how shall I pray?
> It enters into its closet, shuts its door,
> and prays in secret as if not praying,
> and fasts as if not fasting,
> till it grows into a flower,
> and prays not with words but through fragrance.
> Pray you like the mute earth
> that revolves ceaselessly round the sun,
> saying: 'Let your will be done on earth as it is in heaven'.

There is more here than a charming play on themes that find their origins in half-remembered readings of the Christian scriptures. Gopal Singh's poem has its own integrity, not a theological formula like the Chalcedonian definition or an incipient version of the Christian creeds, but a statement of reverence and respect to sit alongside texts which think of Jesus as a holy man, spiritual master and prophet. In the introduction to the collection, I speak about the readings as further responses to Jesus' Christological question. The story of the Caesarea Philippi confession is the centre of the Gospel, a turning point, but it is important to remember that Peter only got the answer half right. He did not expect, and certainly did not want, a Messiah who had come to suffer. At the time the disciples were mystified, and it was only later in the light of Resurrection faith they came to understand what Jesus was saying, that he is the touchstone by which their sense of God is to be reckoned.

There is, of course, a paradox here, for that initial conversation both reveals Jesus as the Christ of God and yet confounds the comfortable conviction that an inner elite has received an initiation that separates them off from the rest of unprivileged humankind. Right in the middle of the Gospel a dramatic question mark is raised over all human claims to know God. In this sense alone, the story speaks to all people of faith, for it acts as a salutary reminder that hard-and-fast distinctions between those who do and those who do not understand are difficult to make. What Paul rejoiced in as the 'scandal of the cross' is not a claim to some esoteric intuition into the nature of God, but neither is it an invitation to sheer irrationality; rather is it a reminder that at the heart of all faith lies hesitation and a struggle to make sense of the mystery of the Ultimate touching into our frail earth.

Anyone who listens to that Caesarea Philippi episode with an open mind will be perplexed. Later, of course, Peter has an opportunity to get his answer more than half right. By the Lake of Galilee Jesus asks him three times 'Do you love me?', and he is able to make amends for denying Jesus three times in the darkness of Holy Thursday night. Peter is the first of the Twelve, not because he has been initiated into the Divine Mystery, but quite simply because he has learned how to love. That is not to say that the conversation

Jesus begins is ever finished. Before the Passion story, the Fourth Gospel records the great farewell discourse. This acts firstly as a reminder of everything Jesus has said and will shortly accomplish in fulfilment of his predictions of the Passion. But it's also a looking forward, not just promising the consolation of the Spirit to those left behind, but assuring them that in the Spirit, 'another advocate', they will do 'greater things'. Always aware of a promise still to be fulfilled, they are exhorted to look forward with hope.

## God at the Heart of Humanness

To what extent was that event in Farm Street, indeed any interreligious meeting, an example of theology as a 'craft', the forging of new relationships between persons of faith after the manner of Christ? The second week of the *Spiritual Exercises* is often understood as an invitation to Christian mission. That is no doubt true. 'Election' – a generous choice of life in response to the Gospel – is central to the intentions of Ignatius. More exactly, however, a rich dynamic of carefully constructed considerations and Gospel stories builds up a contemplative sensibility formed around the person of Christ himself. In an introductory meditation, which sets the mood of the prayer, the parable of the earthly king acts as 'a help towards contemplating the life of the eternal king'. At this point, the exercitant is expected to pray for the grace 'not to be deaf to his call' [91]. The relationship with the compassionate Lord is key but, like the Caesarea Philippi episode itself, the deeper truths of the Gospel take time to settle.

The texts about Jesus we celebrated on that millennium day had this much in common with the *Exercises*: they revered the human Jesus and felt inspired by his qualities of courage and compassion. The wider Trinitarian perspective of Ignatius's Christology – 'Christ our Lord' who became one with us in order to 'save the human race' [102] – was very much absent. None of our texts fitted the canons of Chalcedonian orthodoxy. Nevertheless, it was possible, without too much effort of the theological imagination, to detect hidden or unnamed traces of how, to put it in familiar Christological terms, God's Eternal Word can become Flesh, revealed at the very heart of our humanness. Coming from a Zen Buddhist, the following words of Thich Nhat Hanh are quite remarkable:

> When we look into and touch deeply the life and teaching of Jesus, we can penetrate the reality of God ... God made himself known to us through Jesus Christ.

Ignatius, of course, had no interest in granting 'theological space' to the other. Beginning with feelings of disorder and dissatisfaction, he unfolds the Gospel narrative, moving from the personal invitation of the King, through the Paschal Mystery of Death and Resurrection, to a contemplative vision of all things descending 'from on high ... as rays descend from the sun and waters from a fountain' [237]. It is hardly surprising that at this point in the text any distinction between Christ and 'the Divine Majesty' becomes very difficult to draw. The theological instincts of Ignatius are always Trinitarian, always concerned to integrate every aspect of human experience back into the mystery of 'God our Lord', where alone human sinfulness can be resolved. And yet, for all that the story Ignatius tells is never less than the single mystery of Creation and Redemption, the figure of Christ is no divine apparition, no heavenly projection into the world. The humanity of Jesus remains central. Indeed, in the Third Week, which is centred on the passion and death of Christ, Ignatius tells his exercitant to note how the divine nature is deliberately hidden so that the human nature may suffer on behalf of sinful human beings. Jesus is the 'image of the unseen God' (Col. 1:15), not identified with God in any straightforward sense, but a presence-in-absence that forever presses the limits of human understanding of the divine. This Jesus is the source of God's eternal life, the one in whom God's Word breaks open a moment of truth, thus dramatically reframing the categories with which human beings struggle to live in faith, hope and love.

## The Uniqueness and Otherness of Christ

Wherever Christians and other persons of faith meet, the Christological question is asked and the work of 'crafting' the Word-made-Flesh in our midst continues. My point is that this is not a 'disputed question' that fits within the canons of reason, but an invitation to press beyond the limits of reason, to touch into the very mystery of the self-revealing God. It is the particular merit of Karl Rahner's theology of the human person that he manages to address the question, without letting the contemporary context of religious pluralism appear as a problematic appendage somewhat unsatisfactorily tacked on at the end. Indeed, for Rahner it is the very historicity of God's revealing action which allows him to speak of the Mystery of Christ as the divinisation of the world through the Spirit, in which the Paschal Mystery appears as an 'inner moment'.

In *Foundations* Rahner postulates two principles: firstly, the 'universal and supernatural salvific will of God which is really operative in the world' and, secondly, the historical and social nature of the 'event' of salvation. The Incarnation reveals God through that which makes us most human – our rootedness in temporally bound forms. If for Christians God is made manifest in and through the world of our everyday experience, then something analogous must be true for others as well. *For Christian and non-Christian alike*, divine grace is mediated, not apart from, but precisely through the concrete forms of human religious belief and practice. Paradoxically, by stressing the ecclesial form in which grace is mediated, Rahner manages to build a bridge between different communities of faith. God does not deal with human beings independent of those historically bound social and cultural institutions – 'the religions' – which constitute and inform human existence in the world. If God's grace is operative in the everyday world of human experience, and does not somehow work around it or apart from it, then human institutions like the religions *may* be 'lawful', in Rahner's term. At the very least that possibility must be held open.

How does that principle square with Christian claims for the uniqueness of Christ, the 'disputed question' that so much exercises the advocates of the pluralist paradigm? They are right to note that all religions seek to develop a comprehensive view of things. They are wrong to relativise particular accounts of truth as arbitrary or inappropriate in a multi-faith context. For Christians, this comprehensive view is revealed in the 'Christ event'. This is 'unique' in the obvious sense that it is particular to a certain history, but care needs to be taken not to turn claims to 'uniqueness' into polemical comparisons with other 'unique' founders, saviours or revealer figures.

To be more theologically precise, therefore, Christ is unique because in Christ God has effected a self-manifestation which can be neither surpassed nor repeated. The uniqueness of Christ consists in the reiterated belief of the early Church, and especially the *kerygma* taught by Paul, that in the person of Jesus God has revealed God in a way that has a universal significance. Whatever metaphors are used, the meaning of the early confessions – Jesus as Lord, Christ, Son of God etc. – is that in the person of Jesus human beings have been touched by God in a way that puts in question their ordinary expectations of what God is like.

This is *not* to say, however, that there can be no continuity between what has been decisively revealed in Jesus Christ and what is to be discerned of God in the economy of creation and in the history of God's dealings with human beings as a whole. The crucial question for any Christology is not how Christ's 'uniqueness' can be maintained over against other claims to 'uniqueness', but how God can utter a Word that becomes *Flesh*, revealed at the very heart of our humanness. How to speak of Christ as the 'image of the invisible God' (Col. 1:15) while not turning 'image' into a comprehensive symbol that assumes all meaning to itself?

Much depends on what, in Rowan Williams's phrase, 'we expect Christ to do' – how the Paschal Mystery forms the Church for life in a multi-religious world. As Williams notes, the 'foundational myth' of Christianity is all too easily spelled out in terms of the replacement of one system of meaning by another; the failure of 'Judaism' enables the triumph of 'Christianity'. But the terms are anachronistic in the first century. Rather, what Jesus brings to a head is a crisis *within the religious life of a single people*. Jesus redefines what it means to be Israel by enacting a way of holy living which is normative for everyone everywhere. Put more broadly, the crucified Jesus calls into question the human pretension to 'know' God's meaning. It is this question which a 'refigured Israel' can be said to bear for others, what defines the Church as the community of faith actively committed to communicating a particular truth about the God revealed in Christ. Jesus, says Williams, 'is presented as the revelation of God: as God's question, no more, no less. Being a Christian is being held to that question in such a way that the world of religious discourse in general may hear it.' This is where it becomes important to understand the task of Christology, not as critique of another perspective, but as reflection on one's own God-given experience. While Christ may be uniquely decisive in the interreligious dialogue, not even the Christian community can be said to 'possess' the fullness of God's meaning. That is still to come: it is a function of faith, love *and hope*.

The Church exists as a historically bound people on pilgrimage. It continues to craft its own inner and outer life, and at the same time takes responsibility in its witness to the love of God made manifest in Christ for building up and enhancing the life of others. A Christology which would be faithful to the originating story of the Church's own experience of 'God-with-us', while also granting 'theological space' to others, means letting Christ be in some sense 'other' – beyond what 'we' can ever expect to possess. In practice, if the other is not to be totalised into a Christian conceptual strategy, then it is not simply a matter of my representing Christ *to* the other; I must also find some way in which the other can be Christ *to me*. In some way two movements have to be held together. What I say *of Christ* questions the other; but I must also allow that what the other says may well be spoken *about Christ*, questioning me. In this sense, what is said by the other is inspired by the Spirit of Christ. Instead of asking, therefore, how other religions are somehow included or contained within Christian revelation, or – more simply – completed by it, Christians look to the way the Spirit of Christ is active in all religious communities as *revealing* the mystery of Christ, the mystery of what God is already doing in the world.

*The Spirit Within and Without*

This is where Christology as essentially a craft, a learned skill that gives shape to the practices of faith, shifts attention from the imposition of a Christian set of answers towards the God-focused work of compassion and understanding implied in responding to others' questions. Christians are, of course, given a privileged insight into the inner life of God through God's own self-revealing action in Christ. It is through this privileged insight – the nature of God as a Trinity of persons – that Christians come to understand the world. But to have a privileged insight does not mean acquiring a complete knowledge of all things – the 'God's-eye view' of the world. The danger is that any theology, let alone any theology about the action of God in the world of 'other religions', risks saying more than it is possible to say. The craft of building up the Christian community in a radically pluralist context demands, not just a strategy of inculturation, but a discernment which is primarily an activity of listening, taking with utmost seriousness the insight of Ignatius that 'God is in all things' and the Spirit is at work guiding all human beings in this time and place. As I have tried to stress, at work here are typically and profoundly Ignatian instincts.

The Holy Spirit makes no explicit appearance in the text of the *Exercises*. Even in that famous meditation on the Incarnation, the task of redemption is given to the Second Person, with the Third apparently sidelined. And yet the Spirit as the source of understanding, consolation and wisdom is there on every page. When

Peter responded to Jesus' 'Christological question' he was led into an extraordinary journey of faith which had its moments of darkness as well as light. In Peter can be seen a model of the Church which lives, not by producing the right theological formula, but by entering into and learning to live in the presence of the God who is revealed in Jesus' life, death and resurrection. As Jesus himself has to face the darkness of faith in Gethsemane, risking himself before the unknown, so the Church has to learn to *live* in faith before understanding what faith implies. Through the crafting of practices which form the inner life of the Church, Christians gain that sensitivity to the God revealed in Christ that enables them to discern the movements of the Spirit both inside and outside the Church.

Such an account of the action of the Holy Spirit pointing to the Paschal Mystery encourages trust and a willingness to go on listening, a healthy reticence that is very different from a genial agnosticism. It also raises a more profound question. How is it possible to speak? That is the question that lies behind Jesus' Christological question, about how image and symbol can be said to represent that which is beyond words and beyond form. Without the Spirit, says Paul, we could not make our confession of faith. Without the Spirit, we could not know Christ or speak of his Word, for – as St Paul says – 'we do not know how to pray as we ought' (Rom. 8:26). This is not a matter of the Spirit imparting 'information' about Jesus – the Spirit as some divine teacher. Nor is it a question of the Spirit simply continuing the work of the Word in giving voice to the silence of the Father. The Spirit is the Spirit of Love, the 'excess' which flows from the mutual giving and receiving of Father and Son, a revelation in which the whole of creation is caught up and transformed. In biblical terms the Spirit is that God-given force which disrupts yet also provokes the work of human understanding.

While there is something of a painful process of growth in understanding in the Caesarea episode, the archetypal passage is Emmaus (Lk. 24:13ff). The disciples' world is shattered and only the unexpected stranger on the road enables them to put it back together again. They recognise Jesus over a meal, in a borderline between ordinary and extraordinary experience, between the prosaic sharing of bread and the moment in which the broken pattern mends itself and forms again. Understanding would not have been possible without both the stranger made visible to them, the 'outer Word', and the even stranger 'inner Word', the promptings of the Spirit who enables remembrance and recognition and further learning. Ignatius the mystic, who could not encounter triads without tears of joy at the beauty of the Divine Majesty, would have appreciated that the greatest source of *Vestigia Trinitatis* in our contemporary world lies in the coming-together of persons to pray and acknowledge the work of the Spirit.

# CHAPTER TWELVE

## From Francis to Francis

NOT LONG after his election, a book was published which laid out the interreligious credentials of Pope Francis. *On Heaven and Earth* is a record of conversations with a close friend from Buenos Aires, Rabbi Abraham Skorka, about a variety of subjects: the nature of God, the legacy of the Holocaust, the future of religion. The book stands as witness to the rapprochement after the Second Vatican Council between Jews and Christians, testifying to what becomes possible when personal friendship manages to overcome suspicion and allows the integrity of difference to flourish. Pope Francis says that with Rabbi Skorka 'I never had to leave my Catholic identity behind, just as he didn't have to ignore his Jewish identity. Our challenge was to proceed with respect and affection, trying to be above reproach as we walked in the presence of God'.

One little exchange gets something of the flavour of the whole. Both men agree that creation is a gift from God and that human beings are called to work freely and generously for the sake of their world. The problem, interjects the Pope, is that we so easily fall into the 'Babel syndrome', the arrogance which sees everything we achieve as the fruit of our own labour. Rabbi Skorka responds by introducing a Talmudic interpretation of the episode in Genesis (11:1-9): the one who builds the tower is a tyrant who holds so tight a grip on power that he will allow his subjects to speak only one language – his own. The tower is symbolic of human pretension.

*Remembering the Holocaust: cemetery wall faced by smashed tombstones;*
*Remuh Synagogue, Cracow, Poland*

Language in these terms is despotic, not universal: an alien imposition that punishes and oppresses, not a gift that overcomes violence and communicates without hindrance. When one reads Maimonides and St Thomas Aquinas, says the then Archbishop Bergoglio, 'we see that they always start by putting themselves in the position of their adversary in order to understand them; they dialogue from the standpoint of the other.'

Pope Francis's teaching on interreligious dialogue would be the subject of a book in its own right. In gathering up the Ignatian strands that have run through this book, my aim in this chapter is more modest. With the title 'From Francis to Francis', I seek to link the Jesuit pope to the mainstream of the tradition of the Society of Jesus on mission as inculturation, a theme opened up in the first chapter, 'With Ignatius to India'. There I made the point that faith is always shaped by human language. Ignatius and the first companions valued, not just the scholastic and patristic modes of thinking that linked them back to the sacred scriptures and the experience of the early Church, but the humanist culture of the Renaissance through which they learned to communicate their faith. My question here is about what can be learned from the practice of missionary witness established by the first Jesuit Francis which can help us engage with the more politically informed context addressed by the second.

## When Persons Meet

If Francis Xavier's context was the perennial popular culture of India and the sixteenth-century philosophical thought of Japan, the context of Pope Francis owes more to the shifting language of postmodernity and the fractures and convulsions of our twenty-first-century globalised world. What they share is not just the Ignatian spirituality that shaped their vision of God active in the world of human experience, but something about human experience itself, how it is inseparable from the social and political dimensions of life in community. We are formed, not just by language, but by an unruly history of human relations that does not lend itself to easy resolution. As I have noted earlier, the four forms of dialogue rank 'common life' and 'common action' alongside 'religious experience' and 'theological exchange'. While it is always tempting to arrange distinctions in a hierarchy of significance, the truth is usually more diffuse than we might like.

Dialogue, it has been wisely said, begins when persons meet – when, it might be added, the outer political dimension of human living is refracted through the inner or interpersonal manner of our encounters with each other. Today's life-in-community is wracked by a range of destructive 'isms', from forms of fundamentalism to recent explosions of populism. Early Jesuit missionaries experienced a very different world from that which formed the backdrop to conversations between bishop and rabbi in today's Argentina. But they would all have been aware that political tensions and the debates they provoke are often manifestations of very ordinary and very human resentments and jealousies.

Pope Francis has proved himself an articulate critic of all manner of deeply troubling existential questions and political dilemmas, from clericalism to climate change, from globalised poverty to the unbridled capitalism of late modernity. It has not proved a comfortable experience, neither for himself nor for the Church as a whole. Yet Ignatius would have approved; his vision of the Incarnation in which the compassion of the Trinitarian God becomes operative at the heart of the eternal battle for the salvation of humanity seeks always to make an impact on every aspect of our living and loving. Pope Francis has put his personal stamp on the pastoral agenda of the Church, demanding an uncompromising commitment to what the two earlier Francises would have recognised as the 'Joy of the Gospel'.

## Power of a Name

That, of course, is the title of Pope Francis's first Encyclical, which is more exactly an 'Apostolic Exhortation on the Proclamation of the Gospel in Today's World'. We'll have a look at a few key ideas in a moment. By way of introduction, let me stay with today's convulsed political context and the Pope's project of 'political inculturation'.

That image of the tower of Babel draws attention to the fact that the ability to use language promises a more ordered and less threatening vision of the way things are. The risk, of course, is that we become lulled into thinking that by merely naming and defining the objects of experience they become subject to that most dangerous of pretensions, the will to power. And where 'the religious' comes up against 'the political' the potential for violence is enormous. The *joy* of the Gospel lies, not with some alternative political programme, as if the words of the evangelists are to be read as a blueprint for the betterment of society, but in granting us the confidence to reach beyond the limits of language into the ground of our being and the utterance of the Word that is God's very self.

There's an important, if hidden, Ignatian theme here. An earlier chapter was entitled 'Power of the Word' and offered a cross-religious reflection on poetry. Rather than resting content with an account of poetic inspiration as rooted in experiences of overwhelming emotion, I am interested in the ways in which poetry presses the limits of language, confronting us not just with new and evocative constructions but with the impossibility of any adequate representation. In redefining what can and cannot be said, the poetic genre of writing and speaking takes on a prophetic form, warning against an idolatrous use of language that distorts the true nature of humanity. Prophecy is not just about truth speaking to power. It reminds us of a theme that has run through this book. If, as I have argued, we are creatures who use language to communicate the truth about ourselves, we must always guard against a tendency to substitute impersonal forms of strident speech for a humane discourse that is rooted in *interpersonal* acts of living and loving.

The tyrant's Babel appears in many forms, often plausible and persuasive, and for that very reason it has to be treated with caution. Let me turn back one last time to India. Hovering menacingly over the campus of the Jñanadeepa Vidyapeeth, the Jesuit-run faculties of philosophy and theology in Pune, are two massive black monoliths, mini-versions of the ill-fated twin towers in Manhattan that were destroyed at the beginning of the millennium. From a distance they look like blackened hulks, shiny tombstones memorialising some despotic grand project. On closer inspection the sheen turns out to be non-reflective black glass, allowing the owners to look out and preventing prying eyes from looking in. Each tower consists of twenty-two storeys of hyper-expensive apartments.

All around the gated entrance, the glorious anarchy of urban India continues unabated, helpless pedestrians and cyclists locked in unequal conflict with an unstoppable torrent of cars, motorbikes and the ever-present auto rickshaws. The din of a thousand hooters adds a further measure of madness to this modern Babel. Meanwhile, on the battered sidewalks in the shadow of the towers sit dozens of small stalls, peddling everything from fresh fruit and hot drinks to cheap plastic goods. While India has experienced an extraordinary growth in its GDP over the last decade or so, the wealth is unequally distributed. The widening gap between the new wealthy, safely hidden behind the darkened glass, and the hordes of ever-present urban poor is symbolised, not just by the incongruity of these great brash blocks, but by the title splashed in garish gold lettering across the entrance: *Trump Towers*.

According to the pompous website, the towers redefine the Pune skyline, marking 'the entry of the Trump brand of luxury and elegance in India'. In fact, they no more belong to the Trump business empire than the White House is the personal fief of the President of the USA. The name is used on licence; the ownership of the land and the actual buildings lies elsewhere. Yet Trump's baleful presence reaches way beyond well-manicured golf courses and relaxing holiday resorts. It is not money, but the more insidious power of a globalised 'Trump brand', that has so dramatically altered the familiar skyline.

## Modern Myths

When I first came to Pune, the Jesuit college nestled at the end of a long road that snaked out of the city centre, past military barracks, spacious bungalows and some sedate parkland. There was no wall around the campus, and there were no security guards protecting the property. The socialism of the Nehru-Gandhi dynasty kept the clamour for development and social change under some sort of control. Now, in the era of the business-driven *Hindutva* ideology, the sleepy village of Ramwadi has disappeared under concrete and tarmac. The city of the Marathas, a thorn in the side of both the Mughal empire and the British Raj, has begun to reassert itself, but now in league with more dubious market-driven forces.

If there was ever any doubt that Rabbi Skorka's mono-linguistic despot is alive and well, one need look no further than this corner of modern Pune. Ancient myths take contemporary forms (which

*Trump Towers, Pune, Maharashtra, India*

is not to buy into the cliché that history repeats itself). The simple, but never simplistic, truth is that the managing of difference and pluralism, let alone power structures and vested interests, is never a straightforward process of accommodation. There is far more to inculturation than the inclusion of one mode of self-identification within the broader ambit of another. Culture is never value-free; it has a history that makes for fuzzy edges and contentious negotiation. It's not that too much is at stake, with too many competing for a limited array of goods (though that is undoubtedly an issue). Rather, the harmony of the public sphere always demands some measure of coercion, with the attendant risk of an unmanageable degree of resentment that gives way to violence.

To repeat my earlier 'rule': when the 'other' is suppressed it will come back in another way. It is deeply ironic how often national-ism, the identification of people with a specific culture, thrives on – or, more exactly, reacts against – the phenomenon of globalisation, the inexorable movement towards broader economic and financial interdependence. What does it take to ensure the two work togeth-er creatively? Political will and imagination certainly, but also the work of memory, a sense of tradition and the courage to see how things can be done differently.

In the Preface to a collection of his thought, Pope Francis ac-knowledges that our world is capable of the 'best and the worst', an 'ambivalence' revealed most obviously in the material advance-ment of so many people which has been achieved at the cost of the exploitation and depletion of our common resources. In his travels, he has witnessed more of these contrasts than he ever saw in Argentina:

> I have seen the paradox of a globalised economy that could feed, care for and house all the inhabitants who live in our common home, but which – as some worrying statistics show – concentrates the same wealth that would provide for about half the world's population in the hands of very few people. I have seen that the unbridled capitalism of the recent decades has further widened the gulf between the richest and the poorest, generating new kinds of precariousness and slavery.

Francis Xavier and Ignatius, with their background in the po-litical intrigues of early sixteenth-century Spain, would have rec-ognised the issue. Their relationship with power was never easy. Ignatius had his skirmishes with the Inquisition, while Francis did his best to avoid being involved with Portuguese colonial inter-ests. Two hundred years later, the Society, as an international body whose members were committed to a mission that crossed fron-tiers, became high-profile victims of the destructive power-games which led to its Suppression in 1773. Today the relationship be-tween State and Church (or religion) continues to be problematic in many – perhaps most – parts of the world, and the Society with its commitment to the 'faith that does justice' works in solidarity with disadvantaged and displaced peoples.

Jorge Mario Bergoglio was brought up in the Argentina of Per-onist nationalism, and his personal faith is marked not just by lib-eration theology but by 'the religion of the people'. This is no com-forting devotionalism, but a sharp critique of the shrill populism that has swept the planet in recent years, offering cheap slogans in response to complex problems. Where leaders from Trump to Modi set out to construct 'elites' of all kinds as 'enemies of the people', the Pope bases his political and economic thought on the Gospel and the instinctive wisdom of those committed to a life of prophetic virtue.

### The Joy of the Gospel

It is unlikely Pope Francis had the Tower of Babel in mind when he wrote *Evangelii Gaudium*, but he was certainly conscious of the power of names to promote an 'unbridled capitalism'. Like Igna-tius, his life centres round the name of Christ. *Evangelii Gaudium* began as his response to the 2012 Synod on the 'new evangelisa-tion'. That was an initiative of his papal predecessors, for whom the term 'new' – meaning an intense spiritual renewal – was par-ticularly important for the future of the Church. In the hands of Francis, it has become the basis of his vision for the Church of the twenty-first century, a Church in which each and every individual is called to exercise a mission of joyful presence to the world. To-wards the end of this lengthy yet intensely felt text he moves into a rousing peroration by insisting that 'I am a mission on this earth; that is the reason why I am here in this world. We have to regard ourselves as sealed, even branded, by this mission of bringing light, blessing, enlivening, raising up, healing and freeing' (273).

His later encyclical, *Laudato Si'*, may have had a wider impact

– and caused more upset – than *Evangelii Gaudium*. There can be no doubt, however, that in this exhortation, with its reiteration of the Christian call to participate in the joy-filled mission of Christ himself, we hear a quite distinctive voice. Much of what is said is familiar: since the Second Vatican Council, all popes have made evangelisation a central plank of their message. Francis adds something unique, however. For a start, his experience of the Council is very different from that of his predecessors. While the Council was in session, he was a Jesuit student in Argentina. What he learned about the Council was second-hand. This non-participation, suggests John O'Malley, may have been an advantage. While Pope St John Paul II and Pope Benedict could never fully extricate themselves from the battles they fought in the Council, Francis is free of such memories. He invites us to revisit the Council and to see it with fresh eyes, not as the site of an ideological struggle between 'conservatives' and 'liberals', but as a call to an intrinsically missionary Church to work for reconciliation and social justice.

Francis is reassuringly blunt about the danger of what he calls an insidious 'spiritual worldliness', whether in the form of a 'subjective gnosticism', fixated on ideas and inner experience, or a 'self-absorbed promethean neo-pelagianism', caught up in rules and practices from the past. 'In neither case', he says, 'is one really concerned about Jesus Christ or others' (93-94). Like Ignatius in the *Exercises,* he reminds the Church of the first – the most important yet easily ignored – motivation for mission: that every individual is deserving of care and compassion because each is made in the image and likeness of God. It was for the salvation of each individual person that Jesus offered himself on the cross.

Appearances notwithstanding, every person is immensely holy and deserves our love. Consequently, if I can help at least one person to have a better life, that already justifies the offering of my life. It is a wonderful thing to be God's faithful people. We achieve fulfilment when we break down walls and our heart is filled with faces and names (274).

Francis contrasts this attitude, that of 'evangelisers fearlessly open to the working of the Holy Spirit', with the 'pessimism, fatalism and mistrust' that bury the Gospel under a 'pile of excuses' (275-7). To animate the Church with the Spirit of Christ is his intention, a Church committed to 'the social dimension of the Gospel', to 'building up peaceful coexistence between peoples', and to engaging in dialogue with others 'about fundamental issues' that will plot a 'path to peace in our troubled world' (257).

*Evangelii Gaudium* offers brief reflections on the dialogue between faith, reason and science, on ecumenical dialogue, on relations with Judaism and on interreligious dialogue. None of them says anything particularly new or remarkable. What is to be noted is the context out of which Pope Francis speaks. If such dialogues are dimensions of the broader mission of the Church, that mission is itself inseparable from the *pastoral* nature of God's call – and there is more to 'pastoral' than an evocative metaphor from distant tradition. For this Pope, the word speaks of a mode of communication that emphasises the empathetic and interpersonal. 'The smell of the sheep' has become the single most quoted phrase behind all his talks and exhortations. Pastoral ministry, he says, is not a matter of insisting on a 'multitude of doctrines', but adopting a style of engagement with all manner of people, a style that concentrates 'on the essentials, on what is most beautiful, most grand, most appealing and at the same time most necessary. The message is simplified, while losing nothing of its depth and truth, and thus becomes all the more forceful and convincing' (35).

Simplified does not mean relativised. Pope Francis is not denying the need for epistemological principles and careful attention to the claims of truth. Rather he wants something of what O'Malley calls the Council's 'pastoral style' to become typical of the Church as a whole, a Church not just *turned to* the world but set in the *middle of* the world, always learning how to communicate with people *as they are*. Very little in life, he says, is black and white. Shades of grey prevail – a fact that is as true of interreligious dialogue as it is of life in the political sphere more generally. In *Evangelii Gaudium*, and on many occasions since, Francis says he wants a 'discerning Church', made up of people with a capacity for sober judgment. Speaking to a group of Jesuits about priestly formation, he mentions the historian Hugo Rahner, less well-known brother of the eminent theologian, Karl. For Hugo, a Jesuit is a man with a 'nose for the supernatural – a man gifted with a sense of the divine and of the diabolical'. He must be capable of discerning 'both in the field of God and in the field of the devil'.

This is a direct reference to a theme noted earlier, and specifically to the meditation in the *Spiritual Exercises* called Two Standards, in which Ignatius contrasts the desires of Christ the King with those of the 'enemy of our human nature'. On first reading, it sounds as if we are back in the world of black and white: the divine set against the diabolical, the manifest good of the one over against the manifest evil of the other. This is not, however, what Ignatius is commending. He is asking us to recognise that nothing is ever as 'manifest' as we might like. To return to what was said earlier about the first experience Ignatius had of spiritual movements, the 'enemy' appears in disguise as an 'angel of light'; what we experience may be an illusion, and what we take for peace may turn out to be a self-interested satisfaction or a lazy complacency.

Now, to have a nose for the diabolical as well as the divine does not mean treating all aspects of human experience as if they are inexorably subject to the corruption of human sinfulness. Christian faith is a response to Emmanuel, 'God with us', the God who calls a people to himself and promises to accompany them through the tempests of life. Nevertheless, it does counsel caution about the assurance with which we trust in the power of words and the human capacity to navigate a path *unaided* through the grey edges of our existence.

The lessons of Babel are hard to learn. In the dark days, when the Coronavirus first struck and it seemed the entire world was 'locked down' in an attempt to halt the spread of an unseen plague,

Pope Francis addressed 'the Church and the World' before an eerily deserted and rain-swept St Peter's Square. Meditating on Jesus' stilling of the storm (Mk. 4:35-41), he called for a return to the 'essentials' we have forgotten and ignored:

> The storm exposes our vulnerability and uncovers those false and superfluous certainties around which we have constructed our daily schedules, our projects, our habits and priorities. It shows us how we have allowed to become dull and feeble the very things that nourish, sustain and strengthen our lives and our communities. The tempest lays bare all our pre-packaged ideas and forgetfulness of what nourishes our people's souls; all those attempts that anaesthetise us with ways of thinking and acting that supposedly 'save' us, but instead prove incapable of putting us in touch with our roots and keeping alive the memory of those who have gone before us. We deprive ourselves of the antibodies we need to confront adversity. In this storm, the façade of those stereotypes with which we camouflaged our egos, always worrying about our image, has fallen away, uncovering once more that (blessed) common belonging, of which we cannot be deprived: our belonging as brothers and sisters.

In a powerful touch of inculturation into the shared experience of frightening isolation, the Pope asks where we are to find the 'antibodies we need to confront adversity'. It's a precise demand that we retrieve our sense of 'common belonging', an awareness of a common humanity that has been swallowed up by short-term interests and a culture of narcissistic acquisitiveness. The encyclical *Fratelli Tutti*, a second Franciscan-inspired encyclical, 'On Fraternity and Social Friendship', is a lengthy critique of the polarising forces of contemporary populist politics. But it is also characterised by an appeal to the Gospel – and specifically to the parable of the Good Samaritan – which puts the God-given dignity of each and every person at the heart of all human relations *and* political engagement. God invites us all into *friendship* and expects us to develop patterns of hospitality and compassion modelled on the boundary-crossing figure of Christ.

It is possible to detect here an echo of the warm friendship the Archbishop of Buenos Aires had with Rabbi Abraham Skorka. *Fratelli Tutti* is marked by another example of mutual esteem and respect, that which led to the publication of the *Document on Human Fraternity for World Peace and Living Together* which Pope Francis and the Grand Imam of al-Azhar signed in Abu Dhabi in 2019. The encyclical ends with the joint appeal made by the Abu Dhabi statement to promote a 'culture of dialogue', 'mutual co-operation' and 'reciprocal understanding'. What takes both documents beyond bland exhortations to make peace and overcome differences is the insistence of Pope Francis that we become sensitised to God's own truth *wherever it is to be found*. 'Other cultures are not "enemies"', he says, 'from which we need to protect ourselves, but differing reflections of the inexhaustible richness of human life. Seeing ourselves from the perspective of another, of one who is different, we can better recognise our own unique features and those of our culture: its richness, its possibilities and its limitations' (147).

### Using Words Wisely

As creatures of tradition, we tend, of course, to put our trust in human structures, from political institutions and modes of governance to the systems of belief and practice embedded in our most venerable religious cultures. In one way, we are right to do so; at their best these structures are the result of centuries of sedimented wisdom. To cast them aside in favour of a fundamentalist ideology that is always seeking to rewrite tradition in favour of some nostalgic account of what never existed would be foolhardy indeed.

On the other hand, wisdom is wisdom, not because it is inscribed in an authoritative book of that name, but because it has been made subject to centuries of critical scrutiny and careful discernment. Otherwise it risks becoming, not the source of unity and reconciliation, but the inviolable tribal totem that is never in need of repair or attention. The genius of the poet or the prophet is not that they have seen something others have not, or found words that others less imaginative fail to articulate, but – paradoxically – that they have become so sensitised to the fragility of language that they feel deeply the risk of trapping fleeting feelings into the network of words.

The risk must be taken, but it comes at a cost. Pope Francis is never afraid to speak out against a whole swathe of modern seductions. In the introduction to this book I described him as a 'good communicator'. If he has a way with words – more exactly a way with gesture and symbol – it is because he first listens and learns from the voice of experience wherever it is to be found, whether in conversation with Jewish rabbis or through pastoral contact with the ordinary folk of Buenos Aires. His 'theology of the people' is formed, not from the appropriation of a devotional wisdom, but through deep attention to the many ways in which human beings make sense of their lives, habituating everyday practices of faith into typically Christian virtues of fortitude and patience.

This was no straightforward assimilation; his experience as Jesuit Provincial Superior during the years of the Argentinian junta left him isolated and demoralised. His may be an extreme case, but something similar can be said for any process of learning, especially in our increasingly pluralist world, where parties are often separated by a history of trauma and conflict. Whether in the never-ending stand-off between Israelis and Palestinians, the inter-communal strife that has been resurrected in Modi's Hindutva-dominated India, the tragic story of Rohingya Muslims in Myanmar, or the rise in 'hate crime' in cities like my native London, religion plays an ambivalent role in politics and international relations. It is, however, too easy to lay the blame at the door of 'religion', pure and simple. There is no such thing; it is too diffuse a concept to cover the richness of traditions, cultures and ways of life that are spread across the globe. With their Ignatian 'nose for the supernatural' our two Francises would have pointed to something else. To repeat my 'Babel point', names have power to seduce and corrupt. We may be persons defined by our capacity to use language, but language itself does not grant power *over* language; it sensitises us to its limits.

*Beyond Missionary Methods*

This is something the Church, especially the missionary Church, always needs to learn. Let me return to the story of the earlier Francis. If we want a mental picture of Xavier, it is not the indomitable missionary baptising endless queues of submissive natives, but the classic Jesuit ideal of the 'contemplative in action', the man of prayer, a companion of the homeless Christ. When he left Goa for the south of India, he was drawn by concern for fisher-folk who, a few years earlier, had been hastily baptised in return for some sort of protection against Arab raiders, and then left without sacraments or spiritual support.

It was his first experience of trying to communicate in a completely foreign language. In a long letter to the companions in Rome, he explained his method. First he would pick out natives who had a smattering of Portuguese. To these he would teach the Creed, the Commandments, the Our Father and various other prayers and get them to translate them into Tamil. Slowly and painfully Francis learned the Tamil versions by heart and then, he says:

> I went through the entire village with a bell in my hand, in order to assemble all the boys and men that I could. After they had been brought together, I taught them twice a day. Within the space of a month, I taught them the prayers and ordered the boys to teach their fathers and mothers and all those of their house and their neighbours what they had learned at school.

There is much more to Francis's method than a dull teaching by rote. When he goes through the articles of the Creed, he gets the people to use gestures, the sign of the cross, and to recite prayers with him. He teaches them how to pray; in centring the words of faith around the life of Christ they would come to understand the truth of the Gospel. Christian faith, he is saying, is not a matter of blind assent, but involves a moving of the inner spirit, the heart.

Learning to communicate in another language is never a mechanical process. Nor was the success Francis had due to some extraordinary linguistic competence. The Xavier who was the closest companion of Ignatius was a large personality, not exactly given to fits of self-doubt; nevertheless, there were plenty of moments when he was alternately absorbed and mystified by what he found. He could ask puzzled questions, such as why the Japanese wrote the way they did. And he could make mistakes, such as using a quite inappropriate Buddhist term to translate the untranslatable notion of a Creator God. Engagement with 'the other' is not a matter of confrontation and the replacement of one conceptual framework with another, but a genuine and complex process of learning how to enter into an alien world. In November 1549, he wrote to his fellow-Jesuits, 'Let all witness more by their lives and by their works than by preaching', a sentiment, noted earlier, that brings him close to his namesake from Assisi. Xavier translated the words of the Gospel, but I suspect he realised very quickly that he first needed to translate *himself*, to be one with *these* people.

His theology was, of course, a reflection of the times. In that extraordinary period of transition from the late medieval to the early modern world, difference was explained in terms of sin. This is reflected in his letters; time and time again Francis laments the degree of corruption and vice in which so many of the 'pagans' live. Yet there is also in the letters – and much more obviously in the work of the next generation of Jesuit missionaries – another spirit at work, one which can be traced back to the humanism of the Renaissance and the theological questioning which was current in Paris in the first part of the sixteenth century. It had its effect on

Francis. The longer he spent in Japan the more one detects in him a growing respect for the sophistication and curiosity of the people he encountered.

Today, we realise that such respect and appreciation for difference is the *sine qua non* of any inter-religious dialogue. Difference is now explained, not as the effect of human sinfulness, but in terms of cultural diversity. People and the communities they belong to are just different, unique, special. That may seem totally positive, and in many ways it is. It commends a model of interreligious dialogue built on a benign pluralism and peaceful coexistence. Long before 9/11, however, it was clear that such a model had its dangers.

## The Difference Love Makes

Whatever line we take on religiously inspired violence – whether placing the emphasis on the resentment that grows from the experience of injustice and deprivation, or blaming 'religion' itself and the hard-edged oppositions it entrenches – we need to acknowledge the danger of the most sincerely held beliefs becoming toxic; the danger of these beliefs moving from their proper sphere of concern for the demands of an ultimate truth to something bound up with the violent imposition of vested interests.

Peace between the religions is not a given; it requires work and effort. The 'political inculturation' of Pope Francis entails more than a shift of approach, from translating the Gospel message into strange vernaculars to addressing an audience that includes policy-makers, opinion-formers and economists, as well as populist bullies and their cheerleaders. More exactly, it is about bringing the ever-challenging demands of communicating a vital truth into dialogue with the questions raised by contemporary culture in all its richness and complexity. The Holy Spirit works in the middle of the world, consoling, enlivening and pointing to the truth, a source of hope even in the most troubling of times. But that does not absolve persons of faith from acknowledging the dark side of human religiosity and the need to discern carefully the potential of the diabolical – Ignatius's 'enemy of human nature' – subtly to undermine our most sincerely held desires and aspirations.

If there is a model of interreligious difference for our times, it has to do with the political and economic inequalities that feed off deep-seated memories of trauma and conflict. Over the last few decades, attention has shifted from the dialogues of theological exchange and religious experience to the dialogues of common life and common action. Pragmatic considerations about social cohesion and the prevention of extremism in building civic society are central to the negotiation of difference. But that is very far from sidelining theology. Indeed, it makes theology more necessary, and not just because modern societies are notable for their plurality of religious commitments. Any serious effort to think about the way things are – 'the theological' in a broad sense – has political implications. Theology and politics speak not of mutually distinct areas of concern – as if we are juxtaposing a 'craft of the 'spiritual' to match 'the art of the possible' – but a single yet complex determination to keep open a sense of the transcendent at the heart of human affairs.

To fuse the two together is to risk the violence of theocracy; to set them apart is to grant uncritical power to untouchable political and economic institutions. I have proposed Pune's Trumpian version of the Tower of Babel as symbolic of the way in which international capitalism exacerbates rather than overcomes the divisions that plague the contemporary international order. Pope Francis might have been thinking of Modi's India when he says in *Evangelii Gaudium* that '[T]he worship of the ancient golden calf has returned in a new and ruthless guise in the idolatry of money and the dictatorship of an impersonal economy lacking a truly human purpose' (55). Talk of a 'human purpose' should not distract from the underlying message of Francis, that the culture of post-modernity, pervaded by consumerism and complacency, risks blunting that which makes us most human: an interior life that takes delight in all that connects us to the God revealed in the person of Jesus of Nazareth.

This Jesus does not pontificate from a great height, like some heavenly populist leader dismissing the elites while standing safely above the action. He enters into the ordinary world of humanity, engaging with rich and poor, learned and simple, friendly and hostile alike, turning on their head the common religious assumptions that demarcate spheres of 'sacred and profane' which would keep talk of transcendence safely in its place away from the messiness of human relationships. For it is in the ordinary and everyday that creation becomes once again strangely re-enchanted. 'Finding God in all things', to repeat the Ignatian mantra one last time, means *all* things, not just the objects of our experience but the desires and hopes and dreams that give us a 'truly human purpose'.

If there is such a thing as 'Ignatian mysticism' – and I think there is – it is more than an ill-defined 'nose for the supernatural'. It is, rather, bound up with a profound sensitivity to the connections the Spirit enables, a sensitivity which develops, not just a suspicion of easy answers and plausible shortcuts, but also, and more positively, a willingness to risk something new and different.

Pope Francis's twenty-first century 'political inculturation' is guided by the same theological vision that took his Jesuit namesake to India in the middle of the sixteenth At the very end of the *Spiritual Exercises*, Ignatius spells it out in terms of a contemplation 'to attain the love of God'. His two preliminary points – first, that love should manifest itself in deeds rather than words; and secondly, that love consists in a mutual sharing of goods – are both counter-intuitive, which is not to say irrational. This is a love that is totally other-directed, a self-sacrificial love that responds to what is given without any expectation of reward or recompense. What is contemplated is the love that God – the 'Divine Majesty' – reveals at the heart of the mystery of creation and redemption itself.

For all its magnificence, this is not a theological scheme that is to be admired and accepted as a test of faith. Ignatius describes what God is always doing, 'in the heavens, the elements, the plants, the fruits, the cattle, etc. He gives being, conserves them, confers life and sensation, etc.' [236]. He then goes on immediately to make the point that this vision of the Divine Majesty at work in the world is tied to what God has done *for me*. This is what Pope Francis is talking about in *Evangelii Gaudium* when he calls for Christians to 'help at least one person to have a better life'. More exactly this is what *God* does; it is not a personal mission that brings satisfaction to the giver, but a mystery in which human beings are invited to participate, and which promises nothing less than a glimpse of the radiant fullness of God's providential purposes.

## Name and Word

Something of that vision is written on the face of Ignatius when, as in that statue in the Bom Jesus in Goa, he contemplates the Name of Jesus. Such is the Christian vision that is inspired by an Ignatian perspective that has directed the Society of Jesus from St Francis Xavier to Pope Francis, and will no doubt go on doing so for any-one who seeks to follow the way of the wounded soldier.

This is Jesus the prophet who questions self-important 'isms' of all kinds – but he is so much more than a prophet. Even within the brief space of the New Testament, the theological imagina-tion shifts dramatically from a response to Jesus' Christological question in terms of titles – Messiah, Logos, Son of Man – to the breath-taking cosmology of Ephesians and Colossians, in which Jesus' preaching of the Kingdom inaugurates nothing less than a re-creation of all things 'in Christ'. The former Francis spent his life trying to find ways to communicate this truth which, thanks to Ignatius and his little manual of *Spiritual Exercises*, had taken over his life. The latter Francis is similarly committed to being a 'good communicator', but he also knows about the 'Babel syndrome' which would subordinate the diversity of languages about the Di-vine into a despotic imposition. Pentecost reverses that temptation and puts *God*'s power back at the heart of human interaction. To proclaim God's Word in 'the name of Jesus', as Peter does in the early chapters of Acts, is not to make a counter-imposition, one that is only a little less despotic and more reasonable. It is, rather, to insist that the language we use to communicate with each other as human beings is itself a divine gift. This is where we find God at work, not in carefully structured phrases and systems of thought that encourage a comforting security, but in the Word itself that summons us to risk a self-transcending love.

That is not to say that the everyday language we use to form and maintain our communities has a purely utilitarian value, but rather to insist that its purpose – both in the more purely 'religious' sense of gathering for prayer and the 'political' need for organisation of 'common life' and 'common action' – is only truly apparent when we press the limits of what can and cannot be said. When to speak and when to listen? *How* to speak and *how* to listen?

I hope some useful hints have been given in the intervening chapters of this book after we set out with 'Ignatius to India'. A respectful silence is now in order. Enough, perhaps, to conclude with this single point: whatever the differences of language and symbolism, traditional practice and articulated doctrine, religion will always have implications not just for everyday living and our political relations but also for our future before the Mystery that is God's love. Ignatius would remind us that love shows itself in deeds not just words. It's important never to neglect the nexus between inner practice (thought and prayer) and outer practice (the responsibilities of social life and engagement). For that to happen care needs to be taken not to lose those qualities of curiosity and imagination, as well as patience and perseverance, that come from the slow and painstaking work of listening to and learning from the Word manifested in all human beings; for as Francis the Pope says, 'every person is immensely holy and deserves our love'.

# GLOSSARY OF TERMS

***Ahimsa:*** 'non-violence' but with positive connotations of wishing someone well.

***Anekanta:*** literally 'not-oneness'; a principle in the Jain tradition that all hard binary oppositions are to be avoided.

***Atman:*** the essence or inner principle of life, used in the Hindu classical texts known as the *Upanisads* to denote the eternal, non-material centre of personality.

***Avatar:*** literally 'descent' and often used to speak of the appearance or 'epiphany' of one of the great Hindu god figures (particularly Vishnu) in human form – e.g. Krishna, Rama, Kalki – a form still expected to usher in the final age, and even the Buddha

***Bhagavan:*** 'Lord', a generic title used in Hindu devotional traditions to refer to the personal Absolute, as in classic texts like the *Bhagavad Gita* and *Bhagavata Purana*.

***Bhajan:*** a song with a religious or spiritual theme, most often of a popular nature, which expresses devotion to a god-figure.

***Bhakti:*** 'participation' or 'devotion', with the sense of being attached to or sharing in the life of the Lord, *Bhagavan*; hence loyalty; with *karma* ('work') and *jñana* ('knowledge') one of the major divisions into which the practices or spiritualities of contemporary Hinduism are often grouped.

***Bodhisattva:*** literally 'enlightenment-being' or 'being for enlightenment', i.e. a being who is destined to become a Buddha, an enlightened one. In the Mahayana schools represents the ideal quality of the Buddha as the compassionate teacher.

***Brahman:*** 'holy mystery' or 'cosmic or all-pervading power'; in Hinduism generally refers to the Absolute or transcendent state of being; in some of the *Upanisads* the cosmic *Brahman* is conceived of as identical with the personal *Atman*.

***Brahmin:*** (not to be confused with *Brahman*); a member of the first caste in the hierarchy, responsible not just for maintaining the purity of the ritual but also for traditional learning and the orthodox interpretation of the Veda.

***Dharma:*** 'truth, law, justice, teaching'; exact meaning depends on context; from a verbal root meaning to uphold or bear, hence literally referring to that which gives support.

***Dukkha:*** usually translated as 'suffering'; literally that which is difficult to bear; in Buddhism the first of the Four Noble Truth; refers not just to pain but to the unsatisfactory or insubstantial nature of existence.

***Four Noble Truths:*** the basic principles of Buddhist teaching – suffering, the cause of suffering, the end of suffering, the way to the end of suffering (for the Noble Eightfold Path; see below).

***Gurdwara:*** literally 'home of the *guru*', the Sikh Temple which houses the Guru Granth Sahib, the collection of Sikh scriptures.

***Guru:*** 'teacher or spiritual guide'; a personal preceptor, often the object of personal devotion, who initiates the student into the truth inscribed in texts such as the *Upanisad*s and leads them to the light of wisdom.

***Hajj:*** for Muslims the annual Islamic pilgrimage to the *Kaaba*, the 'House of God', in the sacred city of Makka in Saudi Arabia; one of the Five Pillars of Islam, alongside *Shahadah* (the profession of faith), *Salat* (prayer), *Zakat* (almsgiving), and *Sawm* (fasting).

***Hinayana:*** 'the lesser vehicle' of Buddhism; see *Mahayana* and *Theravada* below.

***Imam:*** in Shi'a Islam one of the twelve successors of Prophet Mohammad; in Sunni Islam a title given to the one who leads the prayer in the mosque and to certain members of the *ulema*, the body of scholars and specialists in Islamic sacred law and theology.

***Jñana:*** 'knowledge'; especially with connotations of highest knowledge or insight which leads to *moksha* (see below).

***Karma:*** 'action', from a verbal root meaning to act or do; in early forms of Hinduism originally refers to the action of the sacrificial ritual but then extended, especially in Buddhism, to cover all intentional acts which have moral consequences.

***Karuna:*** 'compassion'; the most important motivation behind the action of the *bodhisattva*.

***Kinhin:*** a Buddhist practice that involves measured walking between long periods of sitting meditation or *zazen*.

***Mahabharata:*** the 'Great Epic of India', a massive text compiled over several centuries which brings together myths and legends about the major god-figures and heroes who are significant for Hinduism.

***Mandir:*** generic term for a Hindu temple; as well as housing the image of a deity and thus providing a focus of devotion for pilgrims, many *mandirs* have a cosmic significance, integrating the powers of the universe around the sanctuary at the centre of the whole complex.

***Mahayana:*** literally the 'Great Vehicle', a school of Buddhism which dates in a developed form from several centuries after the time of the Buddha but which is most probably based on elements that are relatively early; more liberal religiously and more speculative philosophically than the more conservative schools which Mahayanists tend to refer to pejoratively as *Hinayana* – 'the lesser vehicle'.

**Mandala:** a geometric pattern of squares and circles set around a single point or 'sacred space', used especially in forms of *Mahayana* Buddhism to focus attention and act as a mode of spiritual guidance.

**Middle Way:** very often used as a description of Buddhism; a path between extremes, both ascetical (i.e. between types of religious practice) and philosophical, especially between a position that seeks an experience of eternity and one which seeks only annihilation.

**Mindfulness:** in Buddhism, the penultimate stage of the Noble Eightfold Path, referring to a quality of lucid attention to the present moment.

**Moksha:** 'liberation'; in Indian religions the generic term connoting freedom, a transcendental state opposite to *samsara* (see below), which different traditions may specify further; thus Hindu theistic schools may speak of *moksha* as union with the Lord, *Bhagavan*.

**Nirvana:** literally 'blowing out'; the most important Buddhist term for the experience of *moksha*, the height of Buddhist aspirations; the basic metaphor at work refers to the blowing out of a fire and thus of those factors which hinder *prajña*, enlightenment or wisdom, seeing things as they really are.

**Noble Eightfold Path:** the eight interdependent stages of moral, meditative and spiritual practice which make up the Fourth Noble Truth (the Way): Right Understanding, Right Thought, Right Speech, Right Action, Right Livelihood, Right Effort, Right Mindfulness and Right Concentration

**Pali:** see *Sanskrit*.

**Pitaka:** 'basket' or collection of texts. In the *Theravada* Buddhist tradition there are three *pitakas*, the *Vinaya* or code of discipline, the collection of *suttas* or discourses, and *Abhidhamma*, more philosophical summaries of psycho-meditative practice.

**Prajña:** 'wisdom', or 'understanding' of the true nature of things; specifically the ability to understand the three characteristics of all phenomenal reality: suffering, unsatisfactoriness and insubstantiality.

**Pratityasamutpada,** the 'nexus of conditioned origination'; the most important philosophical concept in the early Buddhist tradition, referring to the Buddha's teaching about the coinherence or interaction of all phenomena, as if in a great network of human experience.

**Purana:** literally 'ancient'; within the Hindu *bhakti* tradition referring to vast collections of mythical tales about the ancestry and exploits of the great gods of Hinduism.

**Qur'an:** the Muslim scriptures revealed to the prophet Mohammad (died 632 CE), perceived by him and by Muslims today as the unchangeable word of God, uncreated and eternal, superseding all earlier scriptures.

**Ramayana:** an epic story told about the great Hindu god, Rama, which depicts his great journey in search of his wife Sita who has been abducted to the island of Lanka by the wicked demon, Ravana.

**Rasa:** literally 'sap'; i.e. 'taste' or 'flavour'; generic title for aesthetic qualities of works of literary or dramatic art, from the erotic and compassionate to the marvellous and peaceful.

**Śaiva:** a devotee of god Śiva; hence Śaivism.

**Śakti:** multilayered concept connoting cosmic energy, giving rise to a tradition of devotional Hinduism which focuses on the divine as feminine, the power to give and nurture life that can be said to irradiate the Universe.

**Samatha:** 'calming'; one of two qualities of mind which are developed through forms of meditative practice in Theravada Buddhism. The other is *vipassana* or insight which is based on mindfulness training. Although notionally different, in practice elements of both are necessary for enlightenment and work together.

**Samsara:** 'round of rebirth'; key concept in both Hinduism and Buddhism; from a verbal root meaning to flow and referring therefore to the continuous process of life, death and rebirth or the world of contingent reality.

**Sangha:** literally 'flock' or 'congregation'; the community of the Buddha's followers or disciples, the third of the three jewels and three refuges (along with Buddha and *Dharma*).

**Sanskrit:** the ancient Indo-European language in which the classical scriptures of Hinduism are written; *Pali*, a later derivative from the Sanskrit tradition, is the language in which the canonical scriptures of the early *Theravada* Buddhist tradition are written.

**Sannyasi:** a religious ascetic who has renounced the world and embraced a homeless, wandering stage of life or *ashrama*; according to tradition this is the fourth stage, after *brahmacarya* (studentship), *grhastha* (the life of the householder) and *vanaprastha* (retirement).

**Sati** (in Pali) or **Smrti** (in Sanskrit): usually translated as mindfulness but with connotations of remembrance; *samma sati* or Right Mindfulness is the penultimate stage of the Noble Eightfold Path of Buddhism.

**Shari'a:** 'path'; the Islamic code of law and religious practice, based chiefly on the Qur'an and the Sunna (the practice of the prophet Mohammad), regulating all aspects of the life of Muslims.

**Siddhi:** literally 'perfection' or 'accomplishment'; in some forms of Hinduism and Mahayana Buddhism it refers to 'special powers' which may be acquired through certain forms of tantric practice (see *Tantra* below).

**Śruti:** literally 'hearing'; the revealed knowledge contained in the Vedic corpus of literature, the collections of hymns, the sacrificial commentaries and the philosophical texts, the *Upanishads*.

**Shi'a:** 'the party of Ali'; school of Islam that takes its rise from Ali, the son-in-law of the Prophet Mohammad, who the Shi'a believe carries on his legacy of teaching. For the Shi'a the massacre at Karbala in 680 CE in which the

Prophet's grandson Hussein was killed acts as a sort of foundational moment.

*Sunni:* the majority school of Islam, comprising some 85-90% of Muslims, characterised by a greater emphasis upon the *Sunnah*, the traditions and teachings associated with the Prophet Mohammad.

*Śunyata:* 'emptiness'; in the philosophical schools of the *Mahayana* a term developed from the earlier doctrine of *anatmavada* ('lack of self') to show that all things are relative, that all objects lack inherent or substantial existence.

*Tantra:* from a verbal root meaning 'stretch' and referring to a variety of developments within both Hinduism and Buddhism, from the liturgical to the more obviously esoteric, which incorporate popular and sometimes 'fringe' practices; *tantric* texts expand or shift the norms of the classical tradition.

*Theravada:* 'teaching of the elders'; name of the only surviving early Buddhist school (sometimes called collectively by the pejorative term *Hinayana*, 'lesser vehicle', in contrast to the *Mahayana* or 'great vehicle').

*Umma:* Islamic community; seen as a religious and political unity, transcending national loyalties, owing allegiance to God and to the Prophet Mohammad.

*Upanishad:* the *Vedanta* or 'end of the Veda'; texts which comprise the final part of the philosophical treatises concluding the Hindu *śruti* or revelation.

*Vac:* 'word' or 'speech'; personified as a Vedic goddess.

*Vaishnava:* a follower of god Vishnu or one of his *avatars*, such as Krishna or Rama; hence Vaishnavism.

*Varkari Panth:* a devotional (*bhakti*) cult which engages in regular pilgrimage to the shrine of Vitthoba at Pandharpur in Maharashtra.

*Veda:* 'knowledge'; the religious texts which originated in ancient India and form the oldest scriptures of Hinduism: *Rg Veda*, the *Yajur Veda*, the *Sama Veda* and the *Atharva Veda*.

*Vipassana:* 'insight meditation'; see *samatha* above.

*Yoga:* literally 'yoking or joining together' in order to gain control (of the senses); comes to refer to a system of meditative exercises which are intended to cultivate the faculties of the mind so that the practitioner, or *yogi*, can gain an intuitive mystical experience or *jñana*.

*Zazen:* sitting meditation in the Zen Buddhist tradition which involves long periods of silent attention, whether focusing on a natural movement like the breathing (in the Soto school) or attending to the implications of a *koan*, or riddle (in the Rinzai school).

# NOTES ON SOURCES

## CHAPTER 1

The translation of the text of the *Spiritual Exercises* I have used is by Michael Ivens, *Understanding the Spiritual Exercises* (Leominster: Gracewing, 1996). The translation of the 'Formula of the Institute' I have taken from *The Constitutions of the Society of Jesus and their Complementary Norms* (St Louis: Institute of Jesuit Sources, 1996). The quotations from St Francis Xavier come from *The Letters and Instructions of Francis Xavier*, translated and introduced by M. Joseph Costelloe (St Louis: Institute of Jesuit Sources, 1992).

The translation and interpretation of Romans (12:3) comes from Brendan Byrne's commentary in the *Sacra Pagina* series (Collegeville: The Liturgical Press, 1996).

## CHAPTER 2

For the text of the *Autobiography* (*Reminiscences as heard and written down by Luis Goncalves da Camara*) I am indebted to *Saint Ignatius of Loyola: Personal Writings*, edited by Joseph Munitiz and Philip Endean (London: Penguin, 1996).

The fourfold distinction of types of dialogue is first noted in the 1984 document from the Secretariat for Non-Christian Religions, 'The attitude of the Church towards the followers of other religions'. It is repeated in Pope St John Paul II's 1990 encyclical, *Redemptoris Missio*, and in the 1991 joint document from the Pontifical Council for Inter-religious Dialogue and the Congregation for Evangelisation, 'Dialogue and Proclamation: reflections and orientations on inter-religious dialogue and the proclamation of the Gospel of Jesus Christ'.

For text and translation of the documents of the Second Vatican Council I have normally made use of Norman Tanner (ed), *The Decrees of the Ecumenical Councils* (London: Sheed and Ward; Washington: Georgetown University Press, 1990).

Michel de Certeau is one of the most extraordinary examples of a Jesuit made in the mould of the intrepid missionaries of the early era. Historian and theorist of mysticism, cultural critic and theologian, his most important work includes *The Mystic Fable* (Chicago: Chicago University Press, 1992) and *The Practice of Everyday Life* (Berkeley: University of California Press, 1984). For an excellent personal account of de Certeau as 'the pilgrim', see George B. York, *Michel de Certeau or Union in Difference* (Leominster: Gracewing, 2009).

Emmanuel Levinas's 'Abrahamic journey' is implicit in much of his writing. I rely especially to the intense meditations on Jewish tradition contained in

*Nine Talmudic Readings,* edited by Annette Aronowicz (Bloomington IN: Indiana University Press, 1994); and the short essays and talks on Judaism collected in *Difficult Freedom* (Baltimore: The Johns Hopkins University Press, 1990).

Gwen Griffith Dickson's novel, *Bleedback,* was published by Ismo Books in 2016.

## CHAPTER 3

The principle that theological reflection on religious pluralism and the questions it raises for Christian faith is always done in 'the middle of things' is developed at length in Michael Barnes, *Theology and the Dialogue of Religions* (Cambridge: Cambridge University Press, 2002). I acknowledge my debt to the work of Gillian Rose, particularly *The Broken Middle: Out of our Ancient Society,* (Oxford: Blackwells; 1992).

Karl Rahner's thesis of the 'anonymous Christian' remains influential within in the theology of religions. Amongst his many articles, the most important are 'Christianity and the non-Christian Religions', *Theological Investigations (TI)*, 5, 115-34; 'Thoughts on the Possibility of Faith Today', *TI* 5, 3-22; 'Anonymous Christianity and the Missionary Task of the Church', *TI* 12, 161-78 (London: DLT, 1961-84).

The reflective material now available on Scriptural Reasoning is considerable. Particularly helpful is an issue of *Modern Theology*, 22.3, July, 2006, especially the introductory essay by David Ford, 'An Interfaith Wisdom: Scriptural Reasoning between Jews, Christians and Muslims'.

For Rowan Williams's reflections on the 'integrity of theology', see the collected papers in *On Christian Theology* (Oxford: Blackwell, 2000).

The little parable of the theological dwarf is quoted from Johann Baptist Metz, *Faith in History and Society* (New York: Herder and Herder, 2007; 101). The quotation from Walter Benjamin comes from *The Arcades Project,* edited by Hannah Arendt, translated by Howard Eiland and Kevin McLaughlin (Cambridge MA: Harvard University Press, 1999; 463). It is quoted by Giorgio Agamben in *The Time that Remains* (Stanford CA: Stanford University Press, 2005; 141).

## CHAPTER 4

My article on Buddhism and the *Spiritual Exercises* was originally published as 'The *Spiritual Exercises:* A Zen Perspective' (*The Way Supplement*, 55, 1986). It has recently been reproduced in *The Pilgrim and the Sage: Ignatian Spirituality and Buddhism in Dialogue,* edited by Ary C Dy (Mandaluyong City, Philippines: Anvil Publishing, 2019). This collection includes work from a number of Jesuits who have been involved in sustained dialogue with Buddhism, including Aloysius Pieris, AMA Samy and Javier Melloni. Further mention should be made of Jesuits who have been acknowledged as Zen Masters, most especially Robert Kennedy in the USA and Hugo Enomiya Lassalle in Japan. In the area of the creative encounter between Ignatian spirituality and Buddhism, the name of William Johnston stands out. The quotation is taken from his *Being in Love: The Practice of Christian Prayer* (London: Collins, 1988). For an overview of the Ignatian contribution to interreligious dialogue and a brief account of some of the many contemporary Jesuits involved, see Michael Barnes, 'Interreligious Dialogue', in Thomas Worcester (General Editor), *The Cambridge Encyclopedia of the Jesuits,* (Cambridge: Cambridge University Press, 2017).

The quotations from Xavier's correspondence are taken from Costelloe, *Letters,* 178; 297-8.

For Meister Eckhart, see 'On Detachment', from *Meister Eckhart, The Classics of Western Spirituality,* edited by Edmund Colledge and Bernard McGinn, (London: SPCK, 1981).

## CHAPTER 5

Three editions of the *Kristapurana* were published, in 1616, 1649 and 1654. A scholarly edition was produced in Mangalore by Joseph Saldanha in 1907. It has now been translated and edited by Nelson Falcao SDB (Kristu Jyoti Publications: Bengaluru; 2012), in a comprehensive edition, with accompanying appendices, and Stephens's own prose introduction from which the quotation at the end of this chapter is taken. As well as background material and notes, Falcao presents the text in columns – the Marathi (in Roman script) and his English verse translation facing each other. He also gives us something of the textual tradition, insofar as that can be reconstructed.

The rather fanciful comparison with Shakespeare comes from Francis Correa, 'The "Shakespeare" of the Konkan coast: Fr Thomas Stephens SJ (1549-1619)', *Vidyajyoti,* 83 (2019), 461-71. The letter from Campion to Persons is quoted by Philip Caraman in *Henry Garnet, 1555-1606, and the Gunpowder Plot,* (Longmans, 1964). The comments on the Salcete that Stephens encountered are in Georg Schurhammer, 'Thomas Stephens 1549-1619' (*The Month,* April 1955). The comment by Teutonio de Souza on the Cuncolim Martyrs is published in *Jesuits in India: a Historical Perspective,* (Goa: Xavier Centre for Historical Research, 1991). Ananya Chakravarti's careful assessment of Stephens' achievement is taken from *The Empire of Apostles: Religion, Accommodatio, and the Imagination of Empire in Early Modern Brazil and India* (Delhi: Oxford University Press, 2018).

For the background to the Indian *puranic* culture I am indebted to Friedhelm Hardy's magnificent commentary, *The Religious Culture of India* (Oxford: Oxford University Press, 1994). For the Directory of Fabio de Fabi see the collection edited by Martin E. Palmer SJ, *On Giving the Spiritual Exercises: The*

*Early Jesuit Manuscript Directories and the Official Directory of 1599* (St Louis: The Institute of Jesuit Sources, 1996). Pedro Arrupe's definition of inculturation is taken from his 'Letter to the Whole Society on Inculturation', *Studies in the International Apostolate of the Jesuits,* (Washington DC: 7, June 1978).

## CHAPTER 6

Brother Daniel produced many self-published collections of interreligious prayers, liturgies and readings, the best known being *Transcendence, Prayer of People of Faith* which has now been expanded in a new edition (available through Westminster Interfaith, the Roman Catholic agency for interreligious dialogue).

Comparative Theology boasts an ever-growing bibliography and the on-line Journal of Comparative Theology. The best overview and introduction is Francis X. Clooney, *Comparative Theology: Deep Learning Across Religious Borders* (Oxford: Wiley-Blackwell, 2010). An excellent collection of typical 'case studies', which includes reflections on method, is contained in *How to do Comparative Theology,* edited by Francis X. Clooney and Klaus von Stosch (New York: Fordham University Press, 2017).

The reference to Jung comes from J. J. Clarke, *Jung and Eastern Thought* (London: Routledge, 1994). For the commentary on the *mandala* I am indebted to the brilliant little book, *The Mandala of the Five Buddhas* by Vessantara (Windhorse Publications, 1999).

The quotations from Augustine's *De Doctrina Christiana* are taken from the translation by R. F. H. Green, (Oxford: Oxford University Press, 1997); and from *The Confessions,* translated by Henry Chadwick, (Oxford: Oxford University Press, 1991). For the theme of memory in medieval Christian thought see Mary Carruthers, *The Craft of Thought* (Cambridge: Cambridge University Press, 1998), from which the quotations in the text are taken; see also Carruthers, *The Book of Memory,* (Cambridge: Cambridge University Press, 2nd edition 2008).

## CHAPTER 7

I have accessed a number of websites on contemporary 'secular' adaptations of Mindfulness. These tend, of course, to get updated regularly so the material is likely to change.

The NHS website can be accessed at https://www.nhs.uk/conditions/stress-anxiety-depression/mindfulness/

For the Open University courses see https://www.open.edu/openlearn/health-sports-psychology/mindfulness-mental-health-and-prison-settings/content

For the Mindfulness in schools project (MiSP) see https://mindfulnessin-schools.org/

The Prison Phoenix Trust can be accessed at https://www.theppt.org.uk/about-us/

Professor Mark Williams, a distinguished clinical psychologist working in the area of Mindfulness-based Cognitive Therapy (MBCT), teaches for the Oxford Mindfulness Centre and works on programmes to evaluate the effectiveness of mechanisms underlying the use of mindfulness in schools, particularly with regard to the training of teachers.

Sr Elaine MacInnes first trained as a violinist and joined Our Lady's Missionaries in 1961 in Canada. Her first mission was to Japan, where she learned Zen and became acknowledged as a Master. She has written several books on her experience of Zen and Christianity, including *Zen Contemplation: A Bridge of Living Water* (Ottawa: Novalis, 2001).

For an excellent study of Mindfulness in school context, see Richard Burnett, 'Mindfulness in Secondary Schools: Learning Lessons from the Adults, Secular and Buddhist', *Buddhist Studies Review*, 28.1 (2011). For critical comment on the 'McMindfulness' phenomenon, see the work of Peter Doran of Queen's University, Belfast, especially *A Political Economy of Attention, Mindfulness and Consumerism: Reclaiming the Mindful Commons* (London: Routledge, 2017).

Anthony de Mello's *Sadhana, A Way to God: Christian Exercises in Eastern Form,* has appeared in a number of editions and reprints. It was first published by the Jesuit publishing house, Gujarat Sahitya Prakash, Ahmedabad in 1978.

For the Buddhist practice of mindfulness see the wonderfully wise little introduction by Walpola Rahula, *What the Buddha Taught* (Bedford: Gordon Fraser, 1968). The text I quote as an example of the rooting of wisdom in the affective understanding is a dialogue between two meditative traditions from the Theravada tradition, is to be found in *Samyutta Nikaya* of the Pali Canon, 2.115.

For the discussion on Messianism and the Church which underpins the final quotation of this chapter see Giorgio Agamben, *The Church and the Kingdom,* (London: Seagull books, 2012); the political and theological questions Agamben raises are taken up in a detailed exegesis of the opening section of Paul's Epistle to the Romans in *The Time that Remains* (Stanford: Stanford University Press, 2005).

## CHAPTER 8

Brother Daniel Faivre produced his own privately published 'Pilgrim's guide to Southall at worship'. *Glimpses of a Holy City* first appeared in 1992, and went through a number of editions as the town's interreligious profile shifted and changed. Daniel outlined four different routes for the pilgrim to follow, with a brief history and contact details of the places of worship on the way. The 2001 edition notes some sixty entries. A quick check, twenty years later, indicates that most are still there and – unsurprisingly – more have been opened. Southall has been the subject of one important social anthropological study: Gerd Baumann, *Contesting Culture: Discourses of Identity in Multi-Ethnic London* (Cambridge: Cambridge University Press, 1994). The last chapter of my *Theology and the Dialogue of Religions* (Cambridge: Cambridge University Press, 2002), entitled 'Negotiating the Middle', was written in a small flat above a hairdresser's in the middle of Southall, and attempts to marry the more theoretical elements of what was in origins a PhD thesis with the everyday pastoral reality of places like Southall. I have tried to develop that theme further in my *Interreligious Learning: Dialogue, Spirituality and the Christian Imagination* (Cambridge: Cambridge University Press, 2012).

Pastoral Theology is one of the most important developments within the Catholic Church since the Second Vatican Council, but it also has very strong ecumenical credentials. The particular approach adopted at Heythrop College has been recorded in James Sweeney, with Gemma Simmonds and David Lonsdale, *Keeping Faith in Practice: Aspects of Catholic Pastoral Theology* (London: SCM, 2010). For the broader ecumenical perspective, see also Helen Cameron, Deborah Bhatti, Catherine Duce, James Sweeney and Clare Watkins, *Talking about God in Practice: Theological Action Research and Practical Theology* (London: SCM, 2010). In my own reflective work, both in my Heythrop teaching and in the daily trudging of the Southall streets, I have found myself indebted to the more theoretical overview of developments recorded in James Woodward and Stephen Pattison (eds), *The Blackwell Reader in Pastoral and Practical Theology* (Oxford: Blackwell, 2000); and the practical aids laid out in Elaine Graham, Heather Walton and Frances Ward, *Theological Reflection: Methods* (London: SCM, 2005).

In expanding on the notion of 'reading' as key to my particular version of comparative theology, I find myself taking inspiration from the powerfully stated study by Paul Griffiths, *Religious Reading: The Place of Reading in the Practice of Religion* (Oxford: Oxford University Press, 1999). Griffiths is concerned with religious or 'reverential' reading as a counter to the typically 'consumerist' attitude of contemporary society which sees texts in utilitarian terms as sources of information.

The term 'super-diversity' I take from Trevor Phillips, *Race and Faith: The Deafening Silence*, (London: Civitas, 2016). The distinction between 'side-by-side' dialogue and 'face-to-face' runs through the work of Jonathan Sacks (see particularly *The Home We Build Together* (London: Continuum, 2007) and forms the title and major structuring concept for a significant report from the Department for Communities and Local Government, 'A Framework for Partnership in our Multi Faith Society (HMG, 2008).

# CHAPTER 9

The material in this chapter which focuses specifically on ageing and old age comes from my inaugural lecture at Heythrop College, November, 2013. I am grateful to my old schoolfriend, Professor Peter Coleman, Emeritus Professor of Social Gerontology at the University of Southampton, for honouring me with a response to that lecture. I am indebted to his work and that of his colleagues, especially the studies published in *Belief and Ageing: Spiritual Pathways in Later Life* (Bristol: Policy Press, 2011). For the ideas in that original I am also grateful to Rowan Williams for his insights in 'The Gifts Reserved for Age: Perceptions of the Elderly', a chapter in his *Faith in the Public Square* (London: Bloomsbury, 2012).

The history of the early Society has received a vast amount of attention. I note here the large number of articles in *The Cambridge Encyclopedia*, edited by Thomas Worcester. I am also indebted to John O'Malley, *The Early Jesuits* (Cambridge MA: Harvard University Press, 1992). For an instant overview of the main currents in the history of Jesuit mission, it is difficult to beat O'Malley's brilliant summary: *The Jesuits, a History from Ignatius to the Present* (Lanham MA: Rowan and Littlefield, 2014).

The concept of 'dialogue' is present in all the literature on theology of religions. My distinction between a 'theology for dialogue' and a 'theology of dialogue' runs through all my work, from *Religions in Conversation: Christian Identity and Religious Pluralism* (London: SPCK, 1989), to *Waiting on Grace: A Theology of Dialogue* (Oxford: Oxford University Press, 2020).

The comment on the colloquy comes from a posthumous collection of Michael Ivens's unpublished work, edited by Joseph Munitiz, *Keeping in Touch* (Leominster: Gracewing, 2007).

For the classical Indian religious tradition as inscribed in the law books, see the *Laws of Manu,* translated by Wendy Doniger with Brian Smith (London: Penguin, 1991).

The comment by Emil Facenheim on revelation comes from his philosophical study, *To Mend the World: Foundations of Post-Holocaust Jewish Thought* (Bloomington IN: Indiana University Press, new edition 1994).

# CHAPTER 10

On the two lines of interpretation that run through the Exercises – 'ascetical and mystical' – see the excellent article by Joseph Veale, 'Ignatian Prayer or Jesuit Spirituality', *The Way Supplement* 27 (Spring 1976). On this topic I have myself found much to admire in the detailed exegesis of the text of the *Spiritual Exercises* by William Peters, *The Spiritual Exercises of St Ignatius, Exposition and Interpretation* (Jersey City: PASE, 1967; also published by CIS, Rome, 1980).

The quotation from Śri Aurobindo comes from his commentary on the

Vedic scripture and is quoted in Harold G. Coward, *Sphota Theory of Language* (Delhi: Motilal Banarsidass, 1980). I am indebted to Coward's work for my presentation here of the Sphota theory. For Tamil poetics I have followed the work of Norman Cutler, particularly *Songs of Experience: the Poetics of Tamil Devotion* (Bloomington IN: Indiana University Press, 1987). For the text of the *Bhagavad Gita* I have used the version edited and translated by R. C. Zaehner, (Oxford: Oxford University Press, 1969). For the *Tiruvacakam* of Manikkavacakar I have relied on a number of texts including Cutler and one venerable edition: G. U. Pope, *Tiruvacagam or 'Sacred Utterances' of the Tamil Poet, Saint and Sage, Manikka-vacagar* (Oxford: Clarendon Press, 1900; re-printed by the University of Madras, 1970).

The poems, 'versions' of the Psalms, by Zoketsu Norman Fischer are pub-lished as *Opening to You: Zen-Inspired Translations of the Psalms* (London: Pen-guin, 2003).

## CHAPTER 11

The encounter with the young man in Southall forms the basis of a contri-bution I made to a collection of articles on Christian faith and the *Bhagavad Gita*, itself part of a Comparative Theology project, Christian Commentaries on Non-Christian Sacred Texts. See Michael Barnes, 'With God in the World: A Dialogue between the Bhagavad Gita and the Spiritual Exercises' in, Cath-erine Cornille (ed), *Song Divine: Christian Commentaries on the Bhagavad Gita* (Leuven: Peeters, 2006).

The 'threefold paradigm' in the theology of religions originates from Alan Race's insightful summary, *Christians and Religious Pluralism* (London: SCM,1983), which is based on John Hick's work in the philosophy of religion. It was followed by Gavin D'Costa's, *Theology and Religious Pluralism* (Oxford: Blackwell, 1986), which neatly tells the same story from a different – Roman Catholic - angle. My own contribution to this 'survey' literature is *Religions in Conversation* (London: SPCK, 1989). Among later more comprehensive overviews, I commend Veli-Matti Kärkäinnen, *An Introduction to the Theology of Religions* (Downers Grove IL: InterVarsity Press, 2004).

Coming again from a Catholic perspective, the work of Jacques Dupuis, although very much a magisterial overview of a broad range of opinions, is more constructive and critical. See especially *Toward a Christian Theology of Religious Pluralism* (Maryknoll: Orbis, 1997), and *Christianity and the Religions: from Confrontation to Dialogue* (Maryknoll: Orbis, 2003. For a recent summary of Catholic approaches to theology of religions see Michael Barnes, 'Catholic Theology and Other Religions', in *The Oxford Handbook of Catholic Theology,* edited by Lewis Ayres and Medi Ann Volpe (Oxford University Press, 2019).

For Rahner's later work, which drops the term 'anonymous Christian', see *Foundations of Christian Faith* (London: DLT, 1978). For his theme of 'divinisation of the world through the Spirit', in which the Paschal Mystery appears as an 'inner moment', see Paul Imhof and Hubert Biallowons (eds), *Karl Rahner in Dialogue: Conversations and Interviews, 1965-82* (New York: Crossroad, 1986).

Rowan Williams's essay, 'Finality of Christ', was first presented at a seminar organised by the Sisters of Sion, privately published by Mary Kelly in 1990, and reproduced in a collection of theological papers, *On Christian Theology* (Oxford: Blackwell, 2000).

*Celebrating Jesus, a Multifaith Appreciation,* edited by Daniel Faivre, Michael Barnes, Tony McCaffry and Edgar Lange, was published by Daniel Faivre (Southall, 1999). Quotation from Gopal Singh, *The Man who Never Died* (Himalayan International Institute of Yoga Science and Philosophy: 1990). Quotation from Thich Nhat Hanh, *Living Buddha Living Christ* (London: Ebury Press, 1996).

## CHAPTER 12

For the dialogues between Pope Francis, when he was Archbishop of Buenos Aires, and Rabbi Abraham Skorka, see *On Heaven and Earth* (NY: Random House, 2013). A number of excellent biographies of Pope Francis have now been published. I find the most insightful to be Austen Ivereigh's *The Great Reformer* (London: Allen and Unwin, 2014); see also his more recent *The Wounded Shepherd* (New York: Henry Holt, 2019). The reference to Hugo Rahner was part of a Q and A session with Jesuits in formation in Krakow given by Pope Francis, 30 July, 2016. The question of the financial system's responsibility for the inequalities of the planet is raised by Pope Francis in his Preface to Michele Zanzucchi (ed), *Potere e Denaro. La giustizia sociale secondo Bergoglio,* ('Power and Money. Social Justice according to Bergoglio') (Rome: Edizioni Città Nuova, 2018). The address by Pope Francis, *Urbi et Orbe,* was given to an empty, rain-swept Piazza of St Peter on 27th March 2020.